hawkeye

LITTLE HITS

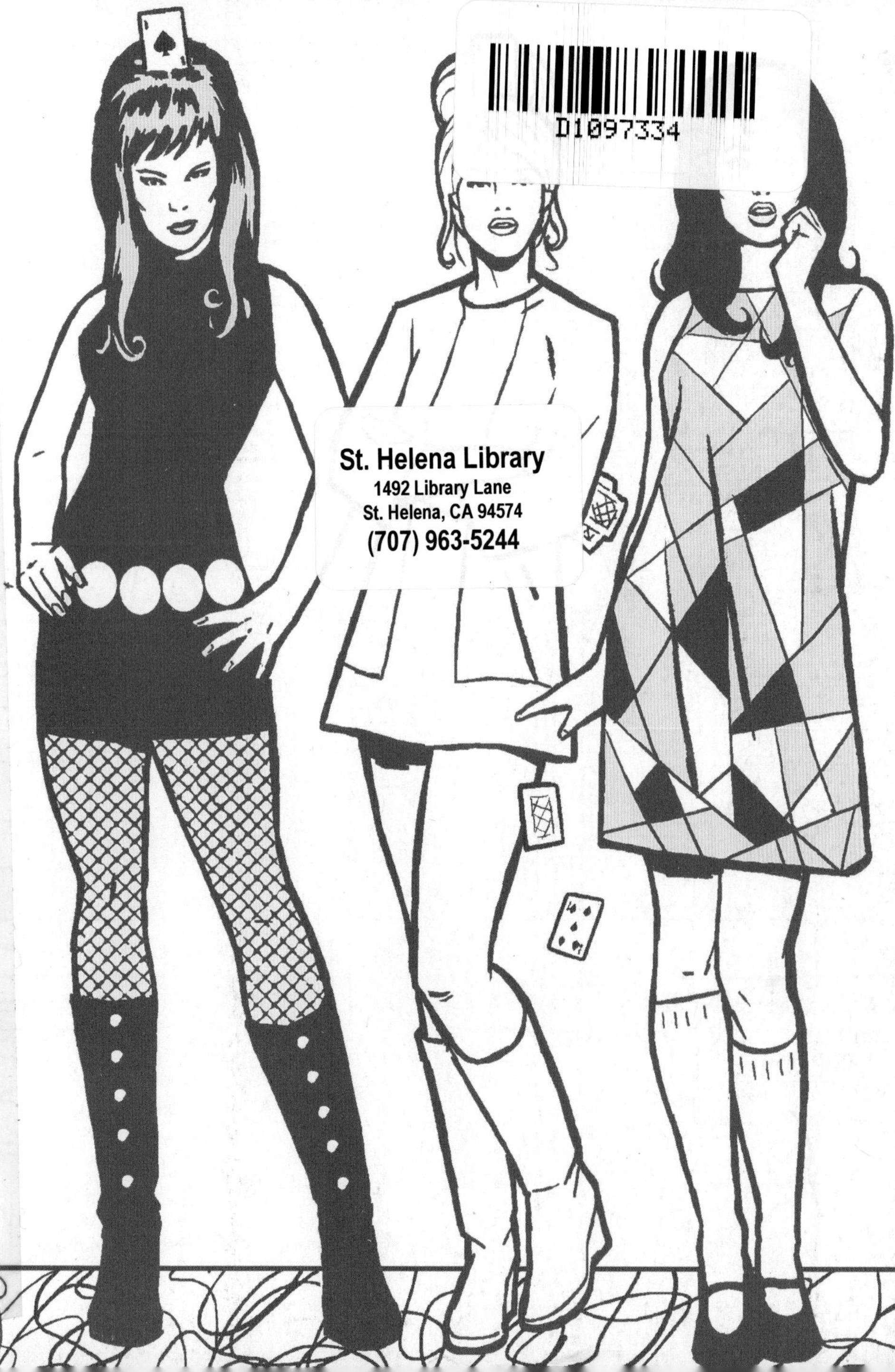

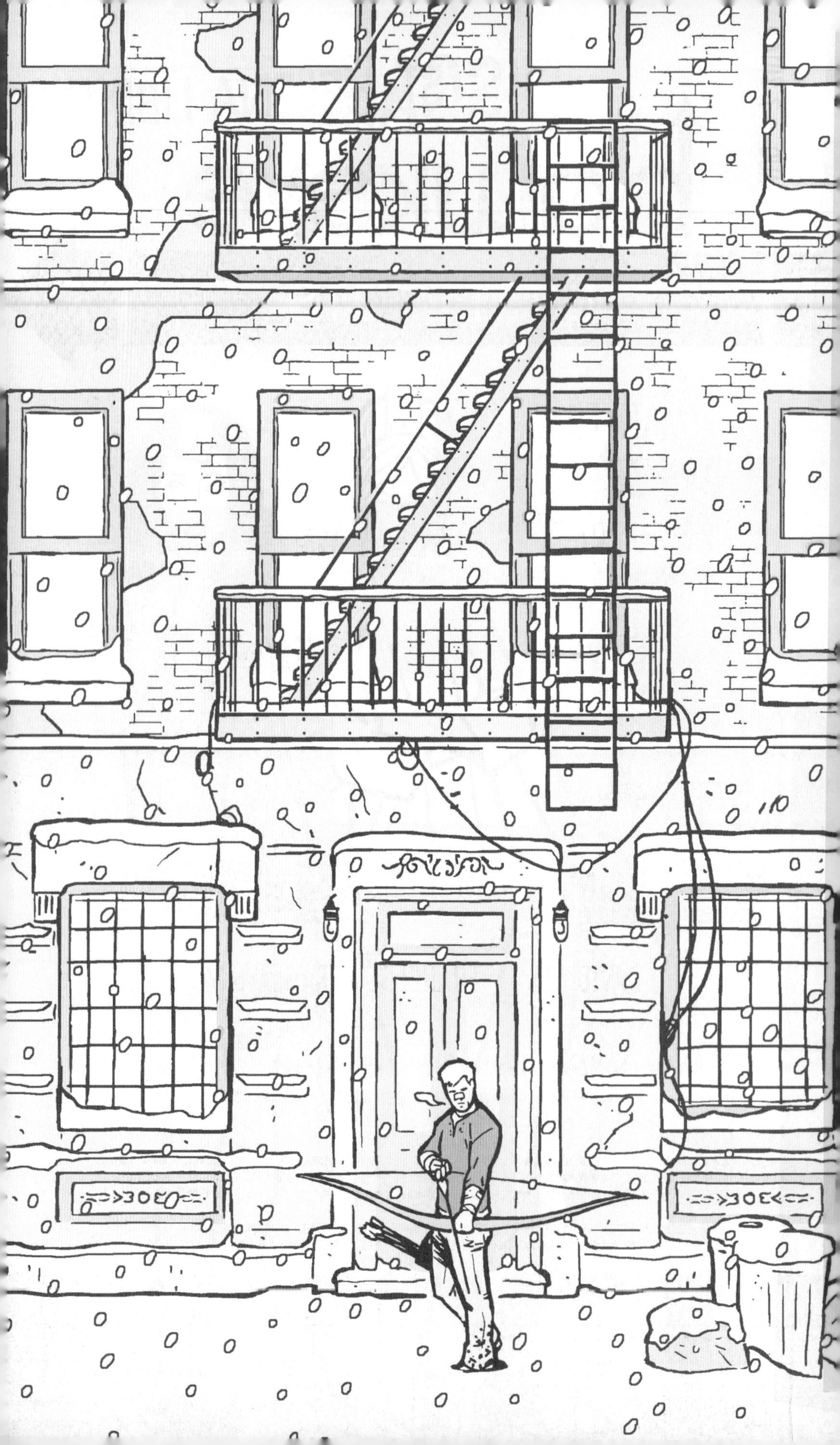

hawkeye

LITTLE HITS

MATT FRACTION
WRITER

DAVID AJA
ARTIST, #6 & #8-11

FRANCESCO FRANCAVILLA
ART & COLOR, #10

STEVE LIEBER & JESSE HAMM
ARTISTS, #7

ANNIE WU
ROMANCE COMIC COVER PAGES, #8

MATT HOLLINGSWORTH
COLOR ARTIST, #6-9 & #11

CHRIS ELIOPOULOS
LETTERER

DAVID AJA
COVER ART, #6-9 & #11

FRANCESCO FRANCAVILLA
COVER ART, #10

SANA AMANAT & TOM BRENNAN
ASSOCIATE EDITORS

STEPHEN WACKER
EDITOR

COLLECTION EDITOR: **JENNIFER GRÜNWALD** • ASSISTANT EDITORS: **ALEX STARBUCK & NELSON RIBEIRO**
EDITOR, SPECIAL PROJECTS: **MARK D. BEAZLEY** • SENIOR EDITOR, SPECIAL PROJECTS: **JEFF YOUNGQUIST**
SVP OF PRINT & DIGITAL PUBLISHING SALES: **DAVID GABRIEL** • BOOK DESIGN: **JEFF POWELL**

EDITOR IN CHIEF: **AXEL ALONSO** • CHIEF CREATIVE OFFICER: **JOE QUESADA**
PUBLISHER: **DAN BUCKLEY** • EXECUTIVE PRODUCER: **ALAN FINE**

E VOL. 2: LITTLE HITS. Contains material originally published in magazine form as HAWKEYE #6-11. First printing 2013. ISBN# 978-0-7851-6563-7. Published by MARVEL WORLDWIDE, INC., a subsidiary of
ENTERTAINMENT, LLC. OFFICE OF PUBLICATION: 135 West 50th Street, New York, NY 10020. Copyright © 2012 and 2013 Marvel Characters, Inc. All rights reserved. All characters featured in this issue and the
e names and likenesses thereof, and all related indicia are trademarks of Marvel Characters, Inc. No similarity between any of the names, characters, persons, and/or institutions in this magazine with those of any
ead person or institution is intended, and any such similarity which may exist is purely coincidental. **Printed in the U.S.A.** ALAN FINE, EVP - Office of the President, Marvel Worldwide, Inc. and EVP & CMO Marvel
s B.V.; DAN BUCKLEY, Publisher & President - Print, Animation & Digital Divisions; JOE QUESADA, Chief Creative Officer; TOM BREVOORT, SVP of Publishing; DAVID BOGART, SVP of Operations & Procurement,
g; C.B. CEBULSKI, SVP of Creator & Content Development; DAVID GABRIEL, SVP of Print & Digital Publishing Sales; JIM O'KEEFE, VP of Operations & Logistics; DAN CARR, Executive Director of Publishing Technology;
RESPI, Editorial Operations Manager; ALEX MORALES, Publishing Operations Manager; STAN LEE, Chairman Emeritus. For information regarding advertising in Marvel Comics or on Marvel.com, please contact Niza
ctor of Marvel Partnerships, at ndisla@marvel.com. For Marvel subscription inquiries, please call 800-217-9158. **Manufactured between 5/1/2013 and 6/3/2013 by QUAD/GRAPHICS, VERSAILLES, KY, USA.**

654321

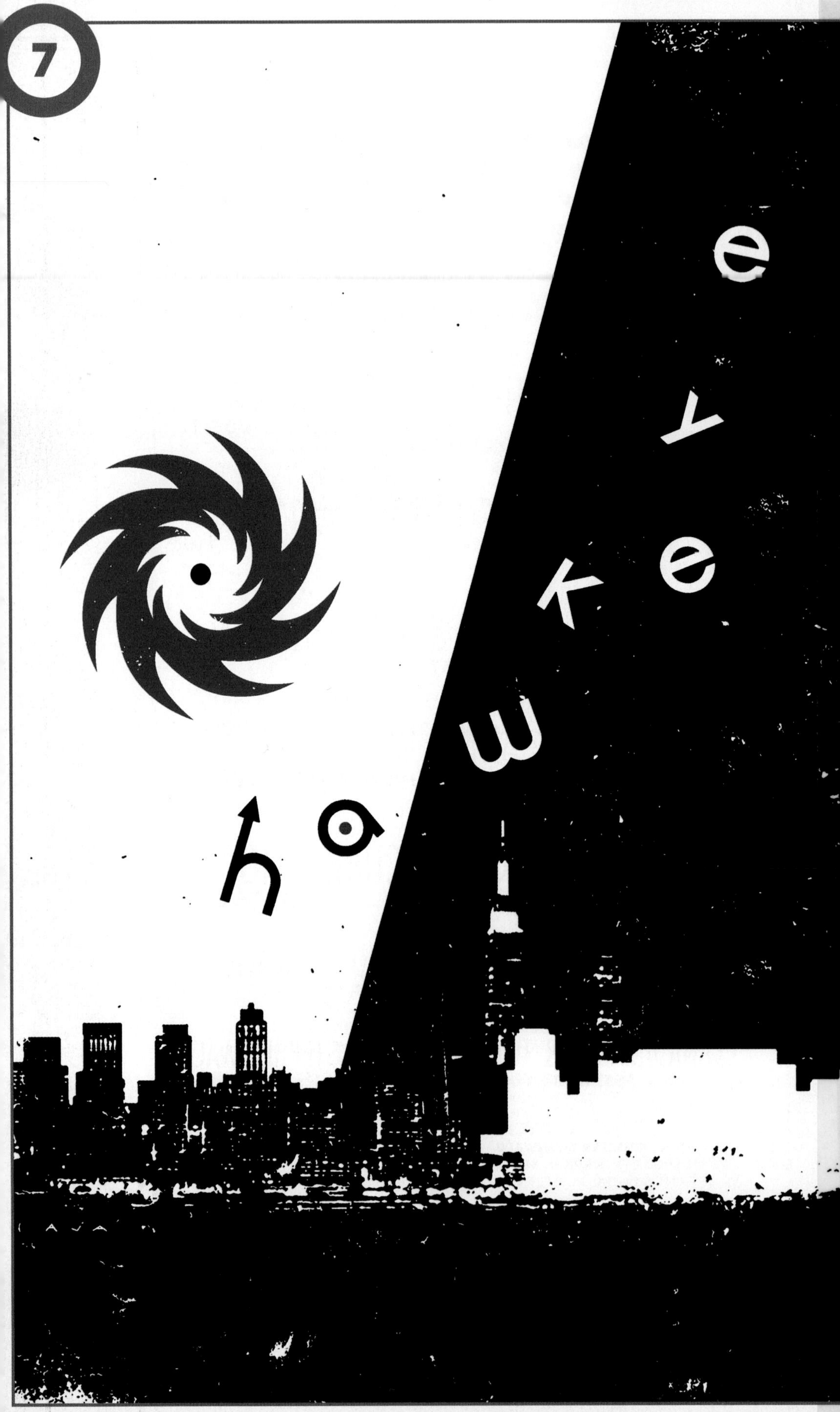
7
hawkeye

clint barton, a.k.a.

hawkeye,

became the greatest sharp-shooter known to man.

he then joined the avengers.

this is what he does when he's not being an avenger.

(enter smug comment here)

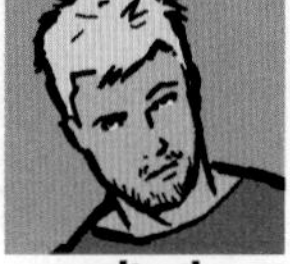

clint barton
(hawkeye)

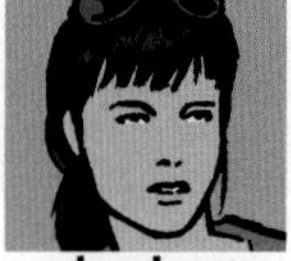

kate bishop
(hawkeye)

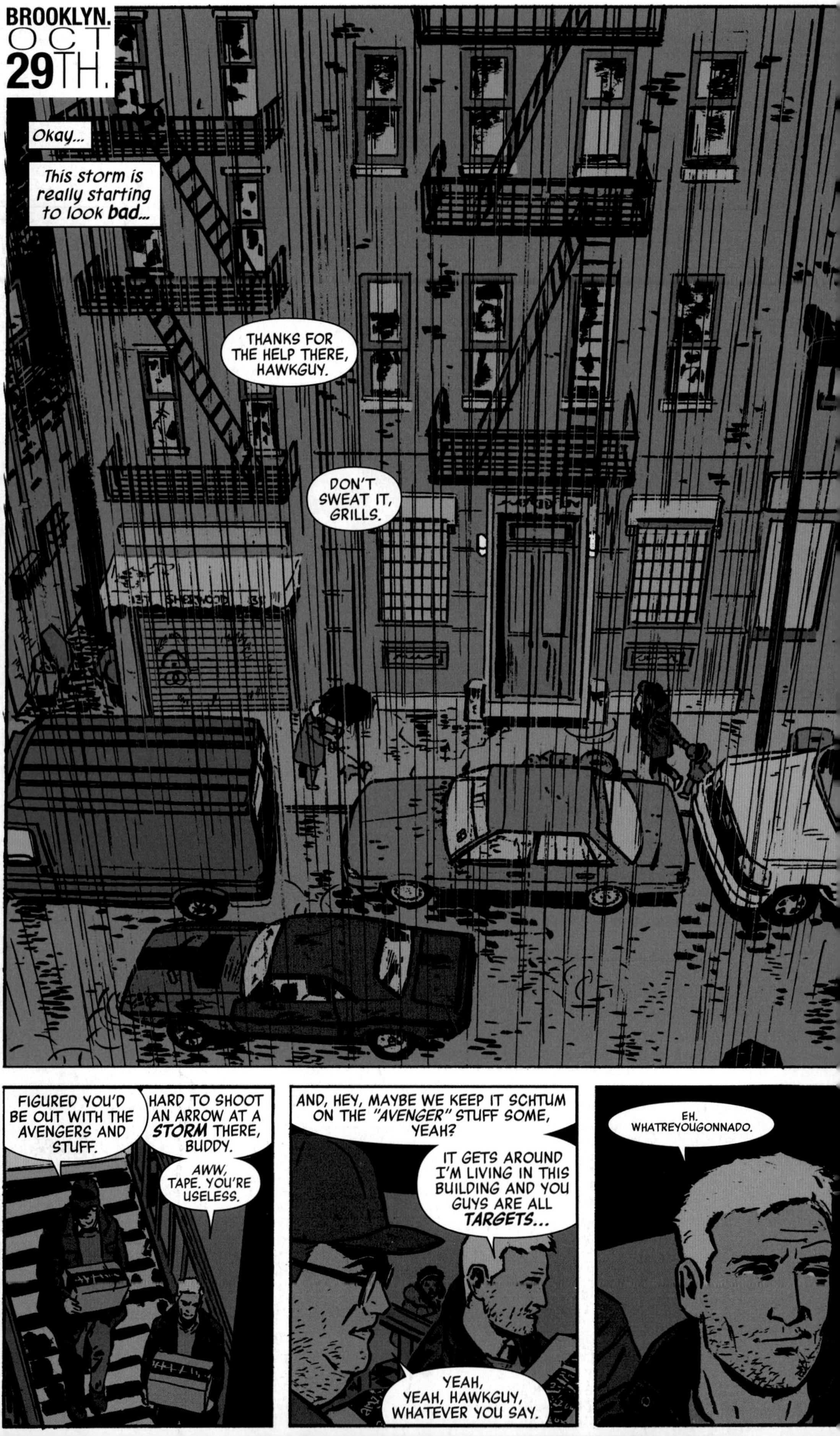
BROOKLYN. OCT 29TH.
Okay...
This storm is really starting to look **bad...**
THANKS FOR THE HELP THERE, HAWKGUY.
DON'T SWEAT IT, GRILLS.
FIGURED YOU'D BE OUT WITH THE AVENGERS AND STUFF.
HARD TO SHOOT AN ARROW AT A **STORM** THERE, BUDDY.
AWW, TAPE. YOU'RE USELESS.
AND, HEY, MAYBE WE KEEP IT SCHTUM ON THE *"AVENGER"* STUFF SOME, YEAH?
IT GETS AROUND I'M LIVING IN THIS BUILDING AND YOU GUYS ARE ALL **TARGETS...**
YEAH, YEAH, HAWKGUY, WHATEVER YOU SAY.
EH. WHATREYOUGONNADO.

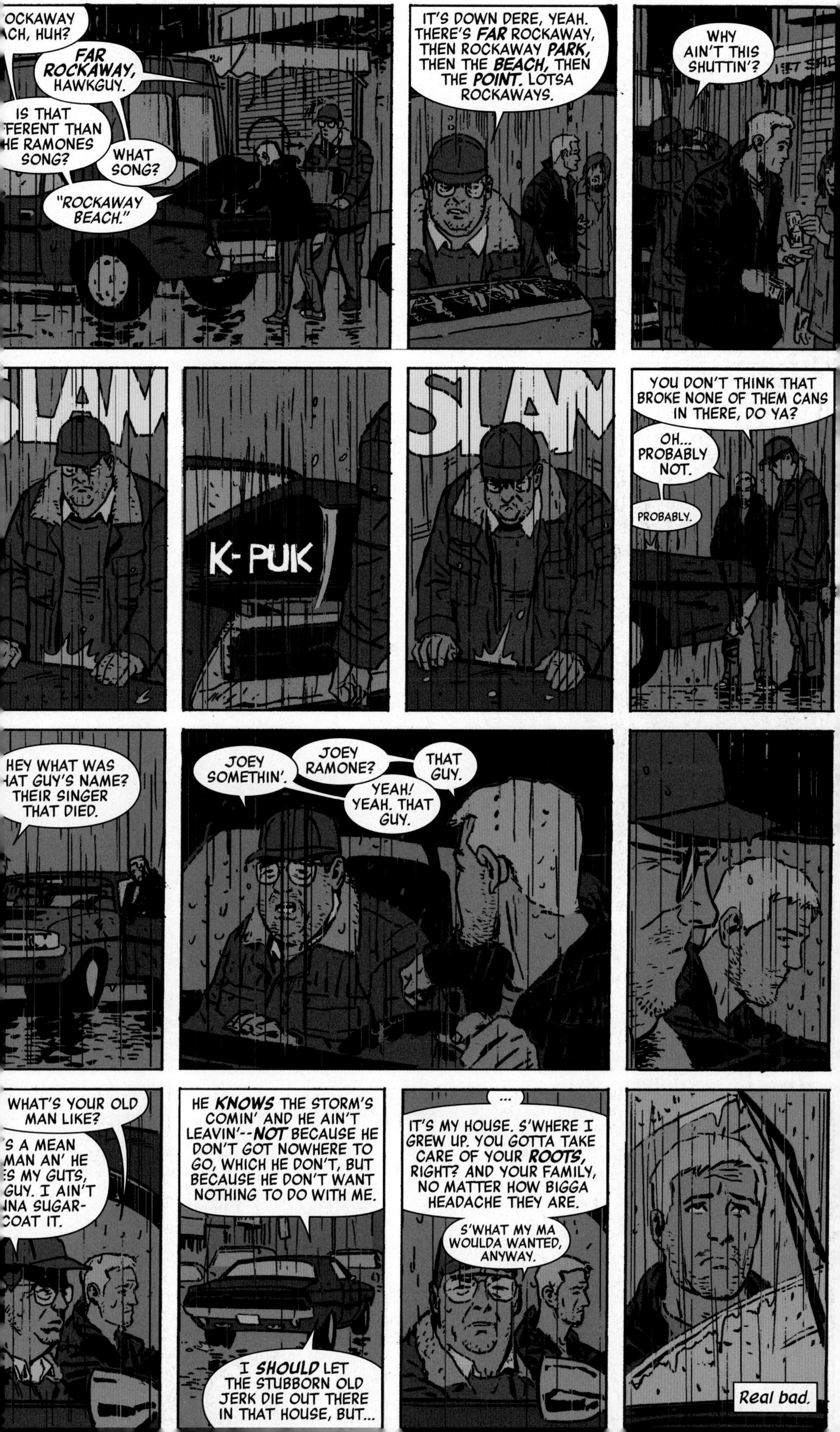
OCKAWAY
CH, HUH?
FAR ROCKAWAY, HAWKGUY.
IS THAT FERENT THAN HE RAMONES SONG?
WHAT SONG?
"ROCKAWAY BEACH."
IT'S DOWN DERE, YEAH. THERE'S FAR ROCKAWAY, THEN ROCKAWAY PARK, THEN THE BEACH, THEN THE POINT. LOTSA ROCKAWAYS.
WHY AIN'T THIS SHUTTIN'?
K-PUK
YOU DON'T THINK THAT BROKE NONE OF THEM CANS IN THERE, DO YA?
OH... PROBABLY NOT.
PROBABLY.
HEY WHAT WAS HAT GUY'S NAME? THEIR SINGER THAT DIED.
JOEY SOMETHIN'.
JOEY RAMONE?
THAT GUY.
YEAH! YEAH. THAT GUY.
WHAT'S YOUR OLD MAN LIKE?
'S A MEAN MAN AN' HE ES MY GUTS, GUY. I AIN'T NA SUGAR-COAT IT.
HE KNOWS THE STORM'S COMIN' AND HE AIN'T LEAVIN'--NOT BECAUSE HE DON'T GOT NOWHERE TO GO, WHICH HE DON'T, BUT BECAUSE HE DON'T WANT NOTHING TO DO WITH ME.
I SHOULD LET THE STUBBORN OLD JERK DIE OUT THERE IN THAT HOUSE, BUT...
...
IT'S MY HOUSE. S'WHERE I GREW UP. YOU GOTTA TAKE CARE OF YOUR ROOTS, RIGHT? AND YOUR FAMILY, NO MATTER HOW BIGGA HEADACHE THEY ARE.
S'WHAT MY MA WOULDA WANTED, ANYWAY.
Real bad.

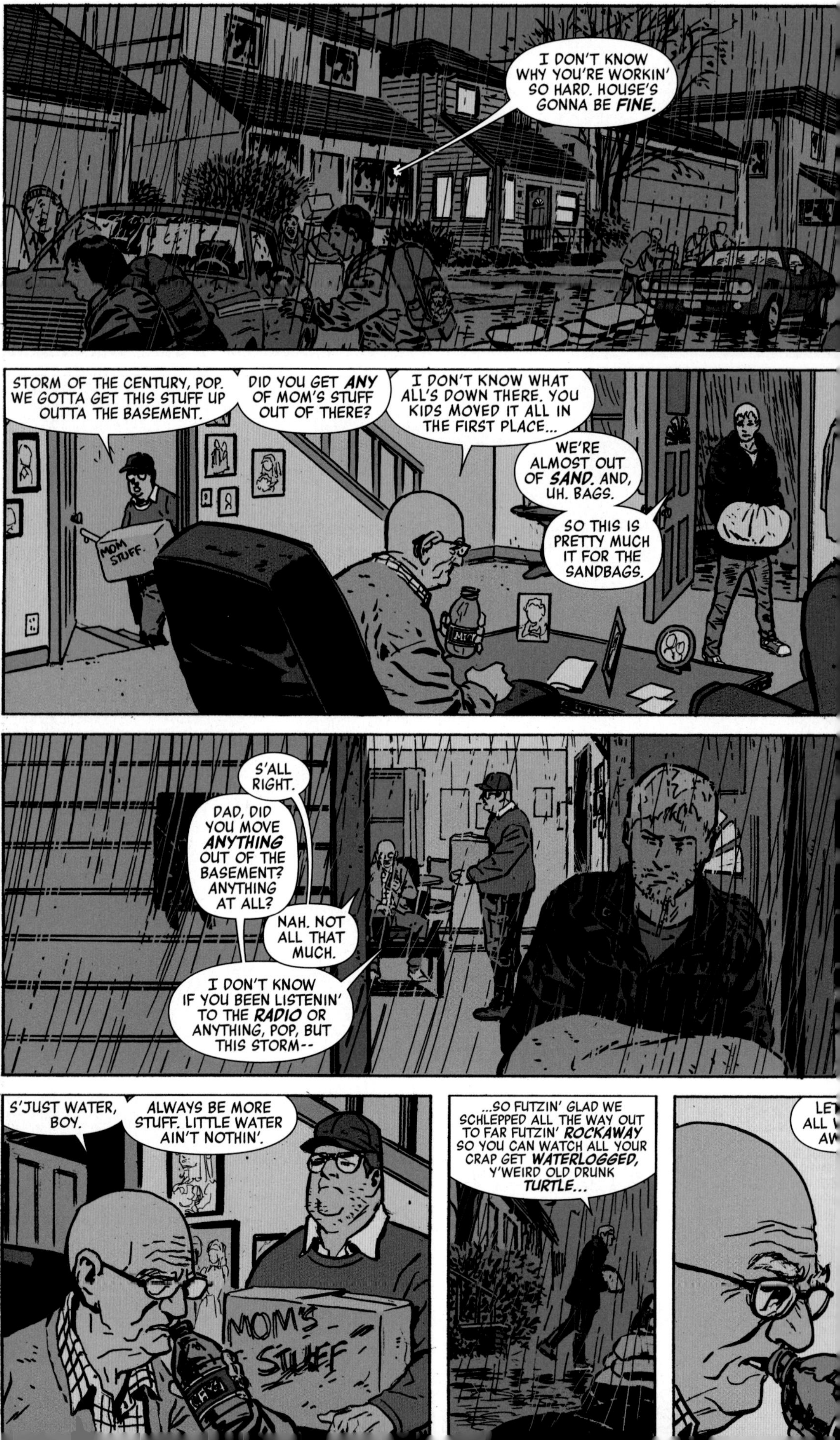

I DON'T KNOW WHY YOU'RE WORKIN' SO HARD. HOUSE'S GONNA BE FINE.
STORM OF THE CENTURY, POP. WE GOTTA GET THIS STUFF UP OUTTA THE BASEMENT.
DID YOU GET ANY OF MOM'S STUFF OUT OF THERE?
I DON'T KNOW WHAT ALL'S DOWN THERE. YOU KIDS MOVED IT ALL IN THE FIRST PLACE...
MOM STUFF.
WE'RE ALMOST OUT OF SAND. AND, UH. BAGS.
SO THIS IS PRETTY MUCH IT FOR THE SANDBAGS.
S'ALL RIGHT.
DAD, DID YOU MOVE ANYTHING OUT OF THE BASEMENT? ANYTHING AT ALL?
NAH. NOT ALL THAT MUCH.
I DON'T KNOW IF YOU BEEN LISTENIN' TO THE RADIO OR ANYTHING, POP, BUT THIS STORM--
S'JUST WATER, BOY.
ALWAYS BE MORE STUFF. LITTLE WATER AIN'T NOTHIN'.
MOM'S STUFF
...SO FUTZIN' GLAD WE SCHLEPPED ALL THE WAY OUT TO FAR FUTZIN' ROCKAWAY SO YOU CAN WATCH ALL YOUR CRAP GET WATERLOGGED, Y'WEIRD OLD DRUNK TURTLE...

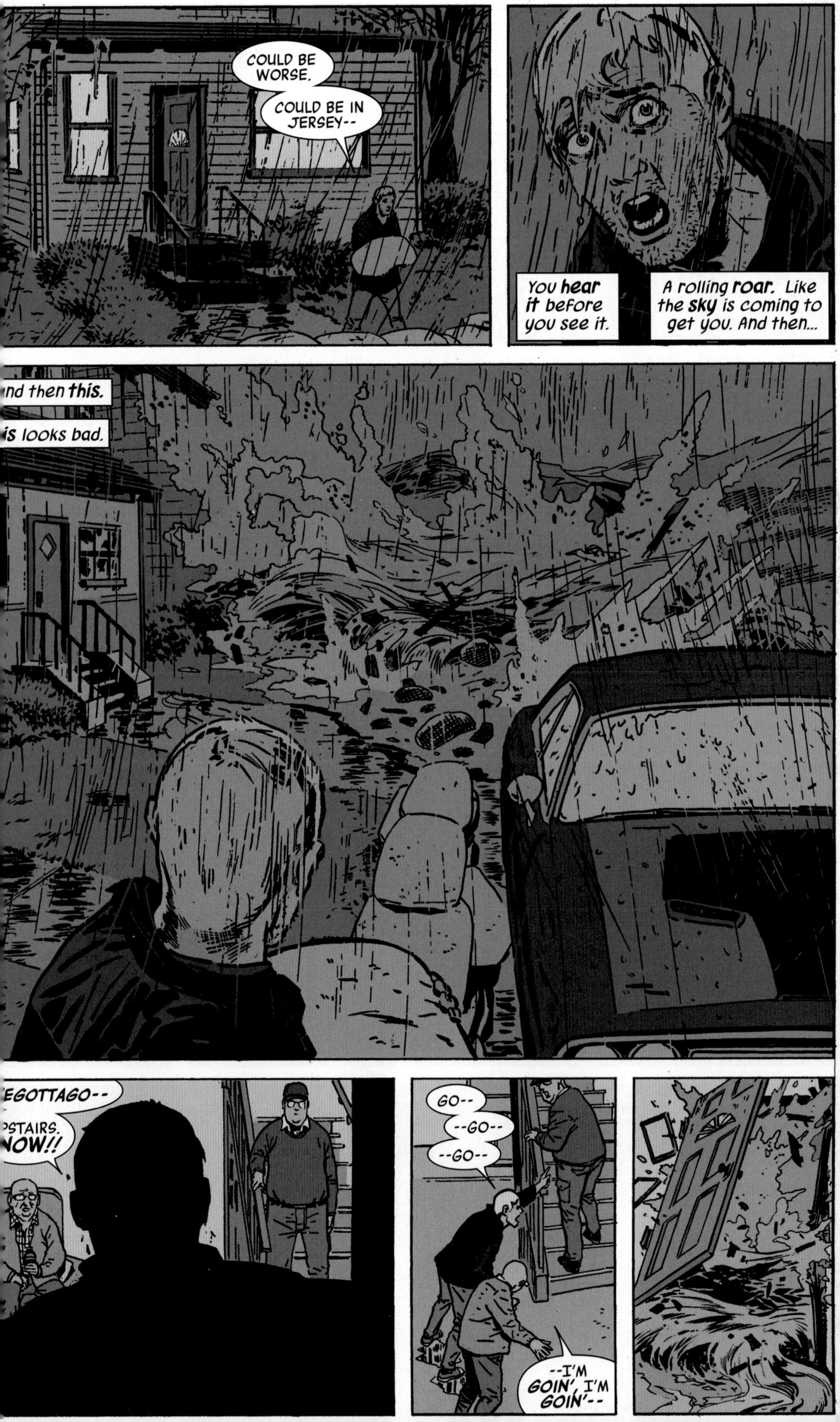

COULD BE WORSE.
COULD BE IN JERSEY--
You hear it before you see it.
A rolling roar. Like the sky is coming to get you. And then...
nd then this.
is looks bad.
EGOTTAGO--
PSTAIRS. NOW!!
GO--
--GO--
--GO--
--I'M GOIN', I'M GOIN'--

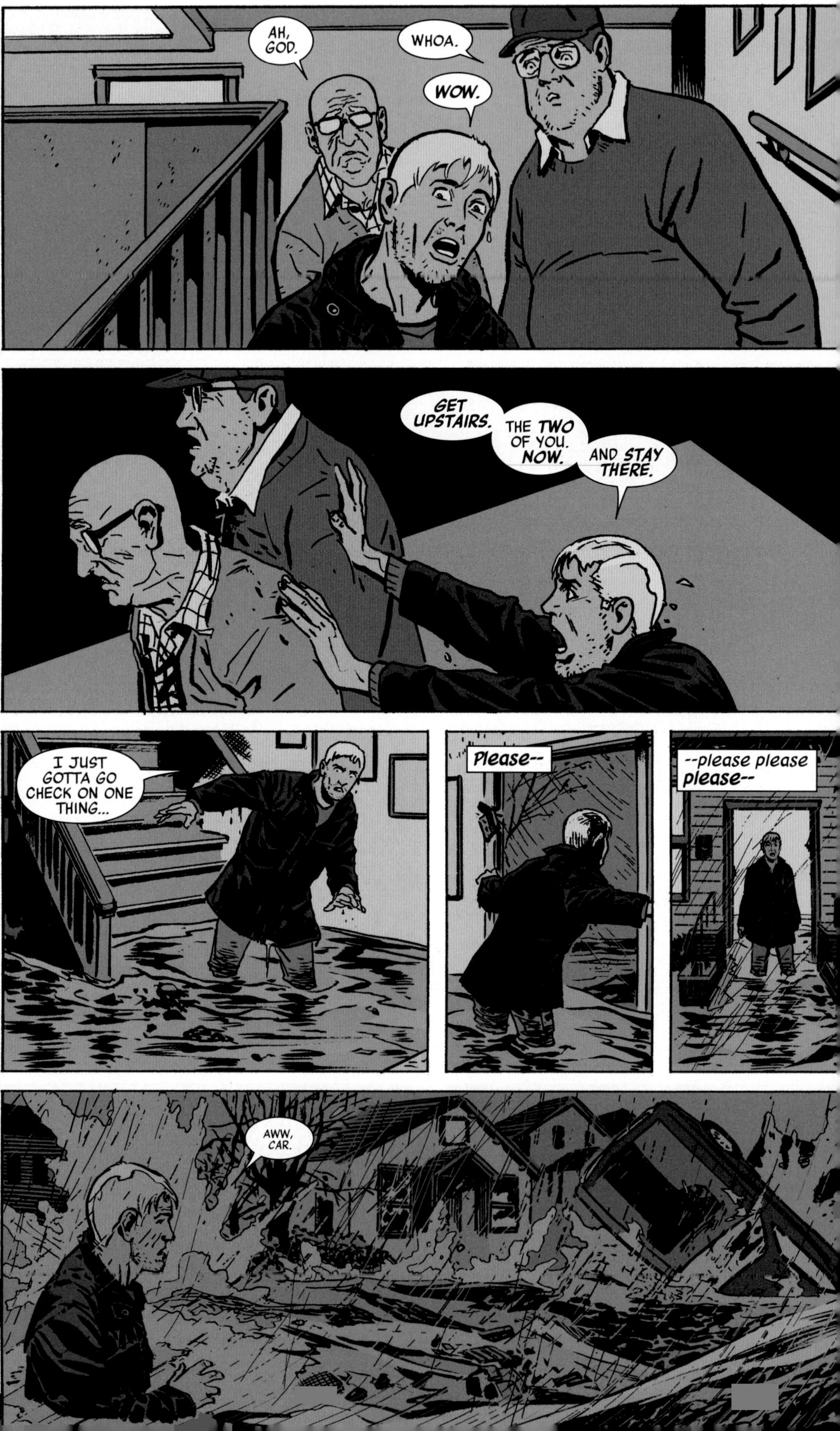
AH, GOD.
WHOA.
WOW.
GET UPSTAIRS.
THE TWO OF YOU. NOW.
AND STAY THERE.
I JUST GOTTA GO CHECK ON ONE THING...
Please--
--please please please--
AWW, CAR.

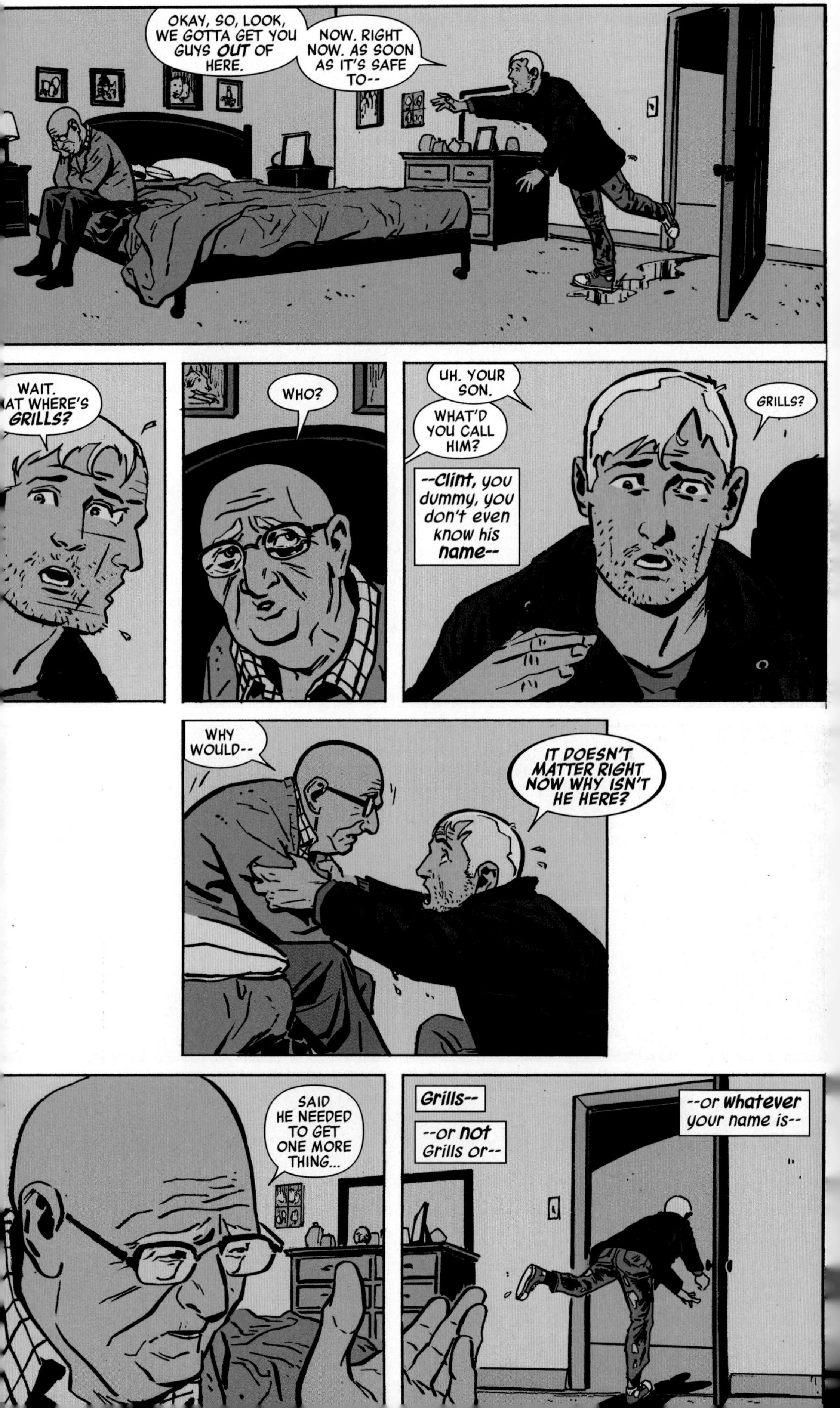
OKAY, SO, LOOK, WE GOTTA GET YOU GUYS OUT OF HERE.
NOW. RIGHT NOW. AS SOON AS IT'S SAFE TO--
WAIT. AT WHERE'S GRILLS?
WHO?
UH. YOUR SON.
WHAT'D YOU CALL HIM?
--Clint, you dummy, you don't even know his name--
GRILLS?
WHY WOULD--
IT DOESN'T MATTER RIGHT NOW WHY ISN'T HE HERE?
SAID HE NEEDED TO GET ONE MORE THING...
Grills--
--or not Grills or--
--or whatever your name is--

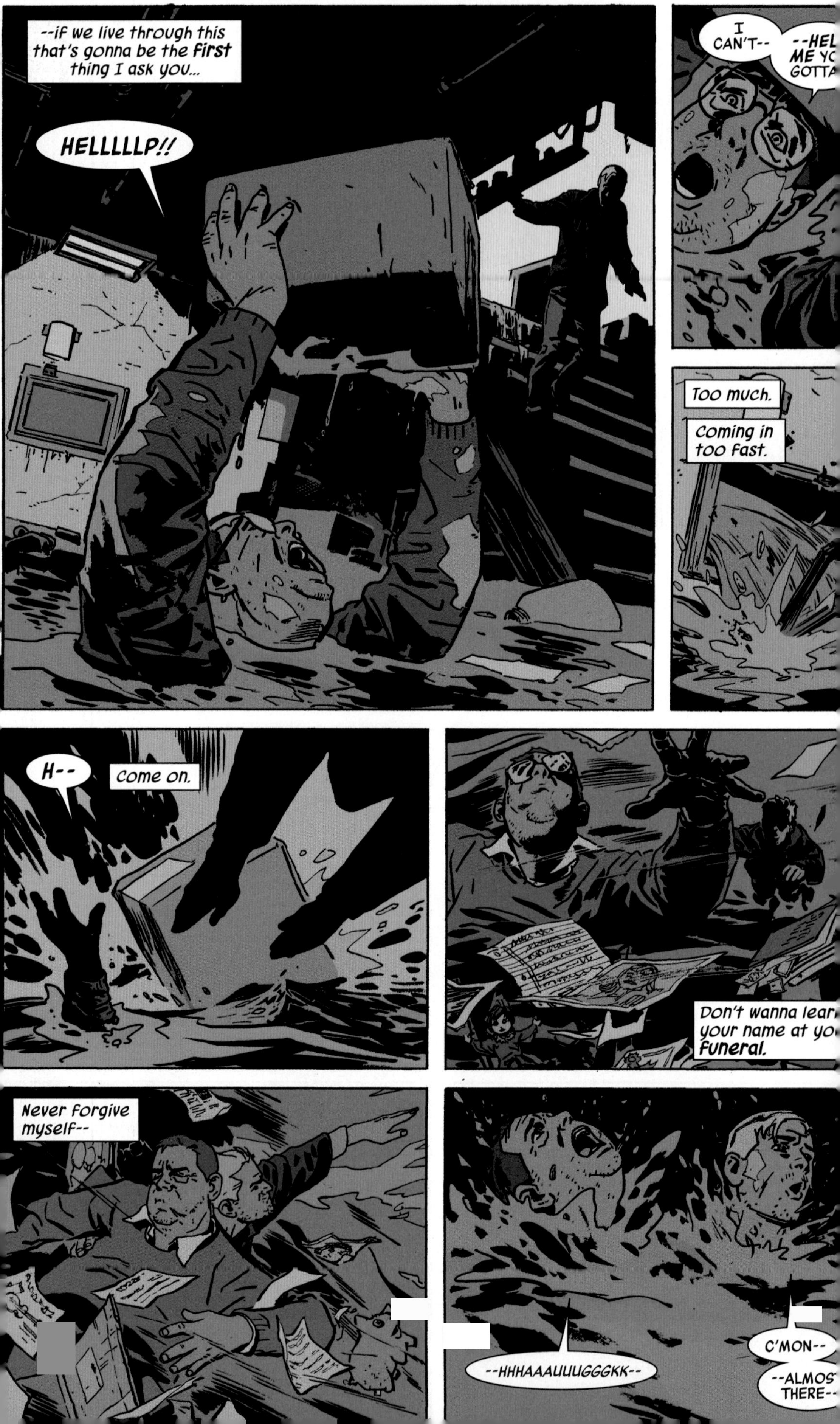
--if we live through this that's gonna be the **first** thing I ask you...
HELLLLLP!!
I CAN'T--
--HEL ME YO GOTTA
Too much.
Coming in too fast.
H--
Come on.
Don't wanna lear your name at yo **funeral.**
Never forgive myself--
--HHHAAAUUUGGGKK--
C'MON--
--ALMOS THERE--

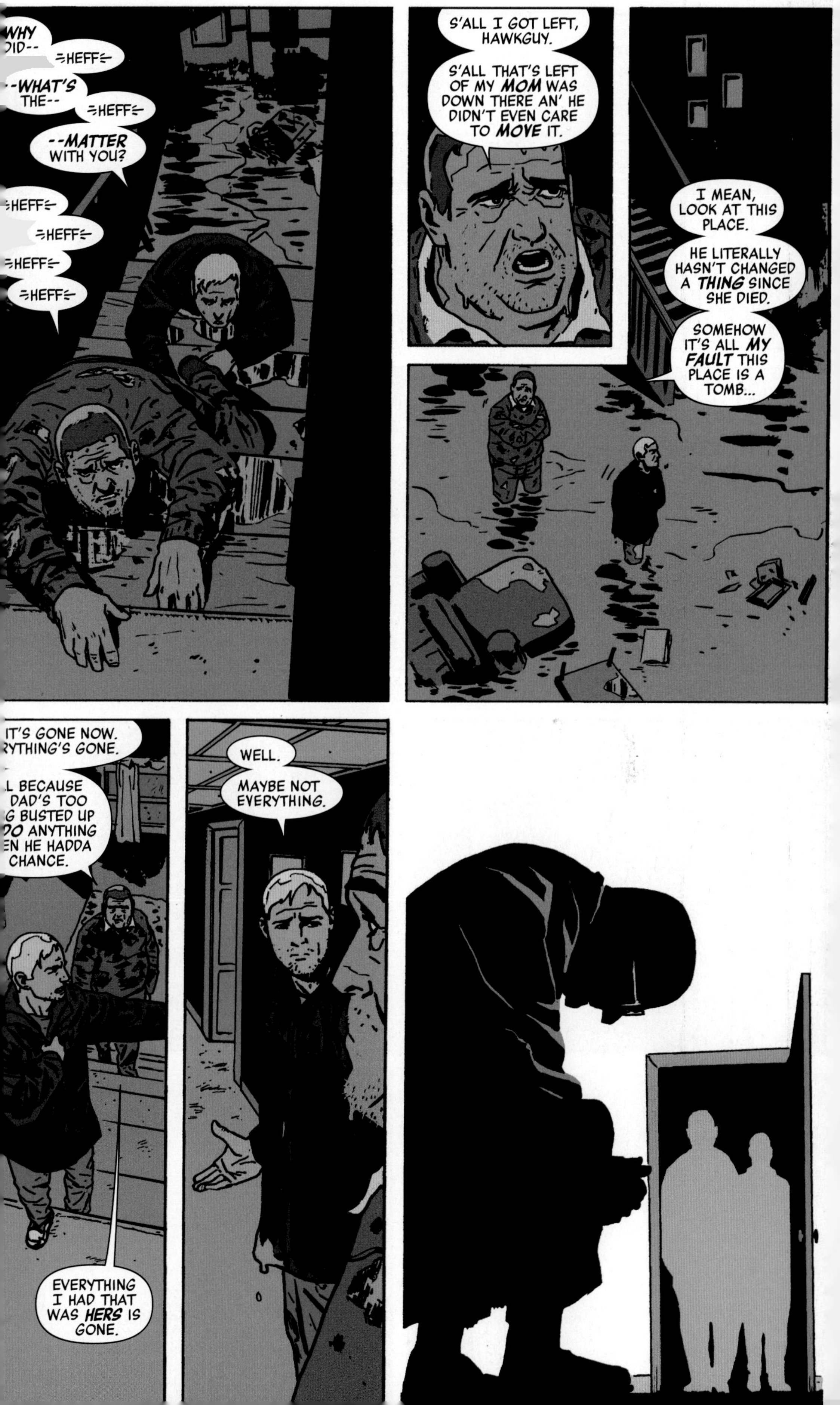
WHY DID--
=HEFF=
--WHAT'S THE--
=HEFF=
--MATTER WITH YOU?
=HEFF=
=HEFF=
=HEFF=
=HEFF=
S'ALL I GOT LEFT, HAWKGUY.
S'ALL THAT'S LEFT OF MY MOM WAS DOWN THERE AN' HE DIDN'T EVEN CARE TO MOVE IT.
I MEAN, LOOK AT THIS PLACE.
HE LITERALLY HASN'T CHANGED A THING SINCE SHE DIED.
SOMEHOW IT'S ALL MY FAULT THIS PLACE IS A TOMB...
IT'S GONE NOW. YTHING'S GONE.
L BECAUSE DAD'S TOO G BUSTED UP DO ANYTHING EN HE HADDA CHANCE.
EVERYTHING I HAD THAT WAS HERS IS GONE.
WELL.
MAYBE NOT EVERYTHING.

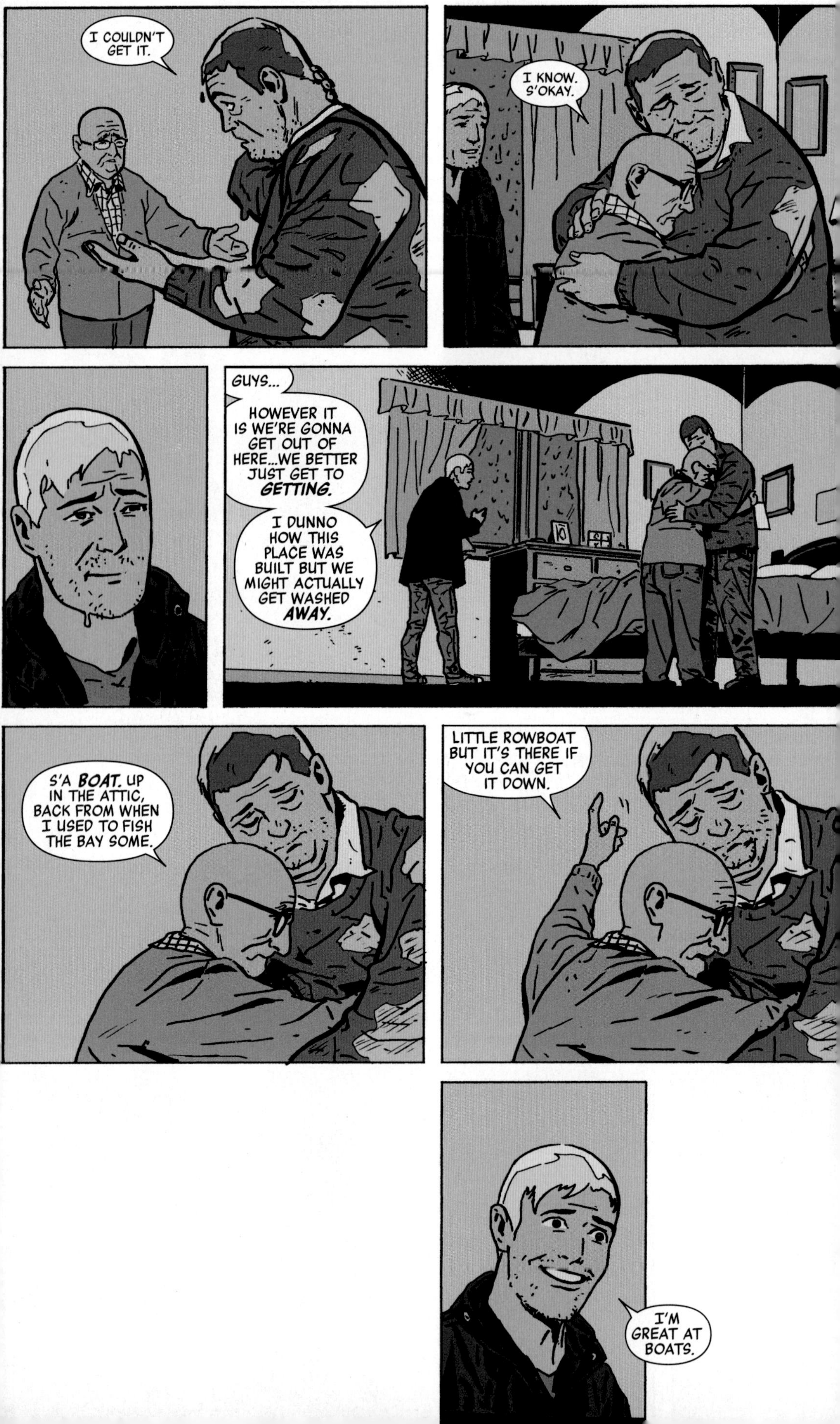
I COULDN'T GET IT.
I KNOW. S'OKAY.
GUYS...
HOWEVER IT IS WE'RE GONNA GET OUT OF HERE...WE BETTER JUST GET TO GETTING.
I DUNNO HOW THIS PLACE WAS BUILT BUT WE MIGHT ACTUALLY GET WASHED AWAY.
S'A BOAT. UP IN THE ATTIC, BACK FROM WHEN I USED TO FISH THE BAY SOME.
LITTLE ROWBOAT BUT IT'S THERE IF YOU CAN GET IT DOWN.
I'M GREAT AT BOATS.

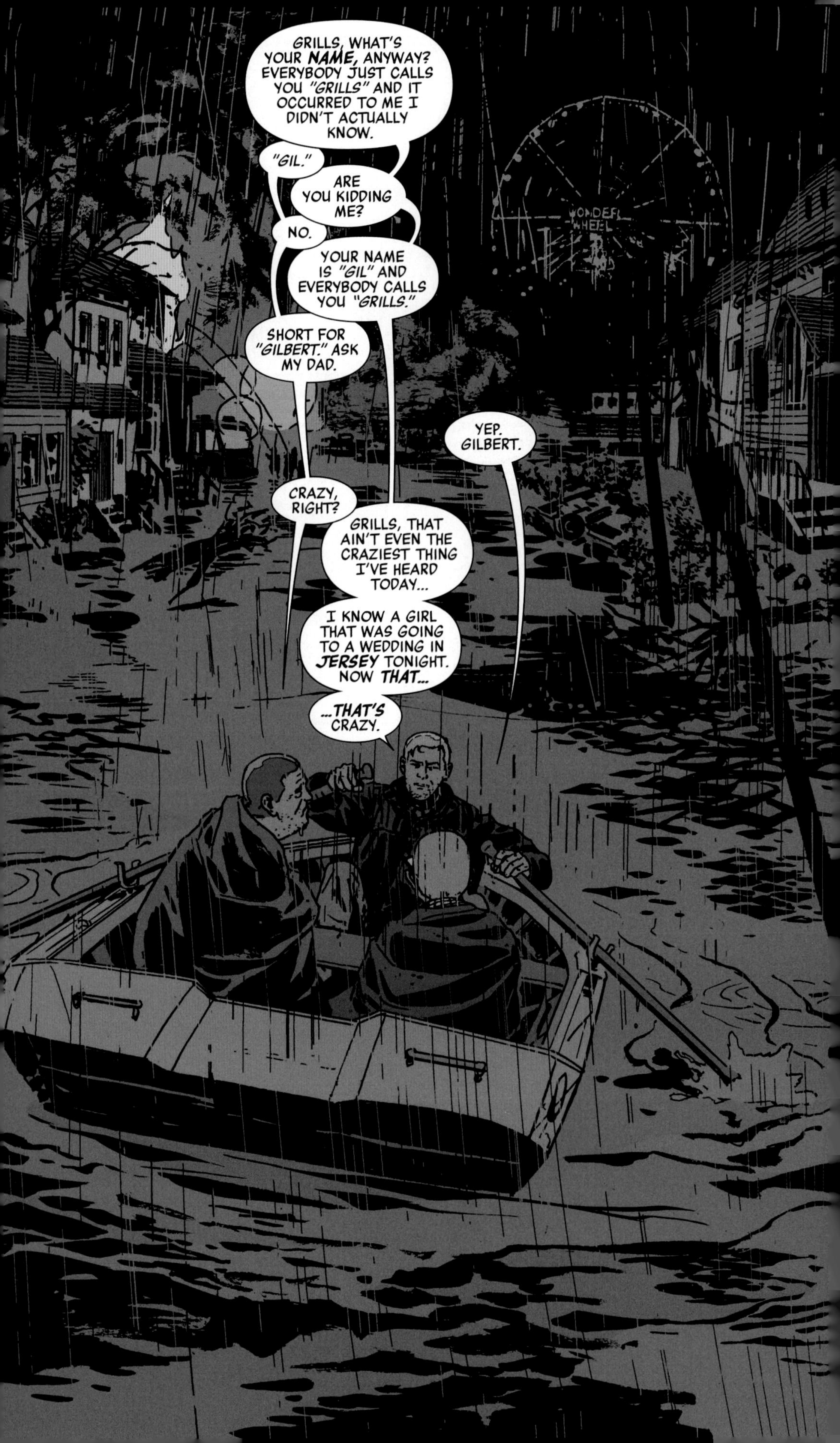
GRILLS, WHAT'S YOUR **NAME,** ANYWAY? EVERYBODY JUST CALLS YOU "GRILLS" AND IT OCCURRED TO ME I DIDN'T ACTUALLY KNOW.
"GIL."
ARE YOU KIDDING ME?
NO.
YOUR NAME IS "GIL" AND EVERYBODY CALLS YOU "GRILLS."
SHORT FOR "GILBERT." ASK MY DAD.
YEP. GILBERT.
CRAZY, RIGHT?
GRILLS, THAT AIN'T EVEN THE CRAZIEST THING I'VE HEARD TODAY...
I KNOW A GIRL THAT WAS GOING TO A WEDDING IN **JERSEY** TONIGHT. NOW **THAT...**
...THAT'S CRAZY.

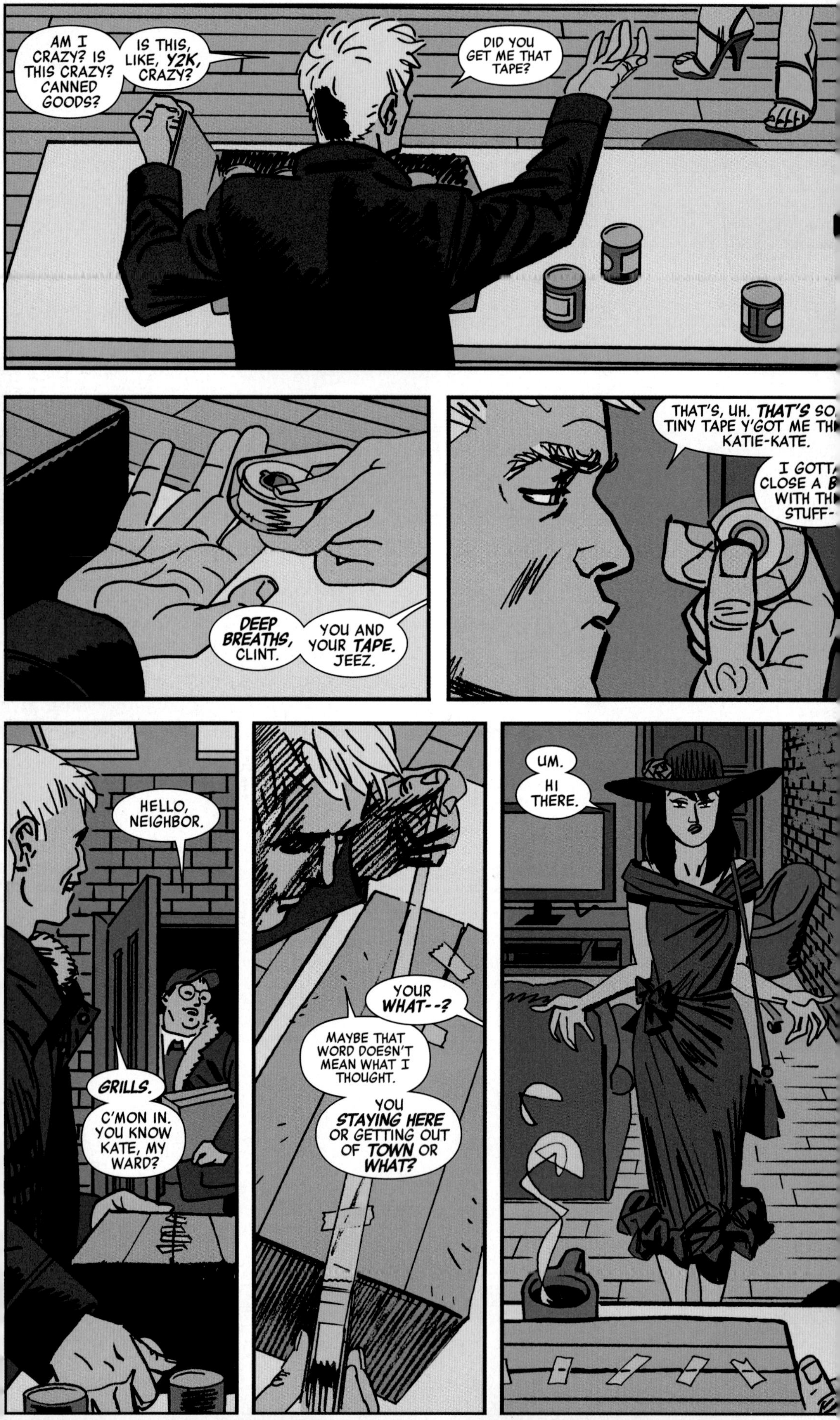
AM I CRAZY? IS THIS CRAZY? CANNED GOODS?
IS THIS, LIKE, Y2K, CRAZY?
DID YOU GET ME THAT TAPE?
DEEP BREATHS, CLINT.
YOU AND YOUR TAPE. JEEZ.
THAT'S, UH. THAT'S SO TINY TAPE Y'GOT ME TH KATIE-KATE.
I GOTT CLOSE A B WITH TH STUFF-
HELLO, NEIGHBOR.
GRILLS.
C'MON IN. YOU KNOW KATE, MY WARD?
YOUR WHAT--?
MAYBE THAT WORD DOESN'T MEAN WHAT I THOUGHT.
YOU STAYING HERE OR GETTING OUT OF TOWN OR WHAT?
UM.
HI THERE.

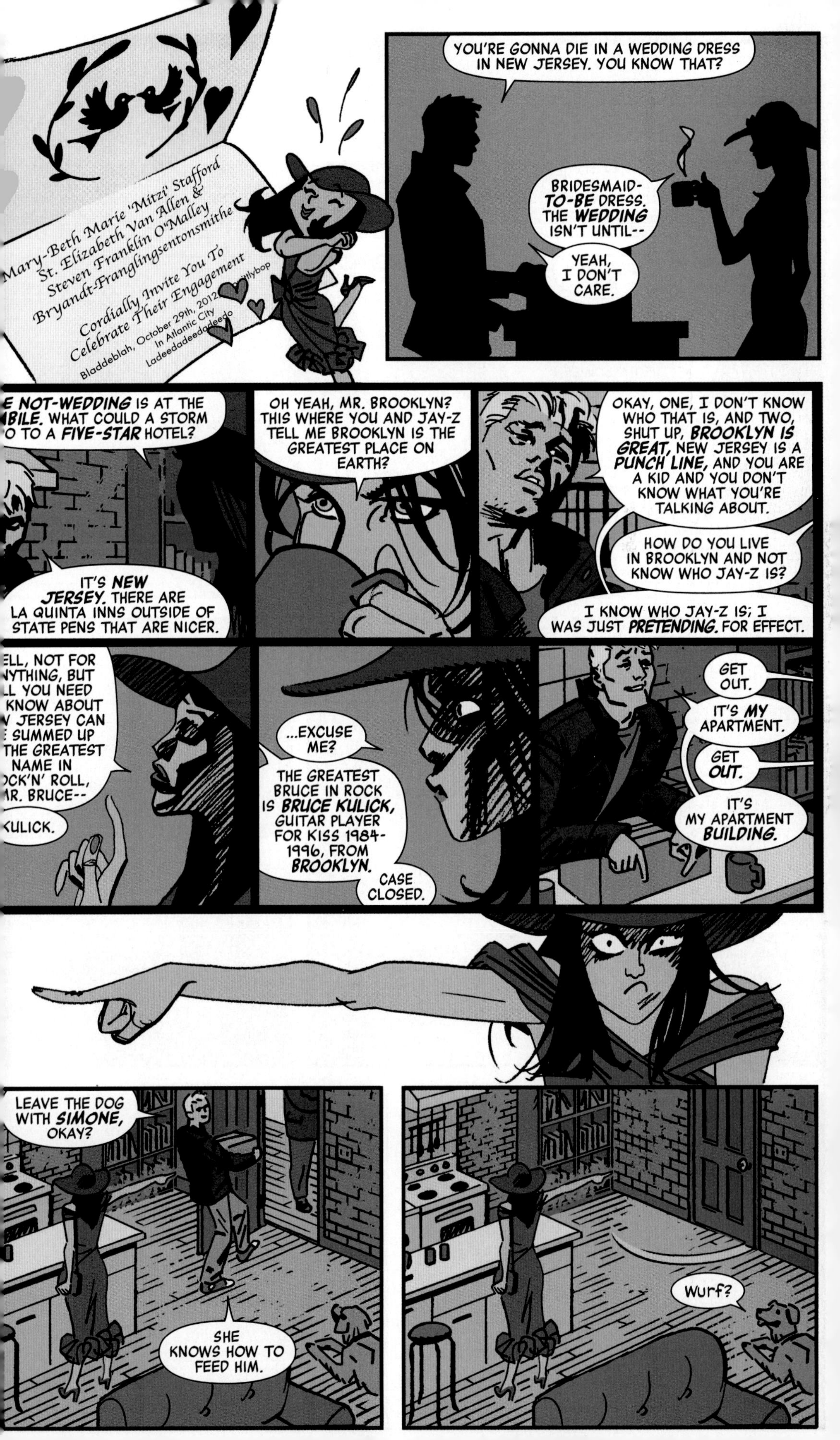
Mary-Beth Marie 'Mitzi' Stafford
St. Elizabeth Van Allen &
Steven Franklin O'Malley
Bryandt-Franglingsentonsmithe
Cordially Invite You To
Celebrate Their Engagement
Bladdeblah, October 29th, 2012
In Atlantic City
Ladeedadeedadeedo
YOU'RE GONNA DIE IN A WEDDING DRESS IN NEW JERSEY. YOU KNOW THAT?
BRIDESMAID-TO-BE DRESS. THE WEDDING ISN'T UNTIL--
YEAH, I DON'T CARE.
NOT-WEDDING IS AT THE BILE. WHAT COULD A STORM O TO A FIVE-STAR HOTEL?
IT'S NEW JERSEY. THERE ARE LA QUINTA INNS OUTSIDE OF STATE PENS THAT ARE NICER.
OH YEAH, MR. BROOKLYN? THIS WHERE YOU AND JAY-Z TELL ME BROOKLYN IS THE GREATEST PLACE ON EARTH?
OKAY, ONE, I DON'T KNOW WHO THAT IS, AND TWO, SHUT UP, BROOKLYN IS GREAT, NEW JERSEY IS A PUNCH LINE, AND YOU ARE A KID AND YOU DON'T KNOW WHAT YOU'RE TALKING ABOUT.
HOW DO YOU LIVE IN BROOKLYN AND NOT KNOW WHO JAY-Z IS?
I KNOW WHO JAY-Z IS; I WAS JUST PRETENDING. FOR EFFECT.
ELL, NOT FOR NYTHING, BUT LL YOU NEED KNOW ABOUT JERSEY CAN SUMMED UP THE GREATEST NAME IN OCK'N' ROLL, R. BRUCE--
KULICK.
...EXCUSE ME?
THE GREATEST BRUCE IN ROCK IS BRUCE KULICK, GUITAR PLAYER FOR KISS 1984-1996, FROM BROOKLYN.
CASE CLOSED.
GET OUT.
IT'S MY APARTMENT.
GET OUT.
IT'S MY APARTMENT BUILDING.
LEAVE THE DOG WITH SIMONE, OKAY?
SHE KNOWS HOW TO FEED HIM.
Wurf?

NO OFFENSE DERE, LITTLE LADY, BUT THE *STABILE* WAS BUILT BEFORE *THE WAR*, EVEN.

THEY REALLY KNEW HOW TO *MAKE 'EM* BACK THEN.

DID THEY NOW.

THE *GREAT ATLANTIC HURRICANE,* THE *ASH WEDNESDAY* STORM, HURRICANE *GLORIA,* THE HALLOWEEN *NOR'EASTER,* FLOYD...

PUDDLES. *NOTHING* TO WORRY ABOUT. THE STABILE IS A *FORTRESS.*

YOU HAVE THE *TIME,* STEVE BUSCEMI'S TINY GRANDPA?

I...ER... IT'S 8:46. WHY?

PARKING

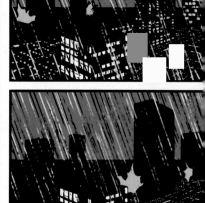

SEE, THOSE *GREEN* EXPLOSIONS WERE *POWER TRANSFORMERS.*

WHAT TIME IS IT *NOW?*

8:47.

WOW. SO IT ONLY TOOK YOU *ONE MINUTE* TO GO FROM HOTEL MANAGER TO COMPLETELY USELESS.

LADIES AND GENTLEMEN, IT'S GONNA BE A LONG NIGHT.

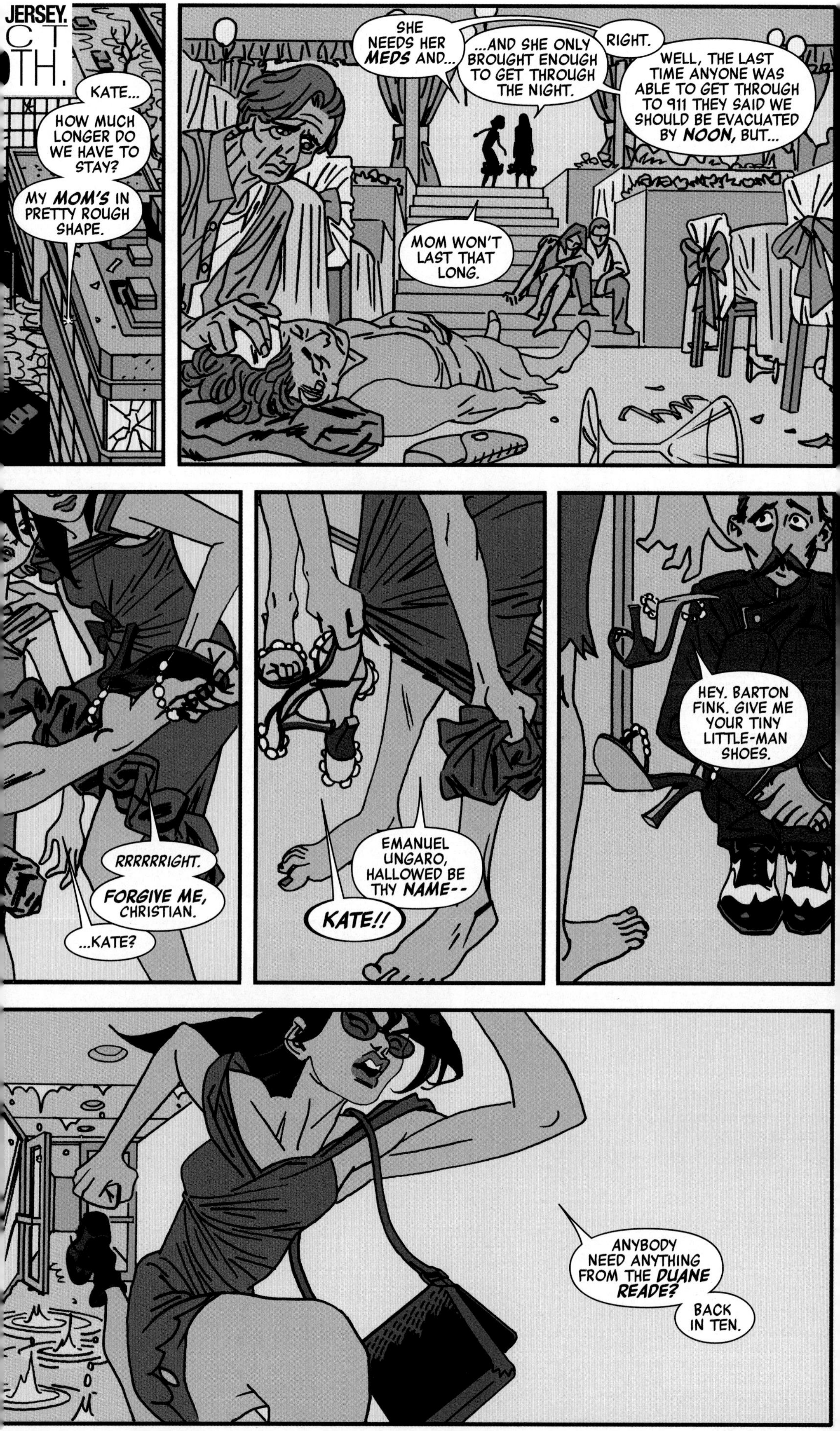
JERSEY.
C T
TH.
KATE...
HOW MUCH LONGER DO WE HAVE TO STAY?
MY MOM'S IN PRETTY ROUGH SHAPE.
SHE NEEDS HER MEDS AND...
...AND SHE ONLY BROUGHT ENOUGH TO GET THROUGH THE NIGHT.
RIGHT.
WELL, THE LAST TIME ANYONE WAS ABLE TO GET THROUGH TO 911 THEY SAID WE SHOULD BE EVACUATED BY NOON, BUT...
MOM WON'T LAST THAT LONG.
RRRRRRIGHT.
FORGIVE ME, CHRISTIAN.
...KATE?
EMANUEL UNGARO, HALLOWED BE THY NAME--
KATE!!
HEY. BARTON FINK. GIVE ME YOUR TINY LITTLE-MAN SHOES.
ANYBODY NEED ANYTHING FROM THE DUANE READE?
BACK IN TEN.

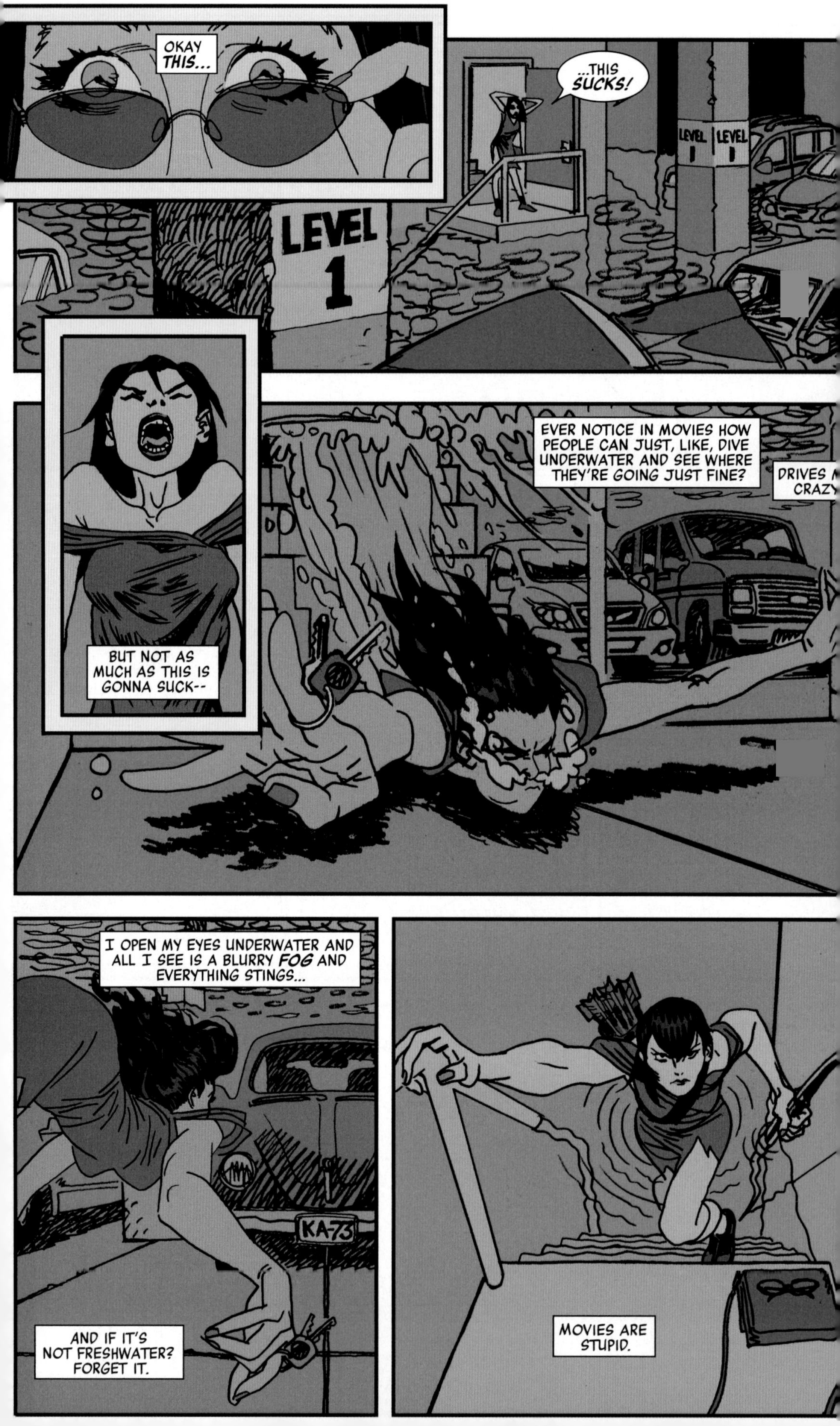
OKAY THIS...
...THIS SUCKS!
LEVEL 1
LEVEL 1
LEVEL 1
BUT NOT AS MUCH AS THIS IS GONNA SUCK--
EVER NOTICE IN MOVIES HOW PEOPLE CAN JUST, LIKE, DIVE UNDERWATER AND SEE WHERE THEY'RE GOING JUST FINE?
I OPEN MY EYES UNDERWATER AND ALL I SEE IS A BLURRY FOG AND EVERYTHING STINGS...
KA-73
AND IF IT'S NOT FRESHWATER? FORGET IT.
MOVIES ARE STUPID.

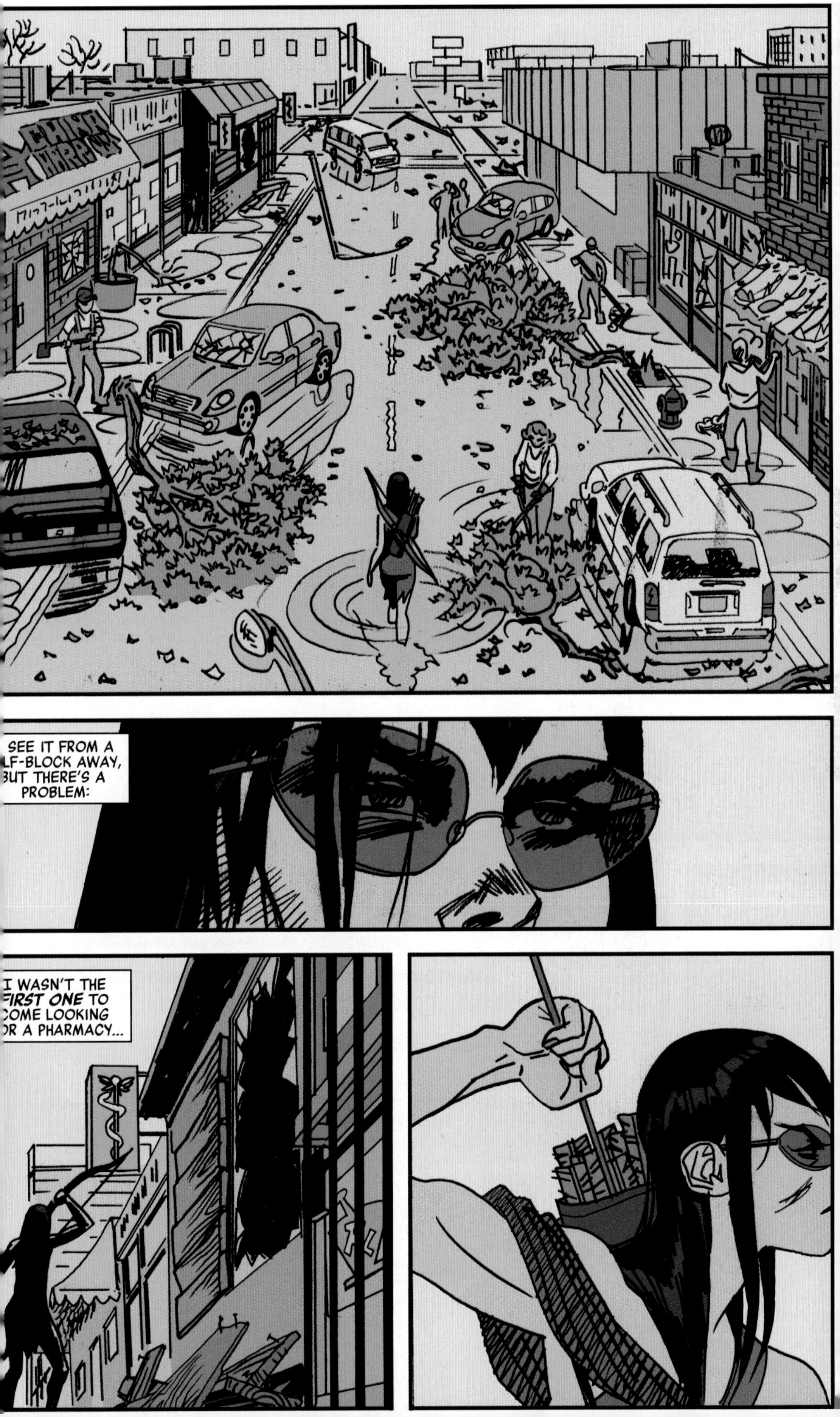
SEE IT FROM A
LF-BLOCK AWAY,
BUT THERE'S A
PROBLEM:
I WASN'T THE
FIRST ONE TO
COME LOOKING
OR A PHARMACY...

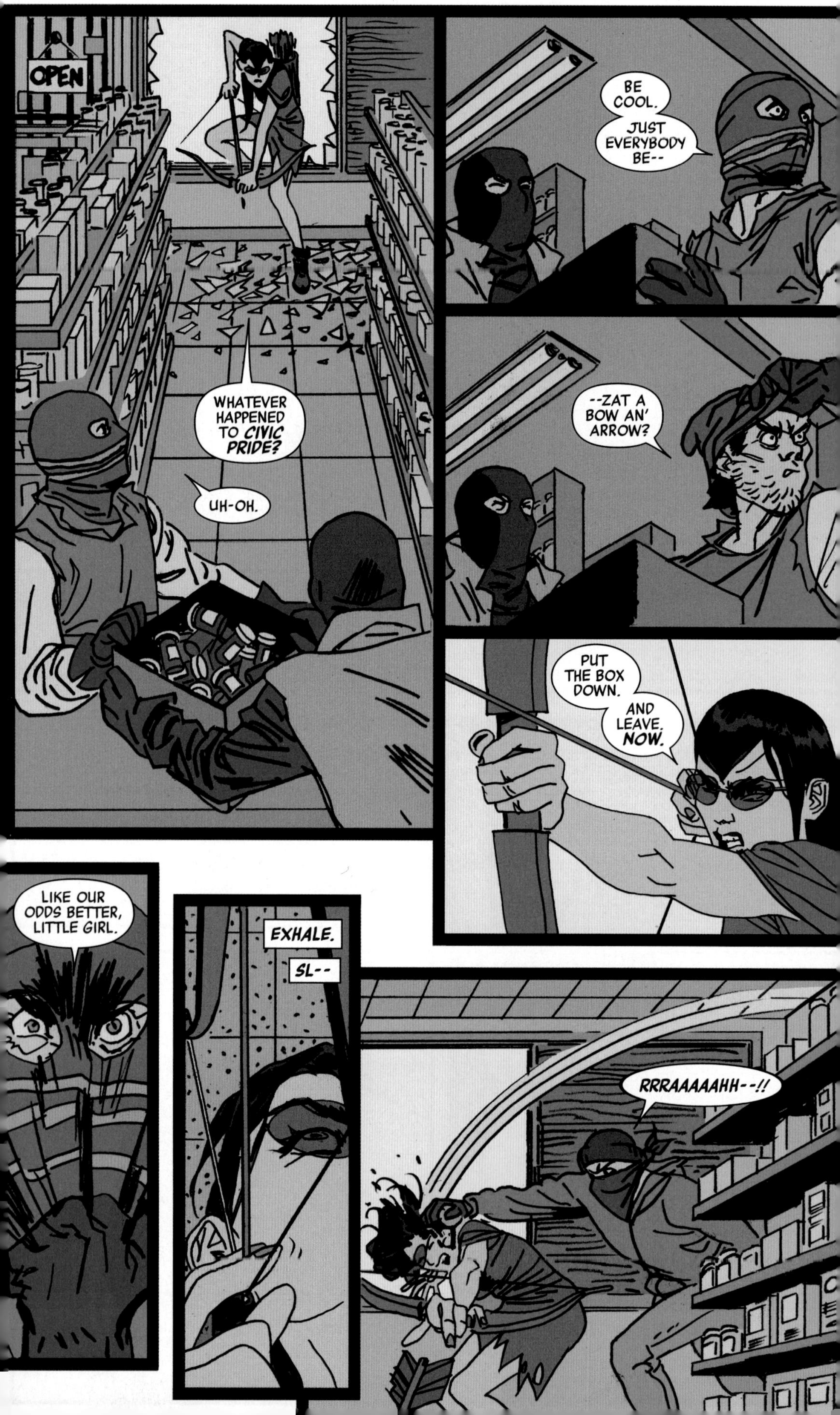
OPEN
WHATEVER HAPPENED TO CIVIC PRIDE?
UH-OH.
BE COOL.
JUST EVERYBODY BE--
--ZAT A BOW AN' ARROW?
PUT THE BOX DOWN.
AND LEAVE. NOW.
LIKE OUR ODDS BETTER, LITTLE GIRL.
EXHALE.
SL--
RRRAAAAAHH--!!

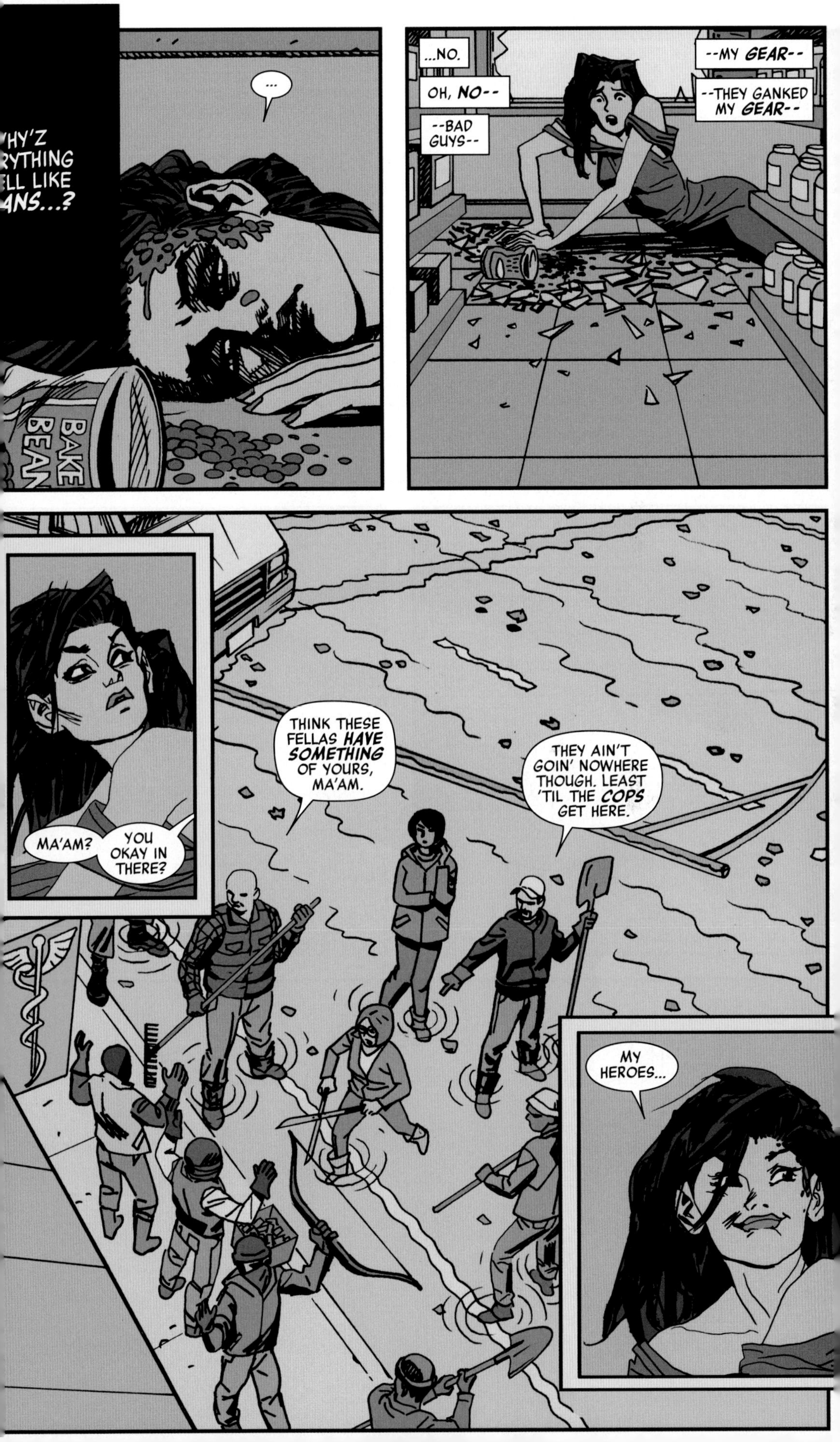

HY'Z RYTHING LL LIKE ANS...?
...
BAKE BEAN
...NO.
OH, NO--
--BAD GUYS--
--MY GEAR--
--THEY GANKED MY GEAR--
MA'AM?
YOU OKAY IN THERE?
THINK THESE FELLAS HAVE SOMETHING OF YOURS, MA'AM.
THEY AIN'T GOIN' NOWHERE THOUGH. LEAST 'TIL THE COPS GET HERE.
MY HEROES...

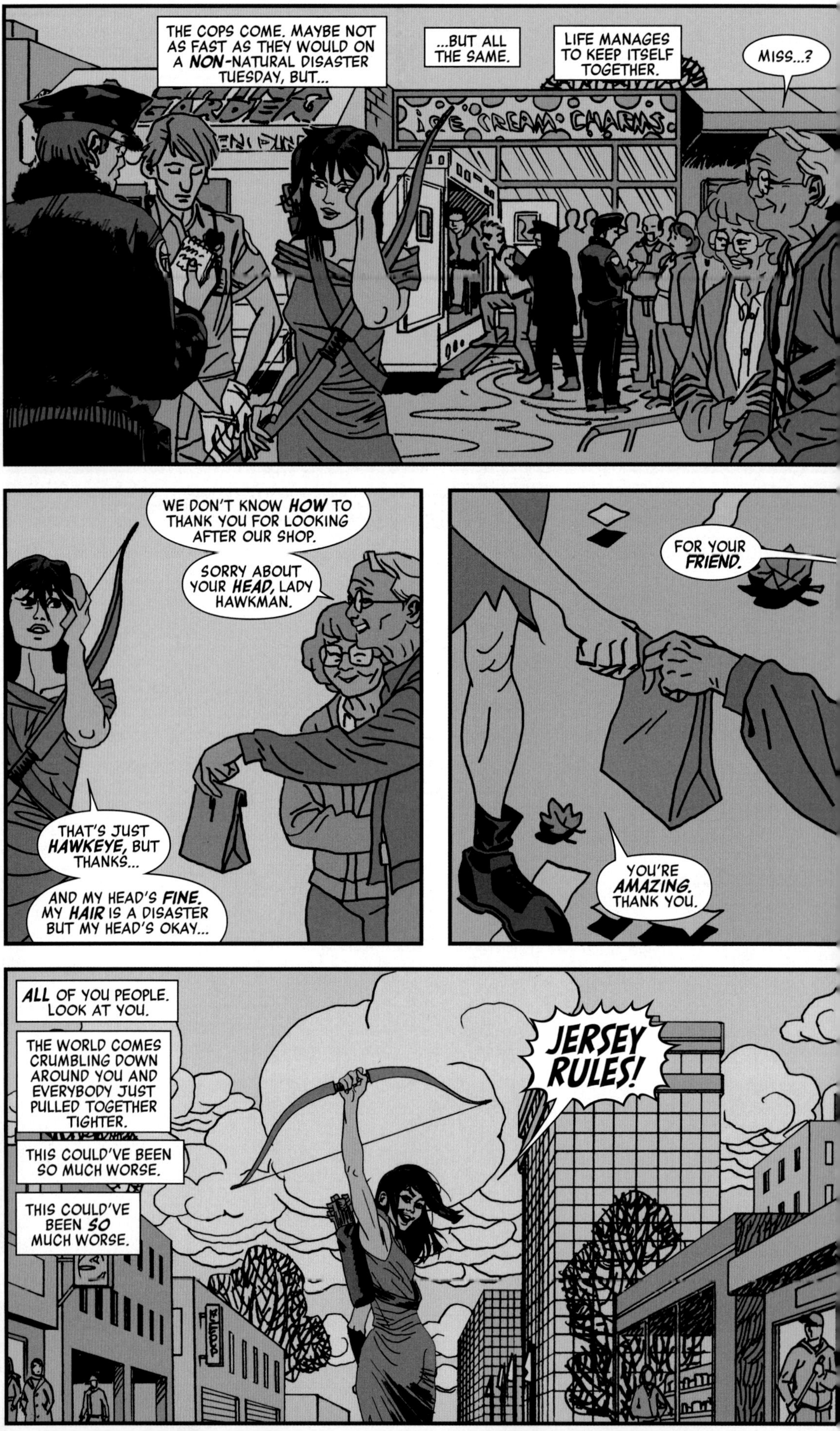
THE COPS COME. MAYBE NOT AS FAST AS THEY WOULD ON A NON-NATURAL DISASTER TUESDAY, BUT...
...BUT ALL THE SAME.
LIFE MANAGES TO KEEP ITSELF TOGETHER.
MISS...?
ICE CREAM CHARMS
WE DON'T KNOW HOW TO THANK YOU FOR LOOKING AFTER OUR SHOP.
SORRY ABOUT YOUR HEAD, LADY HAWKMAN.
THAT'S JUST HAWKEYE, BUT THANKS...
AND MY HEAD'S FINE. MY HAIR IS A DISASTER BUT MY HEAD'S OKAY...
FOR YOUR FRIEND.
YOU'RE AMAZING. THANK YOU.
ALL OF YOU PEOPLE. LOOK AT YOU.
THE WORLD COMES CRUMBLING DOWN AROUND YOU AND EVERYBODY JUST PULLED TOGETHER TIGHTER.
THIS COULD'VE BEEN SO MUCH WORSE.
THIS COULD'VE BEEN SO MUCH WORSE.
JERSEY RULES!

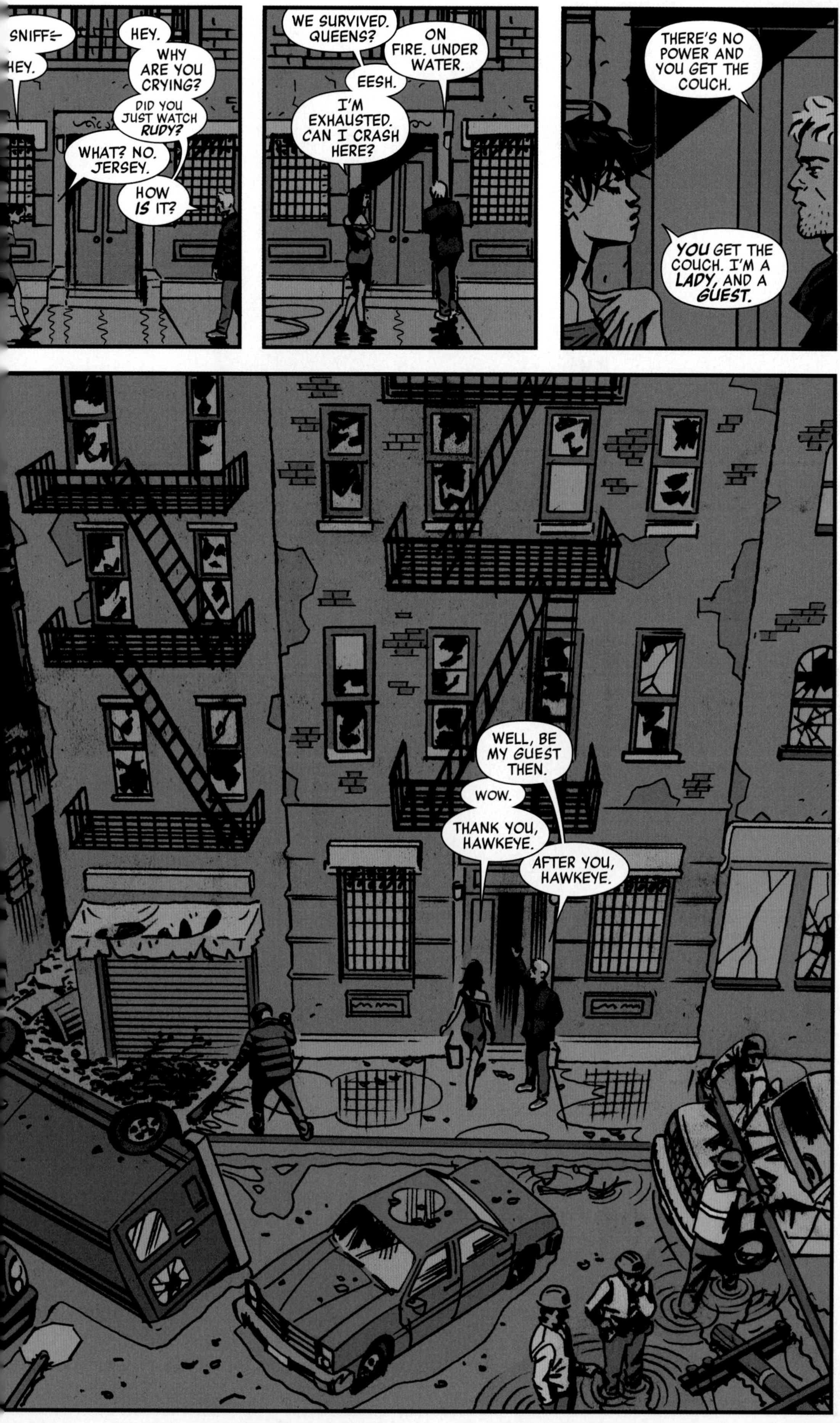
SNIFF
HEY.
HEY.
WHY ARE YOU CRYING?
DID YOU JUST WATCH RUDY?
WHAT? NO. JERSEY.
HOW IS IT?
WE SURVIVED. QUEENS?
ON FIRE. UNDER WATER.
EESH.
I'M EXHAUSTED. CAN I CRASH HERE?
THERE'S NO POWER AND YOU GET THE COUCH.
YOU GET THE COUCH. I'M A LADY, AND A GUEST.
WELL, BE MY GUEST THEN.
WOW.
THANK YOU, HAWKEYE.
AFTER YOU, HAWKEYE.

6

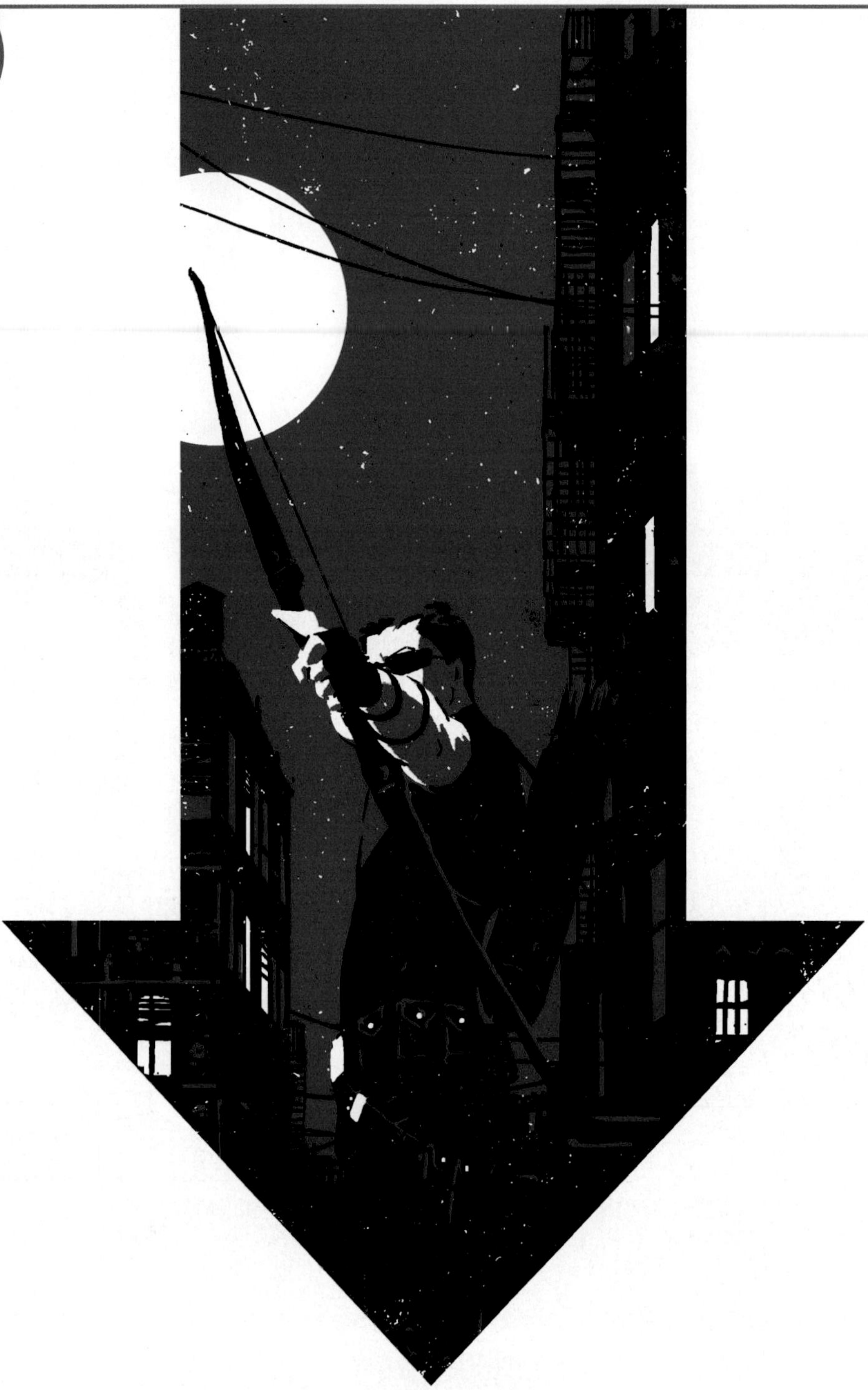

Okay...

...this
looks
bad.

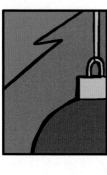

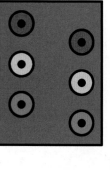

I don't know
what to do
with any of
this stuff.

It's all
knots.

crew
this.

C'MON,
CLINT.

I'M JUST
GONNA *CUT*
THE GREEN
WIRE.

CUT
IT?

WHAT?

THERE'S
PROBABLY
A BETTER
WAY THAN
THIS.

PROBABLY.
AND YET.

CLINT--

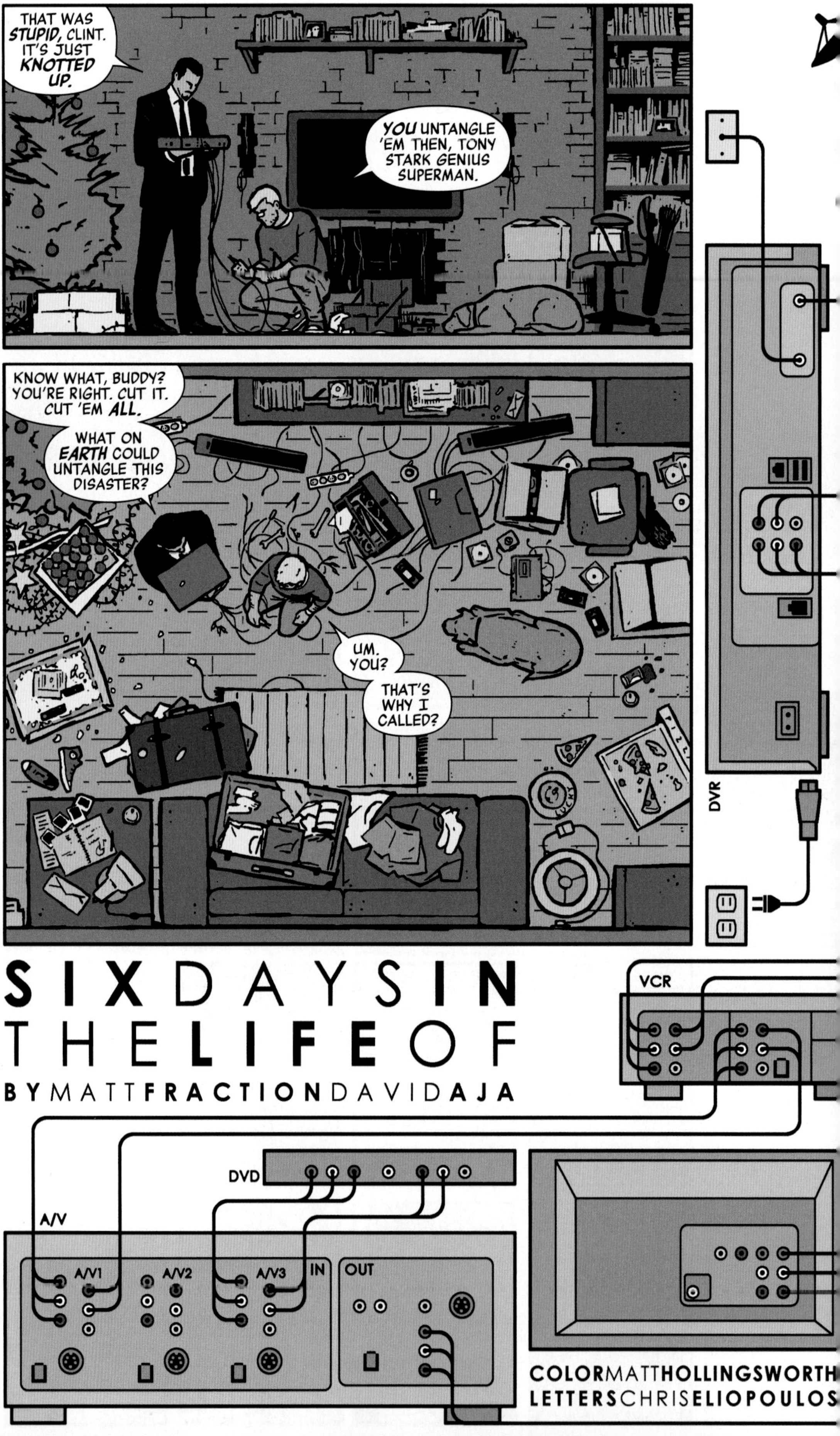
THAT WAS STUPID, CLINT. IT'S JUST KNOTTED UP.
YOU UNTANGLE 'EM THEN, TONY STARK GENIUS SUPERMAN.
KNOW WHAT, BUDDY? YOU'RE RIGHT. CUT IT. CUT 'EM ALL.
WHAT ON EARTH COULD UNTANGLE THIS DISASTER?
UM. YOU?
THAT'S WHY I CALLED?
DVR
VCR
SIX DAYS IN THE LIFE OF
BY MATT FRACTION DAVID AJA
DVD
A/V
A/V1
A/V2
A/V3
IN
OUT
COLOR MATT HOLLINGSWORTH
LETTERS CHRIS ELIOPOULOS

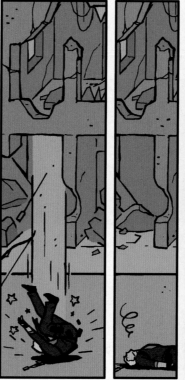

AWW, MAN.

DID I MISS CHRISTMAS AGAIN?

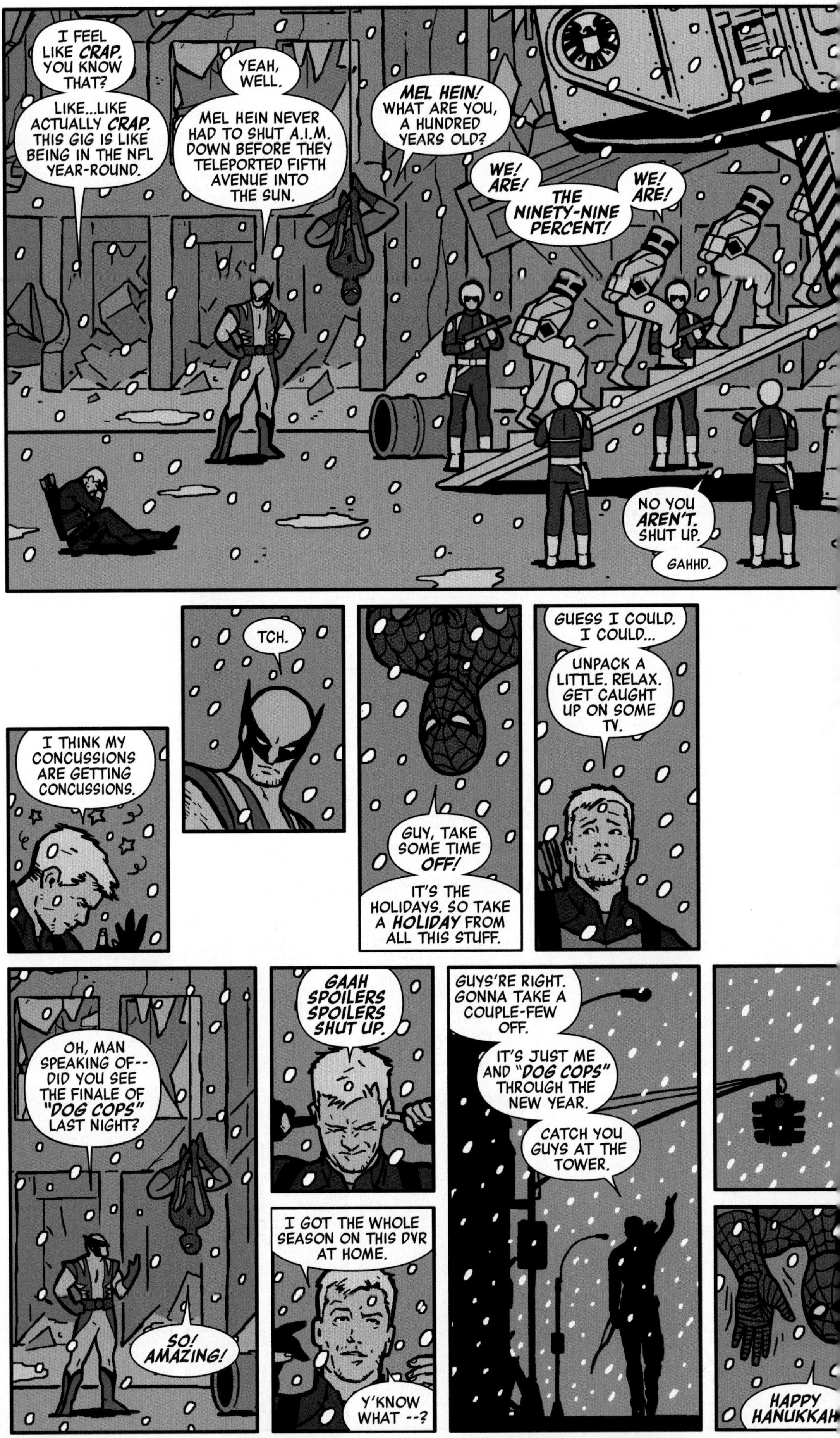
I FEEL LIKE CRAP. YOU KNOW THAT?
LIKE...LIKE ACTUALLY CRAP. THIS GIG IS LIKE BEING IN THE NFL YEAR-ROUND.
YEAH, WELL.
MEL HEIN NEVER HAD TO SHUT A.I.M. DOWN BEFORE THEY TELEPORTED FIFTH AVENUE INTO THE SUN.
MEL HEIN! WHAT ARE YOU, A HUNDRED YEARS OLD?
WE! ARE!
THE NINETY-NINE PERCENT!
WE! ARE!
NO YOU AREN'T. SHUT UP.
GAHHD.
I THINK MY CONCUSSIONS ARE GETTING CONCUSSIONS.
TCH.
GUY, TAKE SOME TIME OFF!
IT'S THE HOLIDAYS. SO TAKE A HOLIDAY FROM ALL THIS STUFF.
GUESS I COULD. I COULD...
UNPACK A LITTLE. RELAX. GET CAUGHT UP ON SOME TV.
OH, MAN SPEAKING OF-- DID YOU SEE THE FINALE OF "DOG COPS" LAST NIGHT?
SO! AMAZING!
GAAH SPOILERS SPOILERS SHUT UP.
I GOT THE WHOLE SEASON ON THIS DVR AT HOME.
Y'KNOW WHAT --?
GUYS'RE RIGHT. GONNA TAKE A COUPLE-FEW OFF.
IT'S JUST ME AND "DOG COPS" THROUGH THE NEW YEAR.
CATCH YOU GUYS AT THE TOWER.
HAPPY HANUKKAH

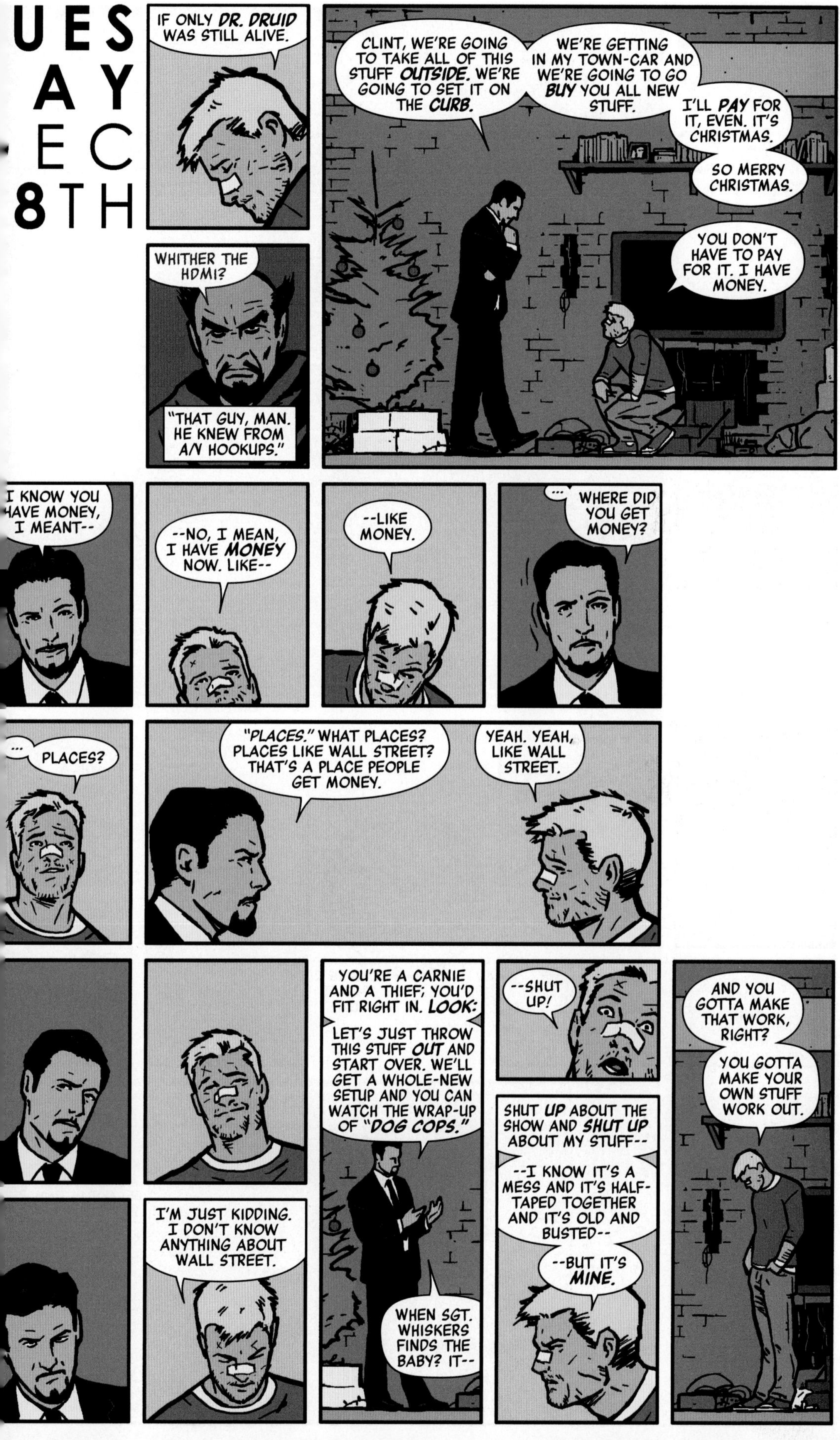
UES
AY
EC
8TH
IF ONLY DR. DRUID WAS STILL ALIVE.
WHITHER THE HDMI?
"THAT GUY, MAN. HE KNEW FROM A/V HOOKUPS."
CLINT, WE'RE GOING TO TAKE ALL OF THIS STUFF OUTSIDE. WE'RE GOING TO SET IT ON THE CURB.
WE'RE GETTING IN MY TOWN-CAR AND WE'RE GOING TO GO BUY YOU ALL NEW STUFF.
I'LL PAY FOR IT, EVEN. IT'S CHRISTMAS.
SO MERRY CHRISTMAS.
YOU DON'T HAVE TO PAY FOR IT. I HAVE MONEY.
I KNOW YOU HAVE MONEY, I MEANT--
--NO, I MEAN, I HAVE MONEY NOW. LIKE--
--LIKE MONEY.
...
WHERE DID YOU GET MONEY?
...
PLACES?
"PLACES." WHAT PLACES? PLACES LIKE WALL STREET? THAT'S A PLACE PEOPLE GET MONEY.
YEAH. YEAH, LIKE WALL STREET.
I'M JUST KIDDING. I DON'T KNOW ANYTHING ABOUT WALL STREET.
YOU'RE A CARNIE AND A THIEF; YOU'D FIT RIGHT IN. LOOK:
LET'S JUST THROW THIS STUFF OUT AND START OVER. WE'LL GET A WHOLE-NEW SETUP AND YOU CAN WATCH THE WRAP-UP OF "DOG COPS."
WHEN SGT. WHISKERS FINDS THE BABY? IT--
--SHUT UP!
SHUT UP ABOUT THE SHOW AND SHUT UP ABOUT MY STUFF--
--I KNOW IT'S A MESS AND IT'S HALF-TAPED TOGETHER AND IT'S OLD AND BUSTED--
--BUT IT'S MINE.
AND YOU GOTTA MAKE THAT WORK, RIGHT?
YOU GOTTA MAKE YOUR OWN STUFF WORK OUT.

MON DAY DEC 17TH

OKAY, CLINT.

YOU CAN DO THIS.

You can actually move in to your apartment like a grown-ass man.

OKAY.

BOXES.

START WITH ALL OF THE BOXES.

DVR

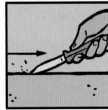

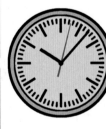

HEY, MY *LASERDISCS!*

BLADE

WHOA!

I *LOVE* THAT MOVIE--

NOK NOK

...ALL THESE MOMENTS WILL BE LOST IN TIME LIKE TEARS IN THE RAIN, LUCKY...

DVR

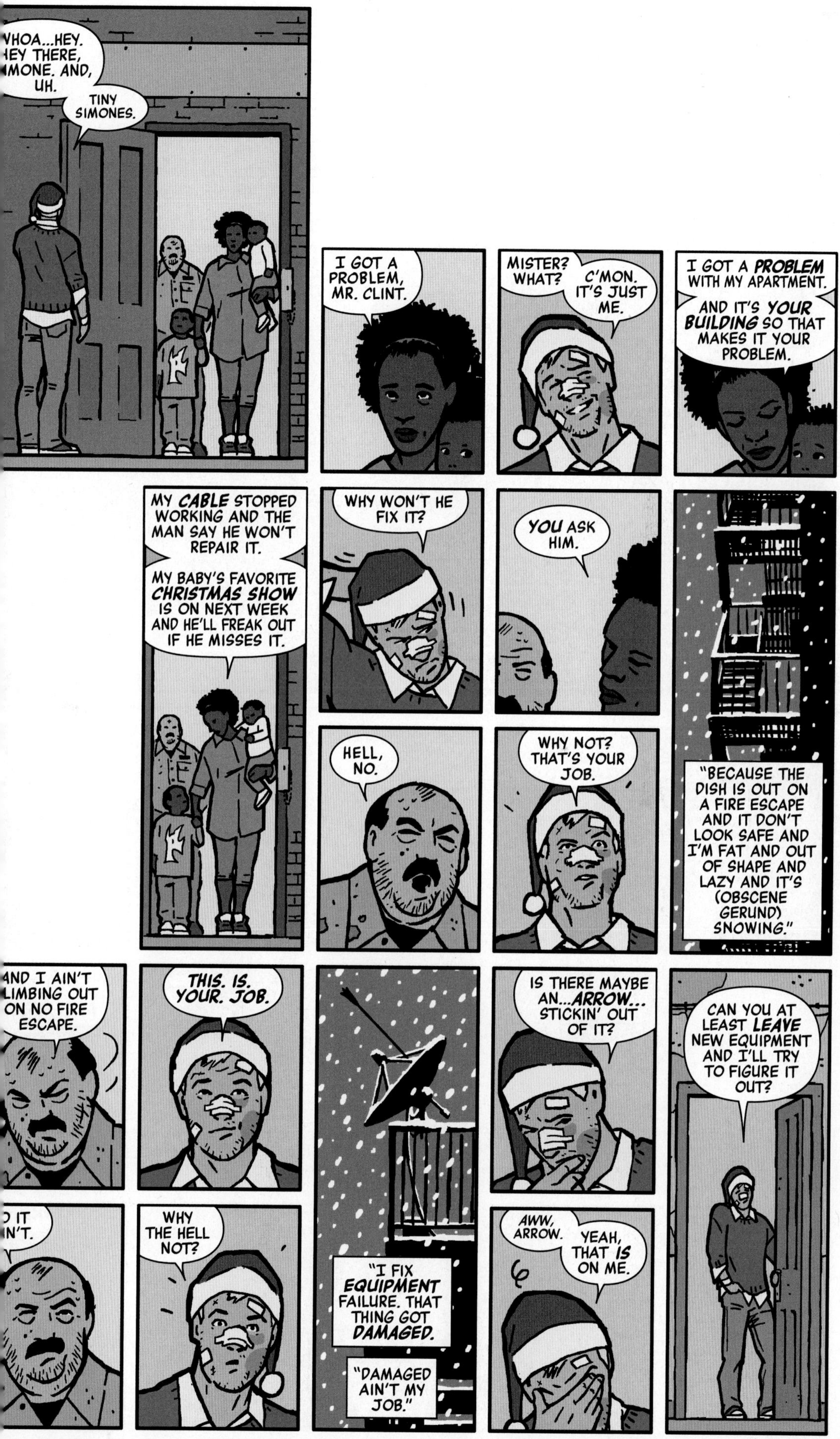
VHOA...HEY. IEY THERE, IMONE. AND, UH.
TINY SIMONES.
I GOT A PROBLEM, MR. CLINT.
MISTER? WHAT?
C'MON. IT'S JUST ME.
I GOT A PROBLEM WITH MY APARTMENT.
AND IT'S YOUR BUILDING SO THAT MAKES IT YOUR PROBLEM.
MY CABLE STOPPED WORKING AND THE MAN SAY HE WON'T REPAIR IT.
MY BABY'S FAVORITE CHRISTMAS SHOW IS ON NEXT WEEK AND HE'LL FREAK OUT IF HE MISSES IT.
WHY WON'T HE FIX IT?
YOU ASK HIM.
HELL, NO.
WHY NOT? THAT'S YOUR JOB.
"BECAUSE THE DISH IS OUT ON A FIRE ESCAPE AND IT DON'T LOOK SAFE AND I'M FAT AND OUT OF SHAPE AND LAZY AND IT'S (OBSCENE GERUND) SNOWING."
AND I AIN'T LIMBING OUT ON NO FIRE ESCAPE.
THIS. IS. YOUR. JOB.
N'T.
WHY THE HELL NOT?
"I FIX EQUIPMENT FAILURE. THAT THING GOT DAMAGED.
"DAMAGED AIN'T MY JOB."
IS THERE MAYBE AN...ARROW... STICKIN' OUT OF IT?
AWW, ARROW.
YEAH, THAT IS ON ME.
CAN YOU AT LEAST LEAVE NEW EQUIPMENT AND I'LL TRY TO FIGURE IT OUT?

FRI DAY DEC 14TH

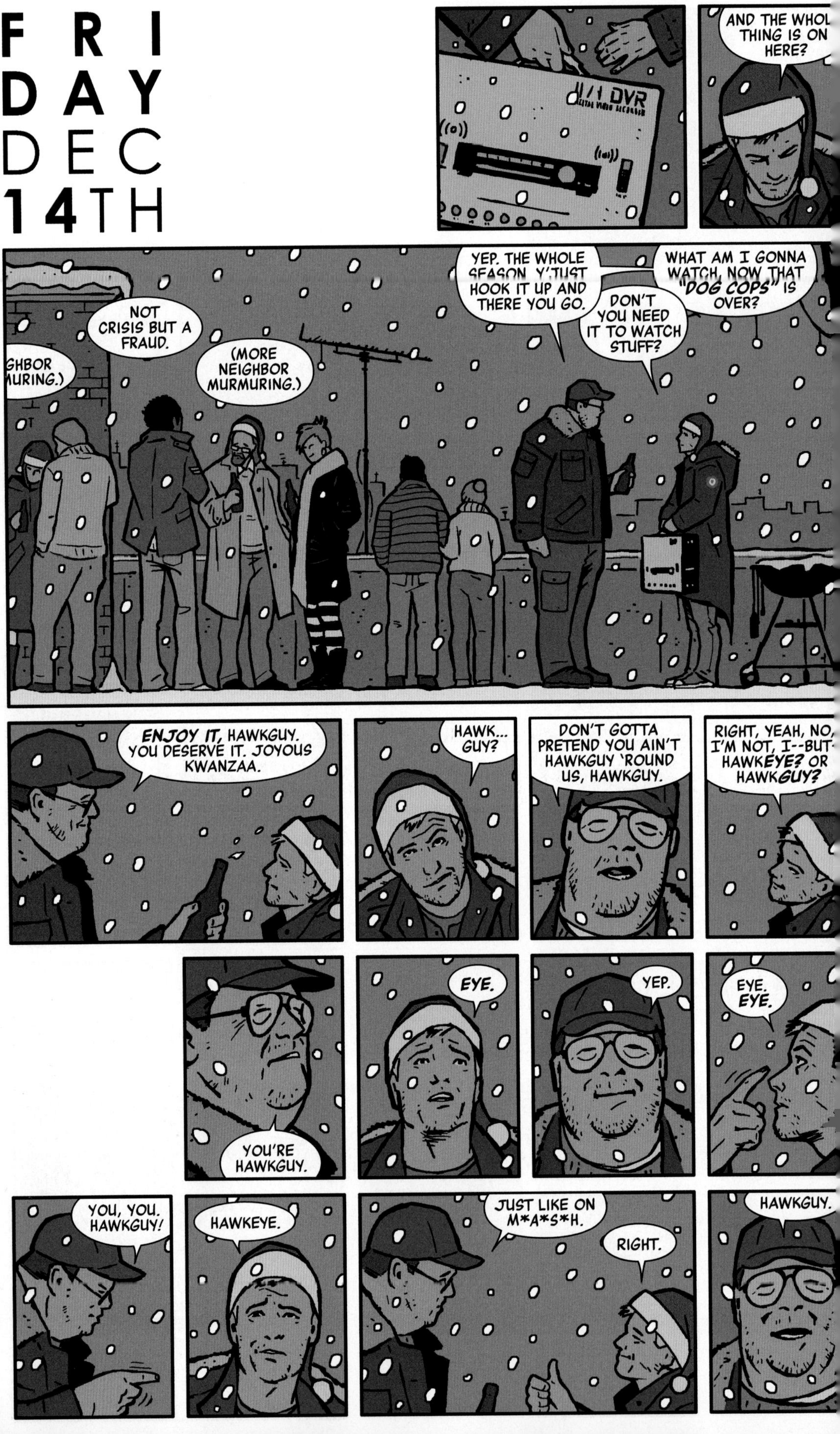

AND THE WHOL
THING IS ON
HERE?
GHBOR
MURING.)
NOT CRISIS BUT A FRAUD.
(MORE NEIGHBOR MURMURING.)
YEP. THE WHOLE SEASON. Y'JUST HOOK IT UP AND THERE YOU GO.
DON'T YOU NEED IT TO WATCH STUFF?
WHAT AM I GONNA WATCH, NOW THAT "DOG COPS" IS OVER?
ENJOY IT, HAWKGUY. YOU DESERVE IT. JOYOUS KWANZAA.
HAWK... GUY?
DON'T GOTTA PRETEND YOU AIN'T HAWKGUY 'ROUND US, HAWKGUY.
RIGHT, YEAH, NO, I'M NOT, I--BUT-- HAWKEYE? OR HAWKGUY?
YOU'RE HAWKGUY.
EYE.
YEP.
EYE. EYE.
YOU, YOU. HAWKGUY!
HAWKEYE.
JUST LIKE ON M*A*S*H.
RIGHT.
HAWKGUY.

'SUP?

YOU TALKIN' ABOUT HULK-GUY?

KWANZAA. JUST HAVIN' ONE JOYOUS-ASS KWANZAA.

WORD. YOU KNOW THERE'S GUYS DOWN FRONT WITH *BATS*, RIGHT?

HEY, BROOOOOOOOOOOOOOOOOOOOO

HE *SEE* US, BRO?

HE *SAW US,* BRO.

IS *ON NOW,* BRO.

BRO, *BRING IT,* BRO.

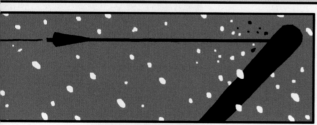

GET THE HELL AWAY FROM MY BUILDING.

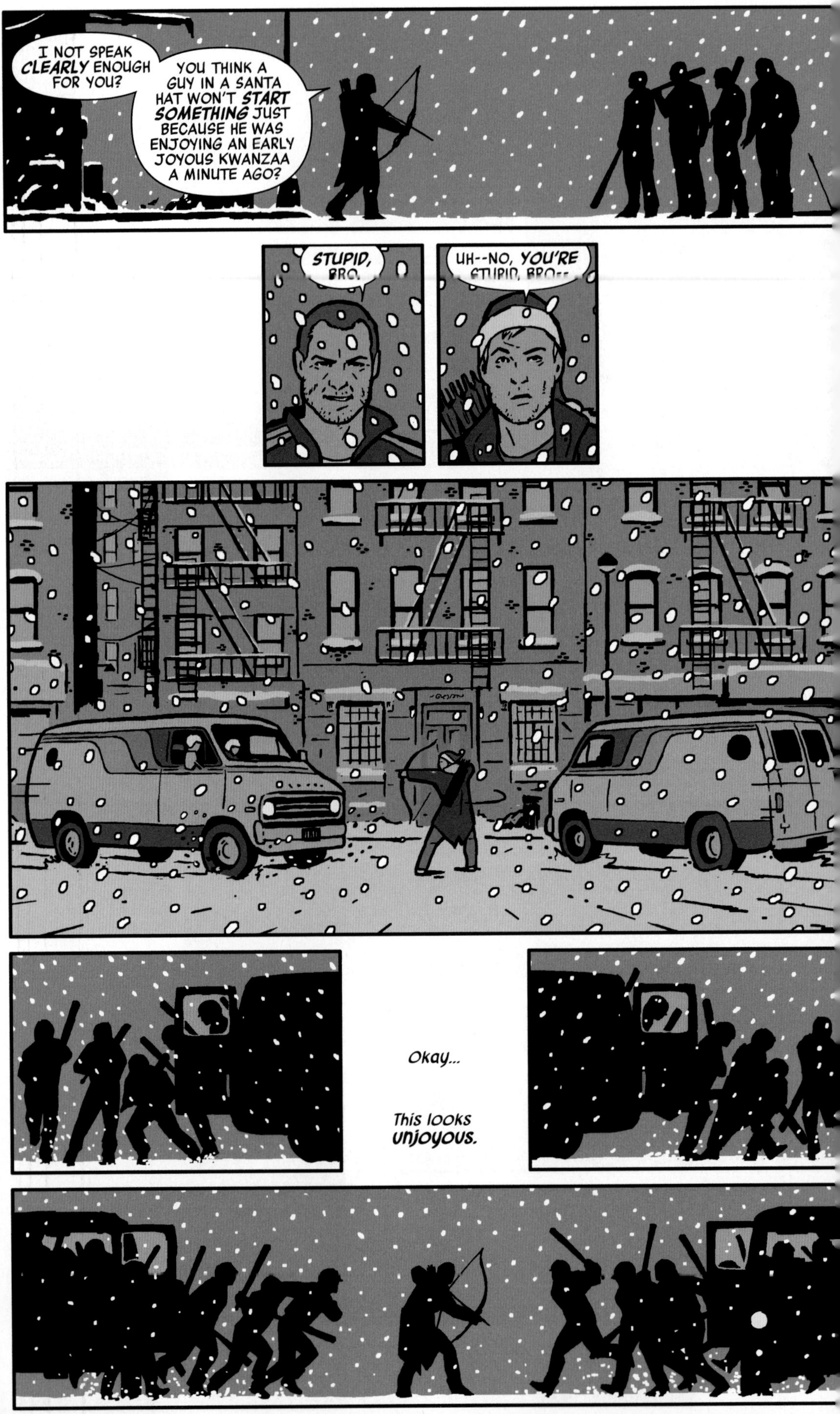
I NOT SPEAK CLEARLY ENOUGH FOR YOU?
YOU THINK A GUY IN A SANTA HAT WON'T START SOMETHING JUST BECAUSE HE WAS ENJOYING AN EARLY JOYOUS KWANZAA A MINUTE AGO?
STUPID, BRO.
UH--NO, YOU'RE STUPID, BRO--
Okay...
This looks unjoyous.

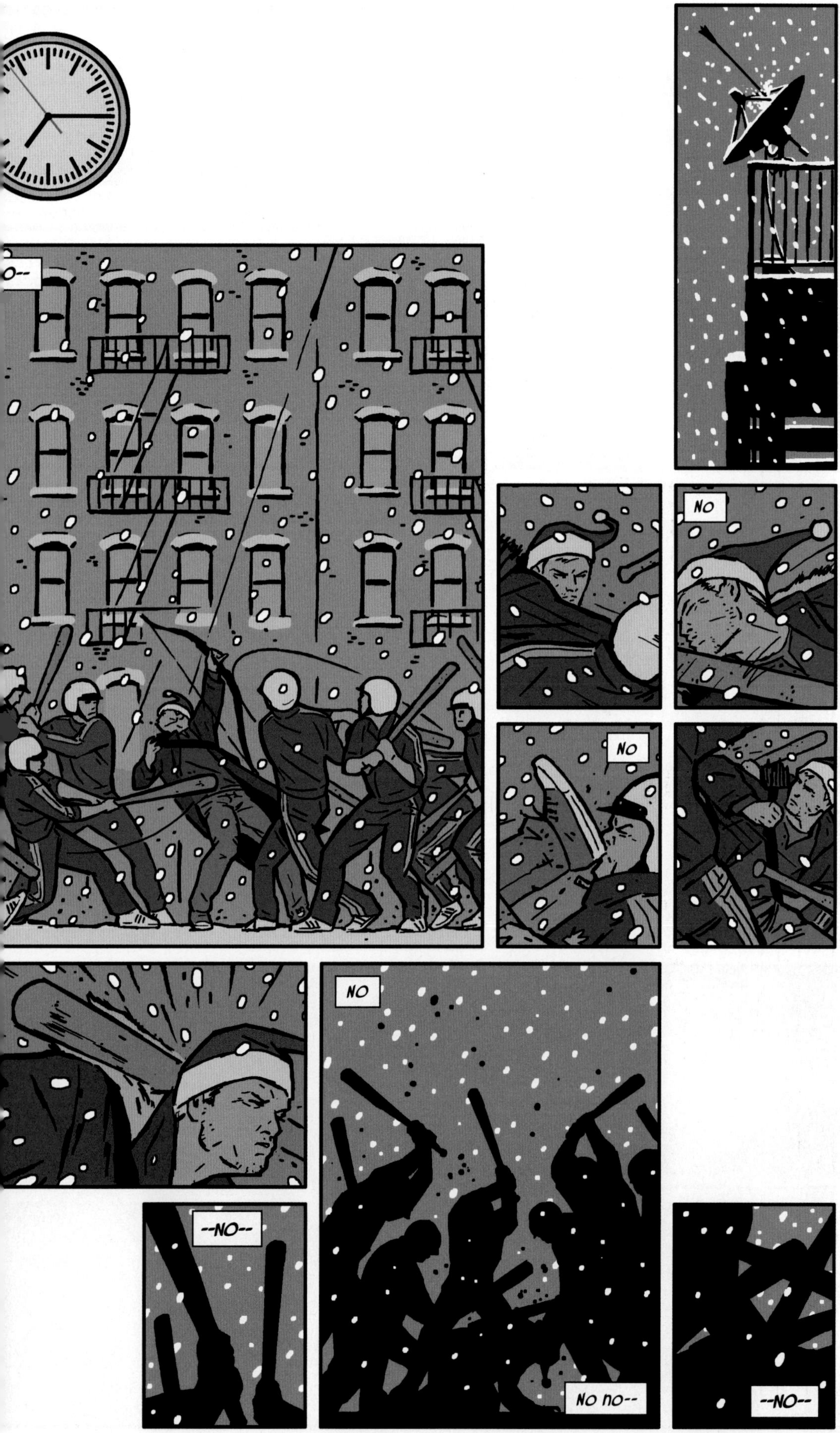

O--
NO
NO
NO
--NO--
NO NO--
--NO--

YYYYYEAH.

GUHHH.

GUH.

GUYS.

I come to an... we're in a tunn...

What's the close... tunnel to--

GUYS, BETTER GO 9E99OMCMORE GUYS.

Brooklyn Battery? They're...

...are we going back into the city?

Wait. Backtrack. Doublebuckli...

They're tryin... to confuse m...

F RI DAY DEC 14TH

After two hours or so it finally works.

When the mask comes off I am completely lost.

SAT RDA DEC 15T

GREAT!

YOU GOT MORE GUYS.

BRO.

YOU MAKE LOT OF BIG BAD PEOPLE REAL MAD BRO.

YOU STEAL OUR BUILDING.

IN OUR HOOD, BRO.

YOU AIN'T FOR MONEY.

YOU TAKE BRO'S *WIFE*, GET HER OUT OF TOWN? *FINE*, BRO. ALWAYS MORE WIFE.

BUT YOU STEAL FROM STEALERS, BRO?

IS *ONE THING* TO *FUTZ* WITH US. IS *ANOTHER* TO *FUTZ* WITH GUYS WE *WORK* FOR.

AND, BRO, THOSE ARE SOME VERY SCARY FUTZING BROS, BRO.

THEY WANT US TELL YOU, THEY *DONE WITH* YOU, BRO.

YOU GO WAY N... FUT... OFF...

OR IS *WAR*, BRO. *TWENTY-FOUR HOURS*, BRO.

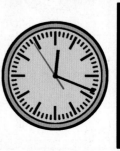

YOU *GONE* OR WE KEELING *EVERYBODY* IN YOU BUILDING, BRO.

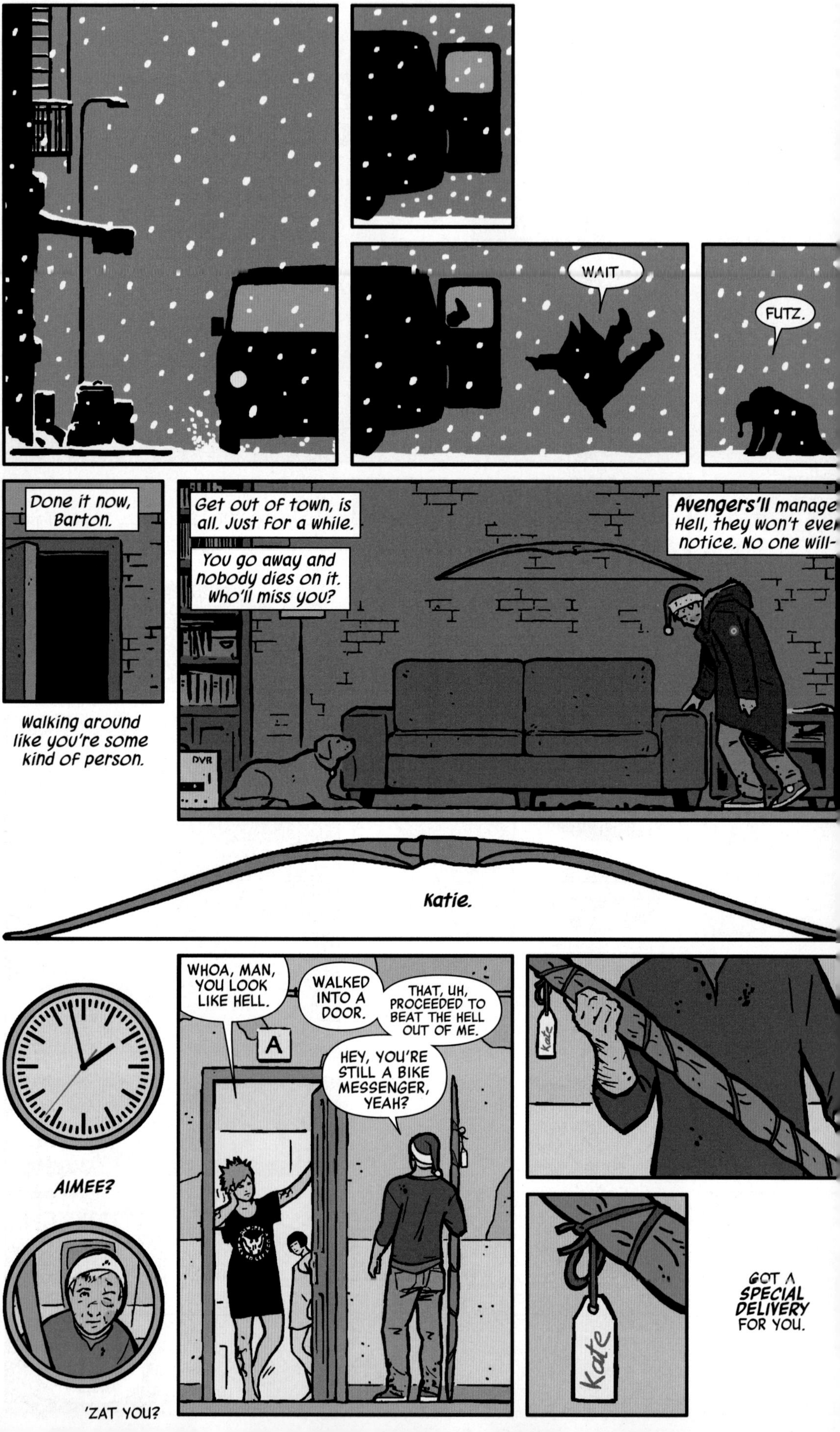
WAIT
FUTZ.
Done it now, Barton.
Walking around like you're some kind of person.
Get out of town, is all. Just for a while.
You go away and nobody dies on it. Who'll miss you?
Avengers'll manage
Hell, they won't eve
notice. No one will-
DVR
Katie.
AIMEE?
'ZAT YOU?
A
WHOA, MAN, YOU LOOK LIKE HELL.
WALKED INTO A DOOR.
THAT, UH, PROCEEDED TO BEAT THE HELL OUT OF ME.
HEY, YOU'RE STILL A BIKE MESSENGER, YEAH?
Kate
Kate
GOT A SPECIAL DELIVERY FOR YOU.

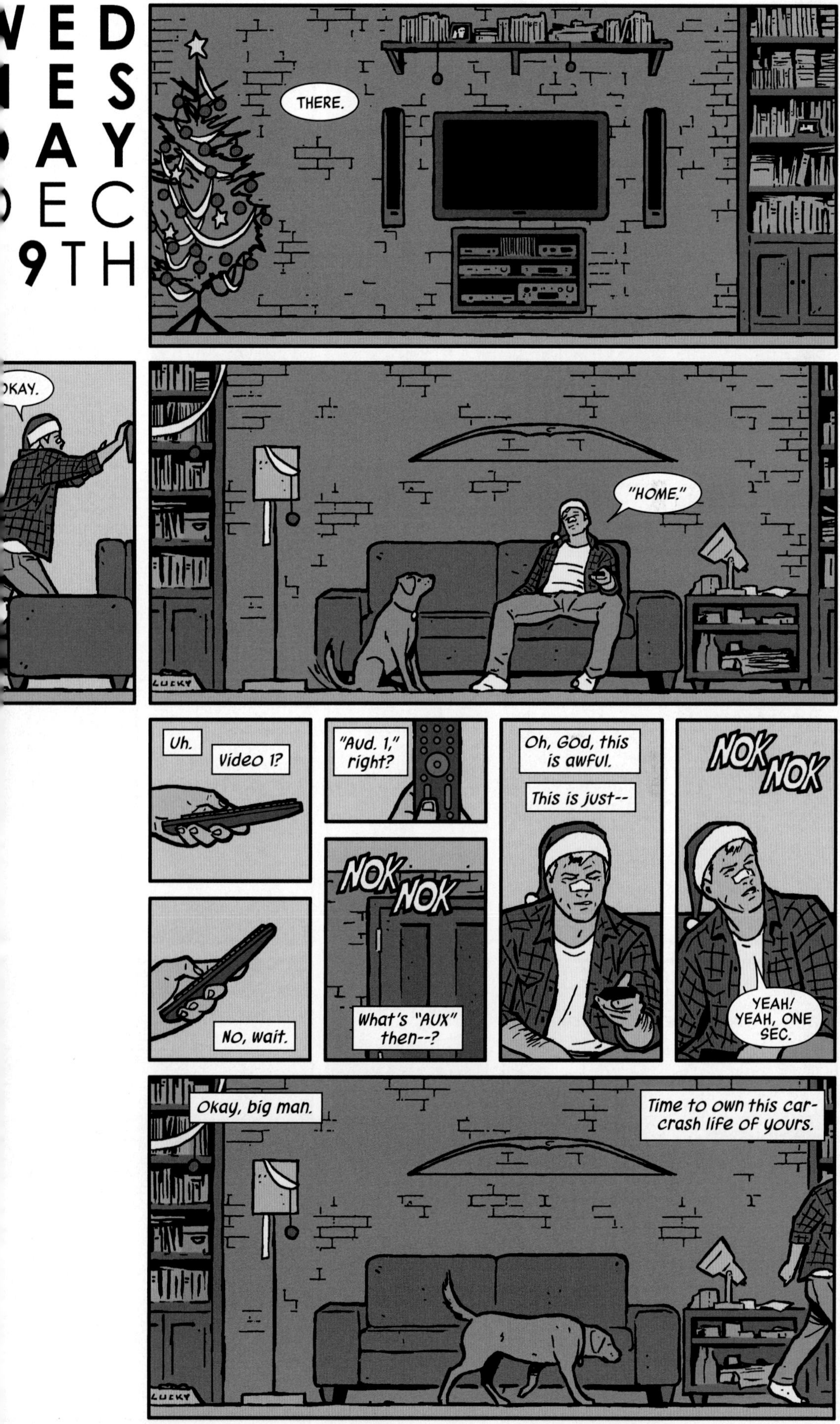
ED
ES
AY
EC
9TH
THERE.
KAY.
"HOME."
Uh.
Video 1?
No, wait.
"Aud. 1," right?
NOK NOK
What's "AUX" then--?
Oh, God, this is awful.
This is just--
NOK NOK
YEAH! YEAH, ONE SEC.
Okay, big man.
Time to own this car-crash life of yours.
LUCKY

SATU RDAY DEC 15TH

ARE YOU *KIDDING* M--

OF... WHAT?

WHAT THE *HELL* IS THE MEANING OF *THIS?*

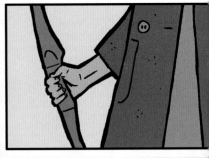

MERRY... Y'KNOW. I JUST--

I WANTED YOU TO HAVE IT.

WHERE ARE YOU GOING?

NUH... NOWHERE?

WHERE. ARE YOU. *GOING.*

THEY'RE GONNA K EVERYONE IN TH BUILDING IF I DO GO, KATIE.

I CAN'T--I SCREWED UP, I COWBOYED AROUND LIKE I *MEANT* SOMETHING TO SOMEBODY AND NOW THEY'RE GONNA KILL EVERYBODY IF I DON'T...

DON'T GO AWAY, I DON'T KNOW.

IS THAT SO.

JUST FOR A *WHILE.* JUST SO THEY FORGET. THE *AVENGERS'LL* BE FINE, EVERYBODY'LL--

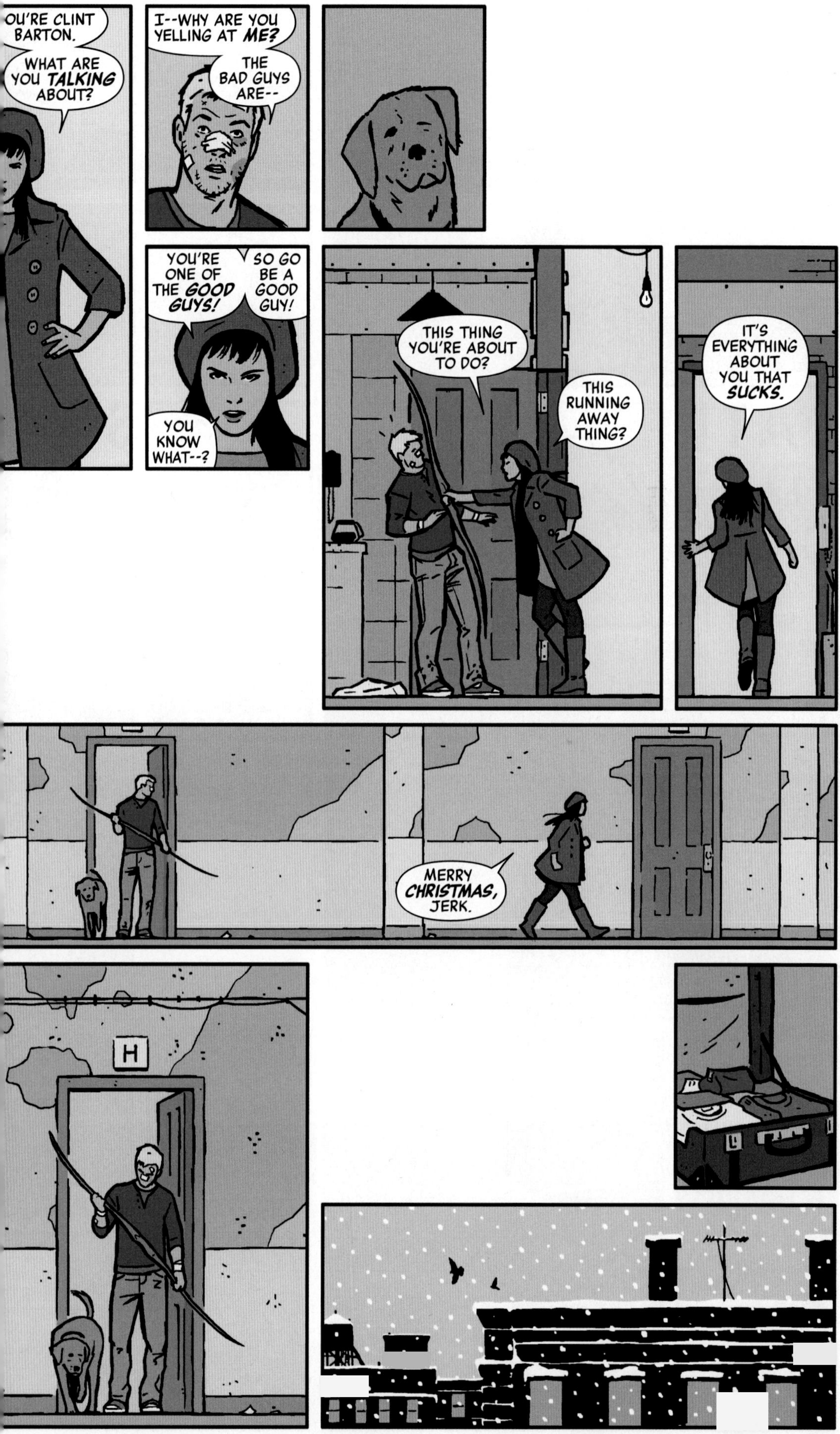
OU'RE CLINT BARTON.
WHAT ARE YOU TALKING ABOUT?
I--WHY ARE YOU YELLING AT ME?
THE BAD GUYS ARE--
YOU'RE ONE OF THE GOOD GUYS!
SO GO BE A GOOD GUY!
YOU KNOW WHAT--?
THIS THING YOU'RE ABOUT TO DO?
THIS RUNNING AWAY THING?
IT'S EVERYTHING ABOUT YOU THAT SUCKS.
MERRY CHRISTMAS, JERK.
H

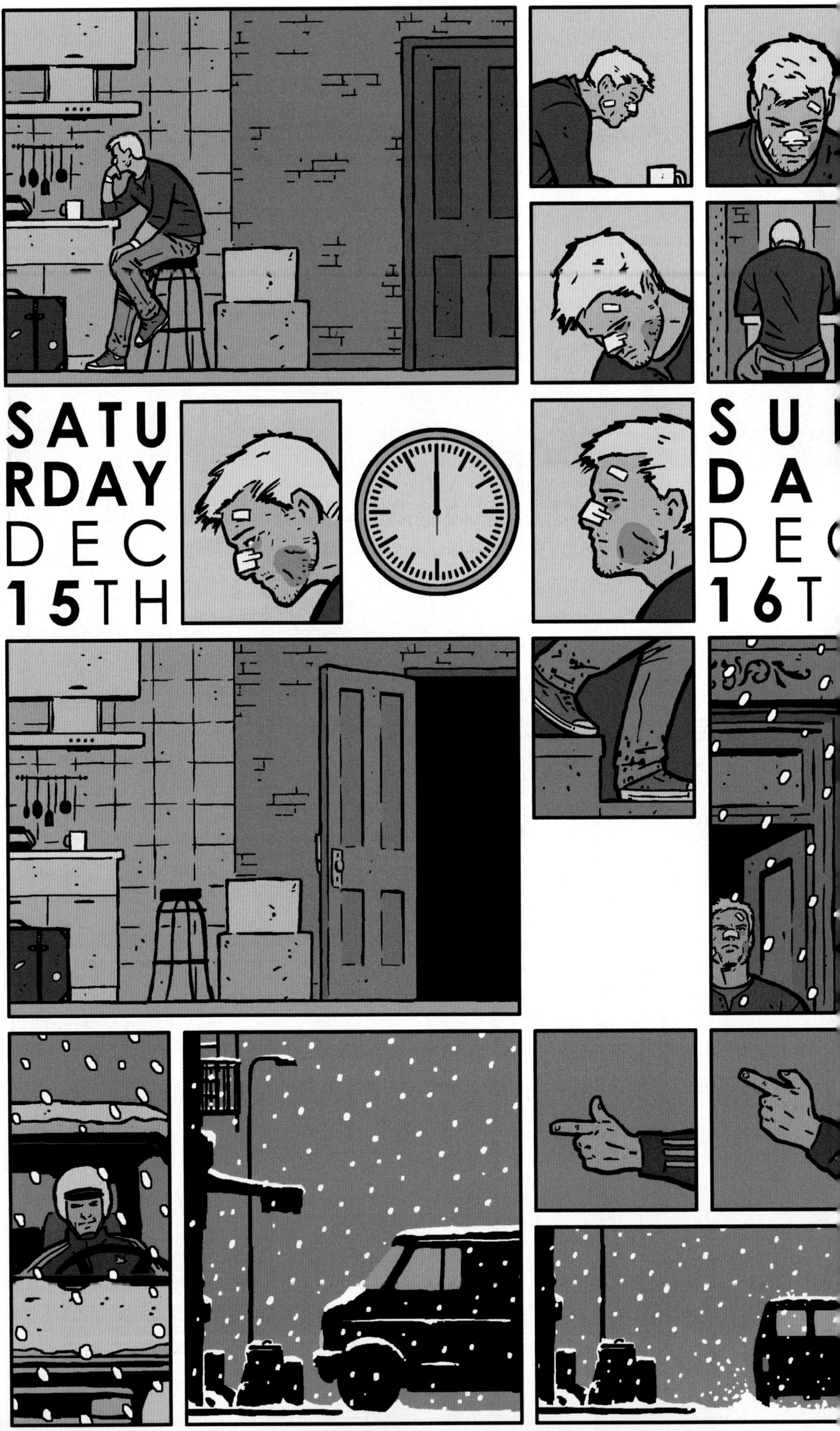
SATU
RDAY
DEC
15TH
SU
DA
DE
16T

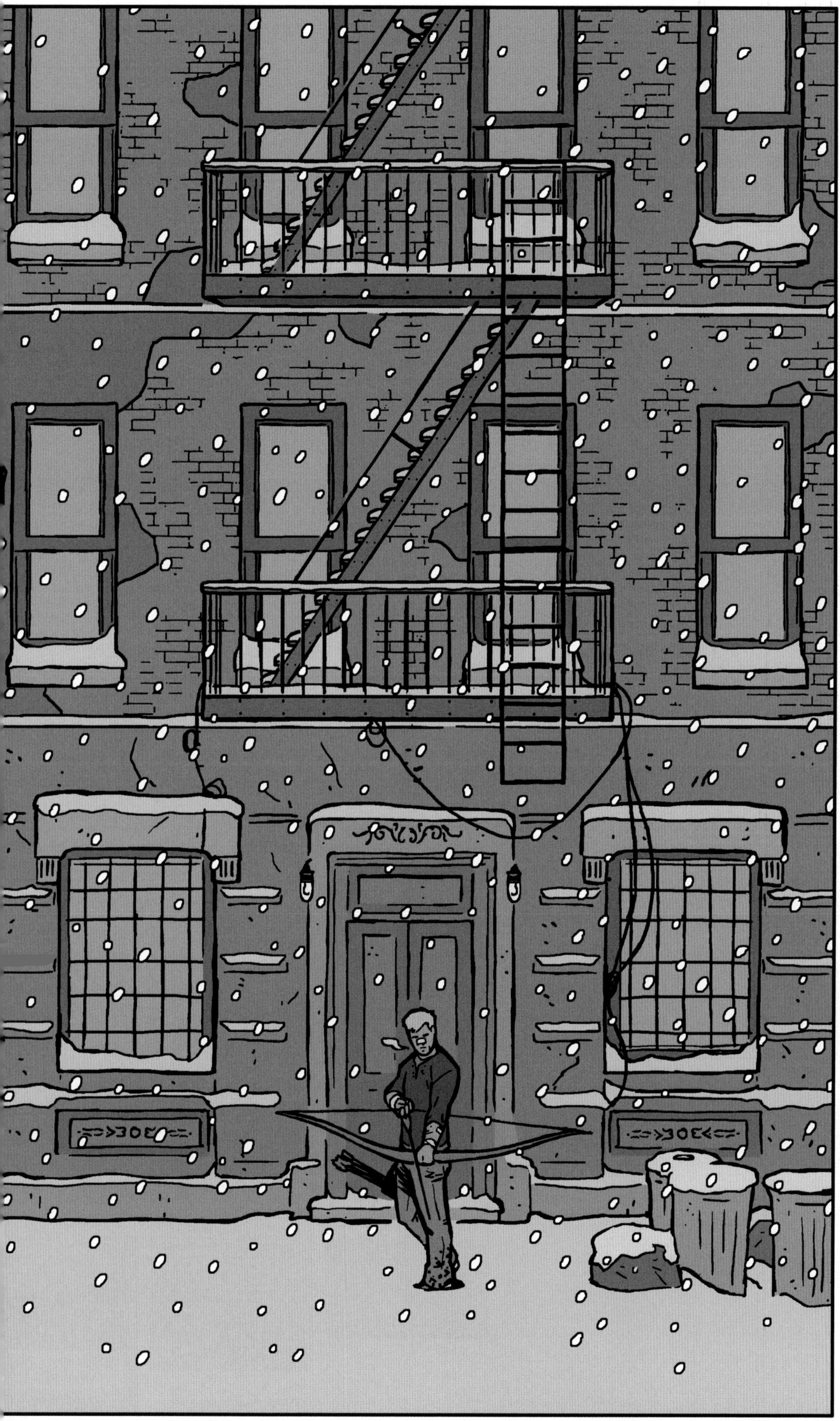

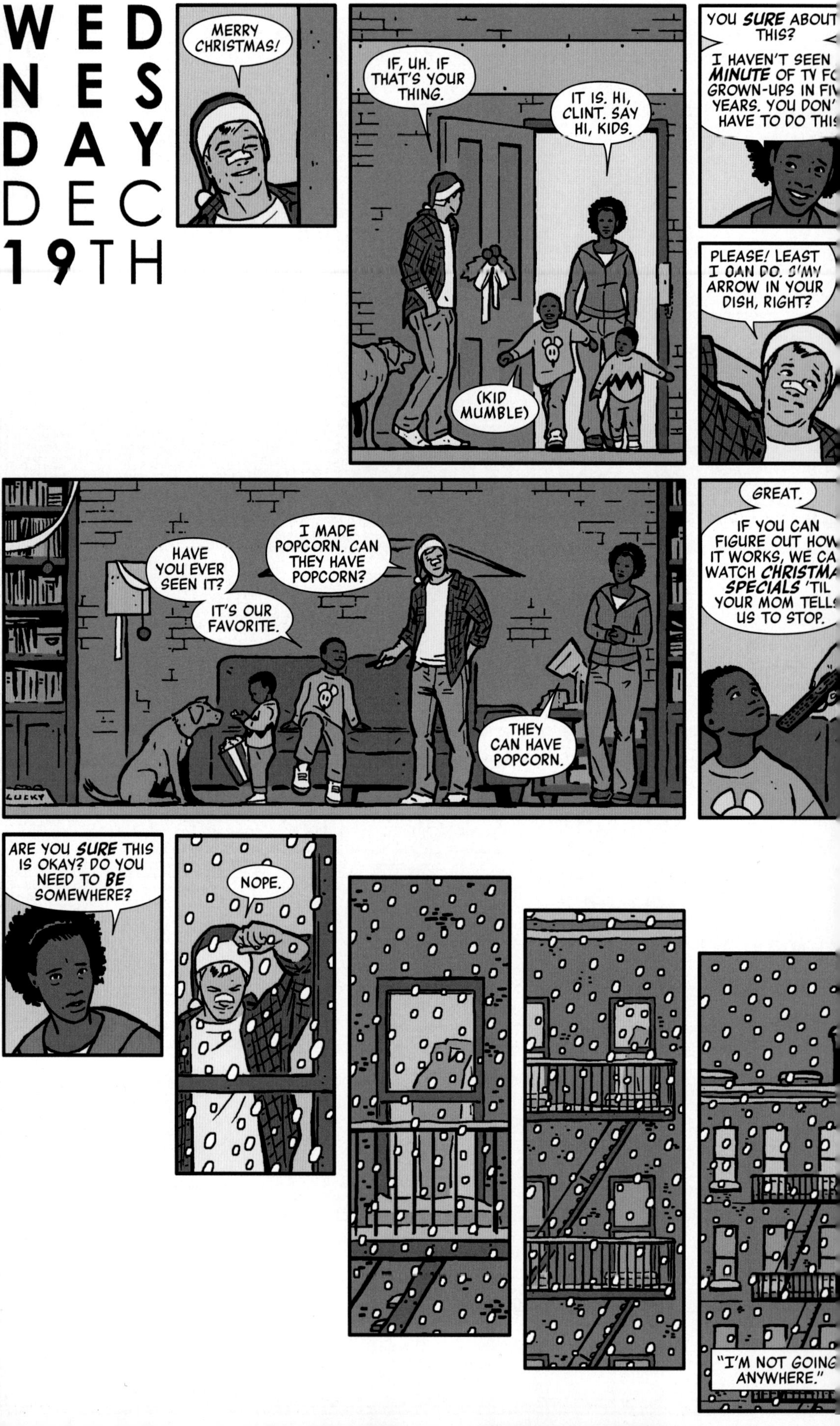
WED NES DAY DEC 19TH
MERRY CHRISTMAS!
IF, UH. IF THAT'S YOUR THING.
IT IS. HI, CLINT. SAY HI, KIDS.
(KID MUMBLE)
YOU SURE ABOUT THIS?
I HAVEN'T SEEN MINUTE OF TV FC GROWN-UPS IN FIV YEARS. YOU DON' HAVE TO DO THIS
PLEASE! LEAST I CAN DO. S'MY ARROW IN YOUR DISH, RIGHT?
HAVE YOU EVER SEEN IT?
IT'S OUR FAVORITE.
I MADE POPCORN. CAN THEY HAVE POPCORN?
THEY CAN HAVE POPCORN.
LUCKY
GREAT.
IF YOU CAN FIGURE OUT HOW IT WORKS, WE CA WATCH CHRISTMA SPECIALS 'TIL YOUR MOM TELLS US TO STOP.
ARE YOU SURE THIS IS OKAY? DO YOU NEED TO BE SOMEWHERE?
NOPE.
"I'M NOT GOING ANYWHERE."

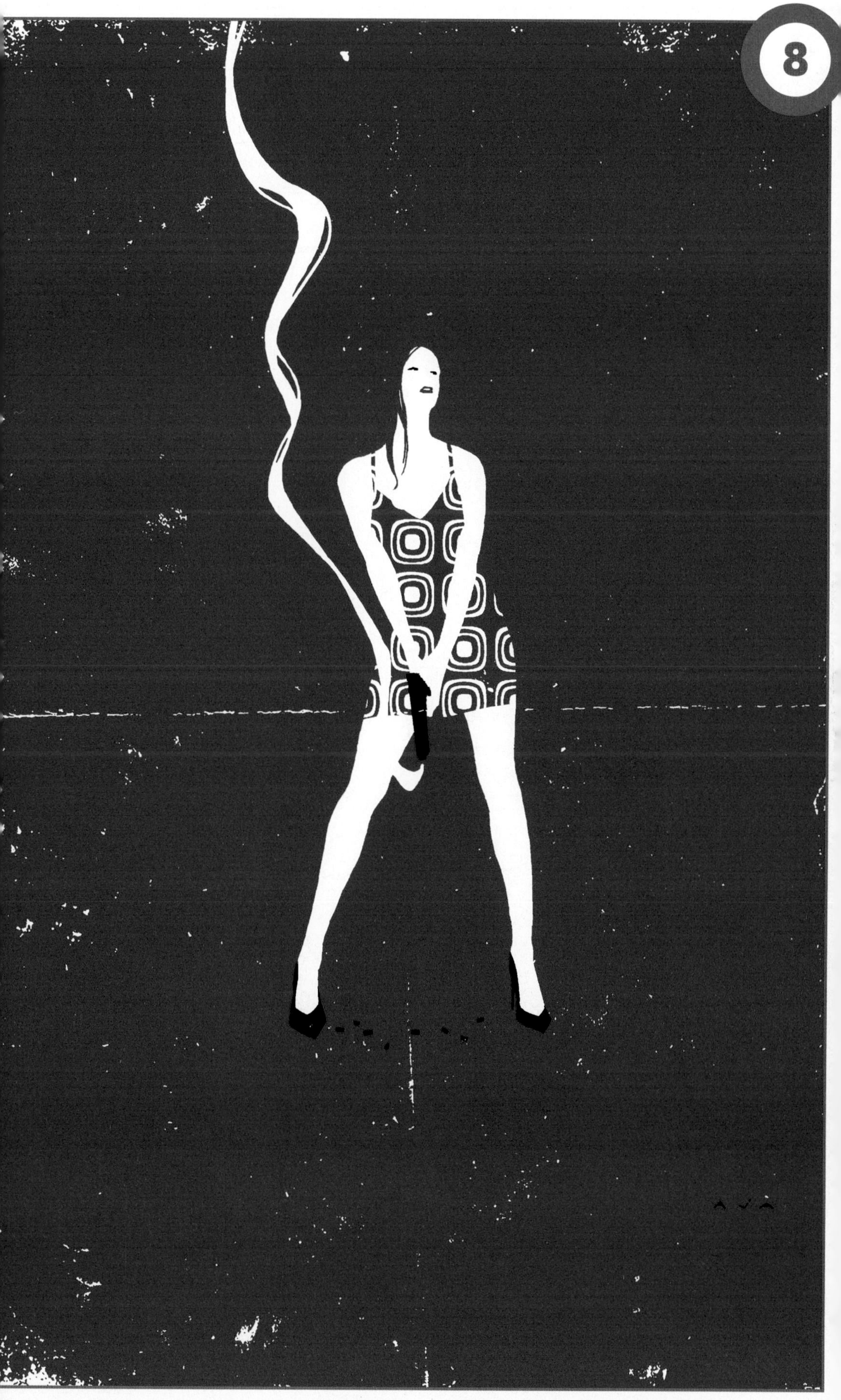
8

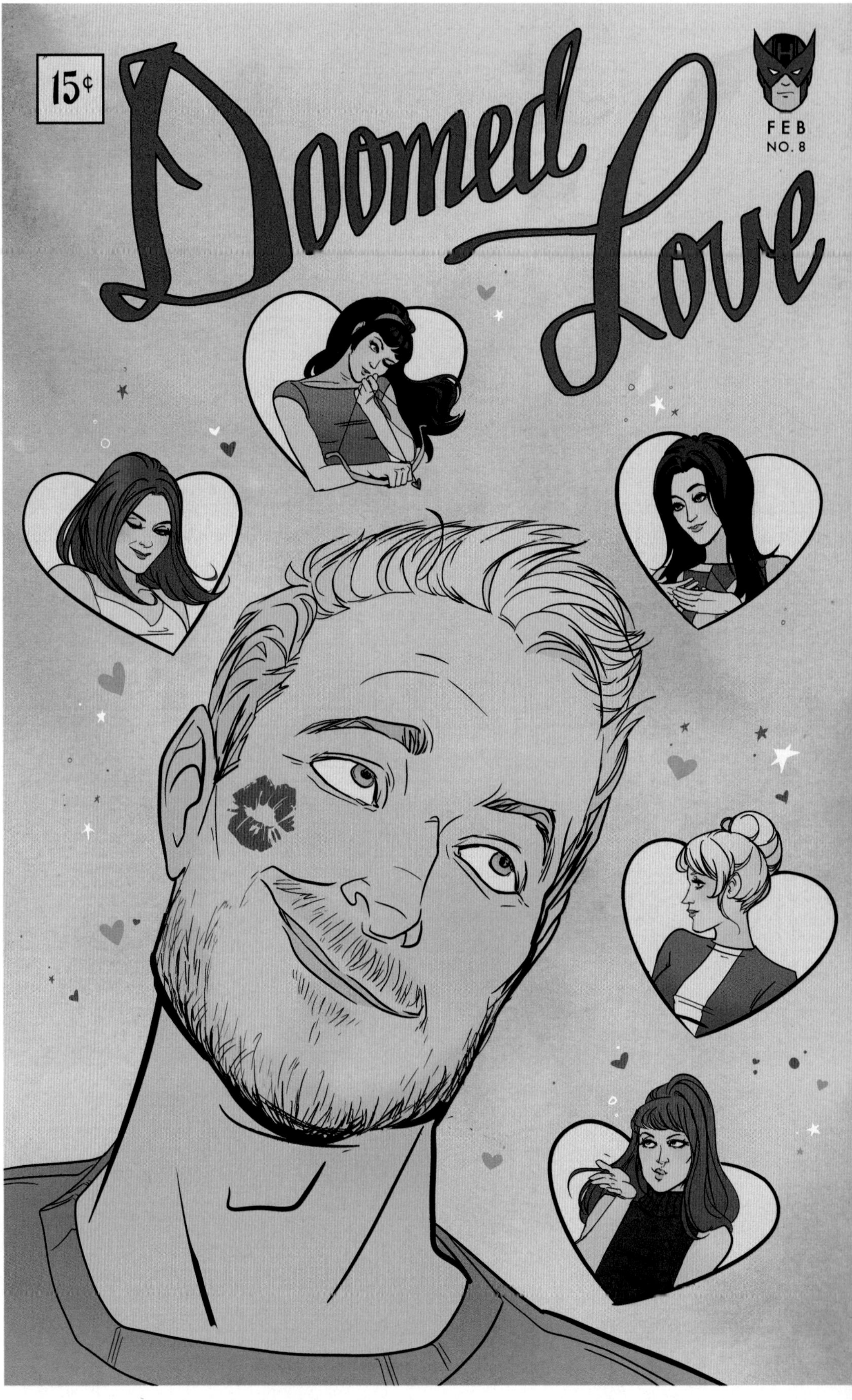

15¢
Doomed Love
FEB
NO. 8

ce upon a time...

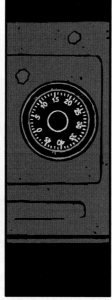

And then...

My Bad Penny

BY MATT FRACTION AND DAVID AJA WITH ANNIE WU, MATT HOLLINGSWORTH AND CHRIS ELIOPOULOS

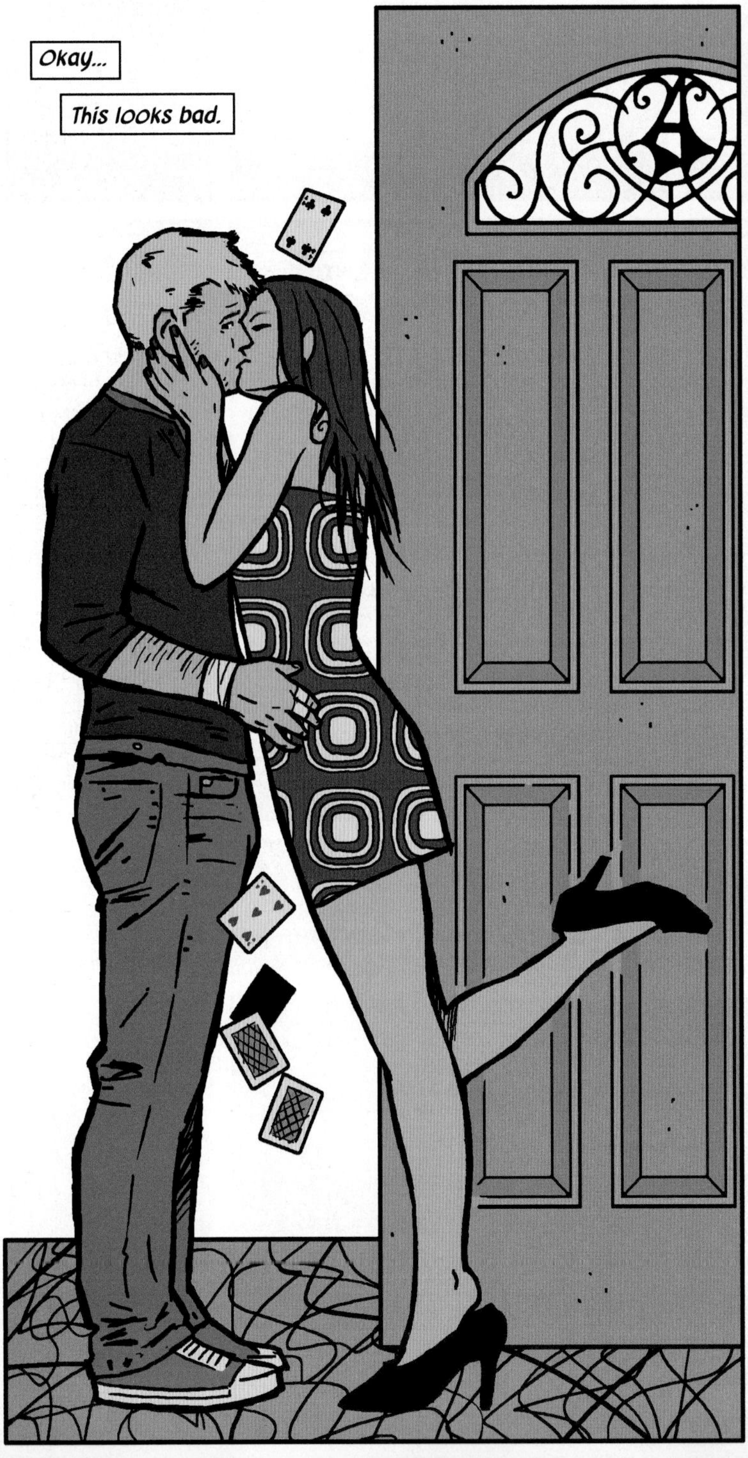
Okay...
This looks bad.

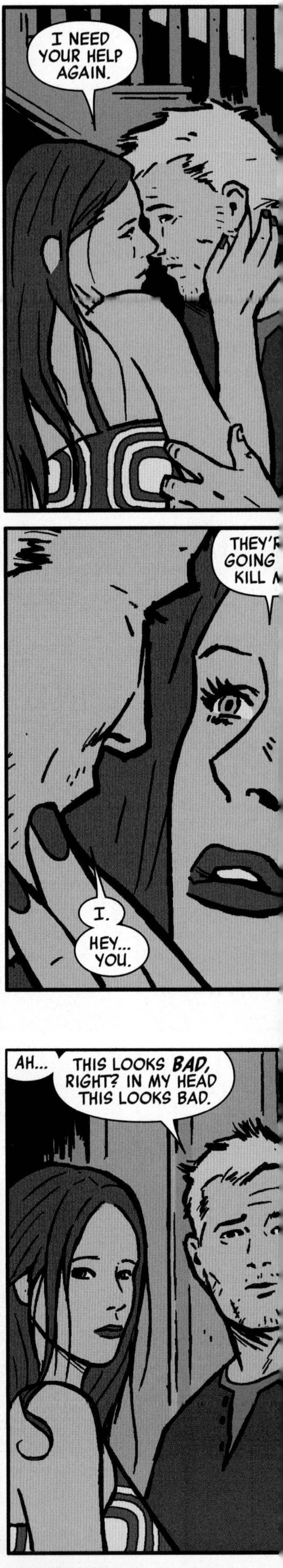
I NEED YOUR HELP AGAIN.
THEY'R GOING KILL
I.
HEY... YOU.
AH...
THIS LOOKS BAD, RIGHT? IN MY HEAD THIS LOOKS BAD.

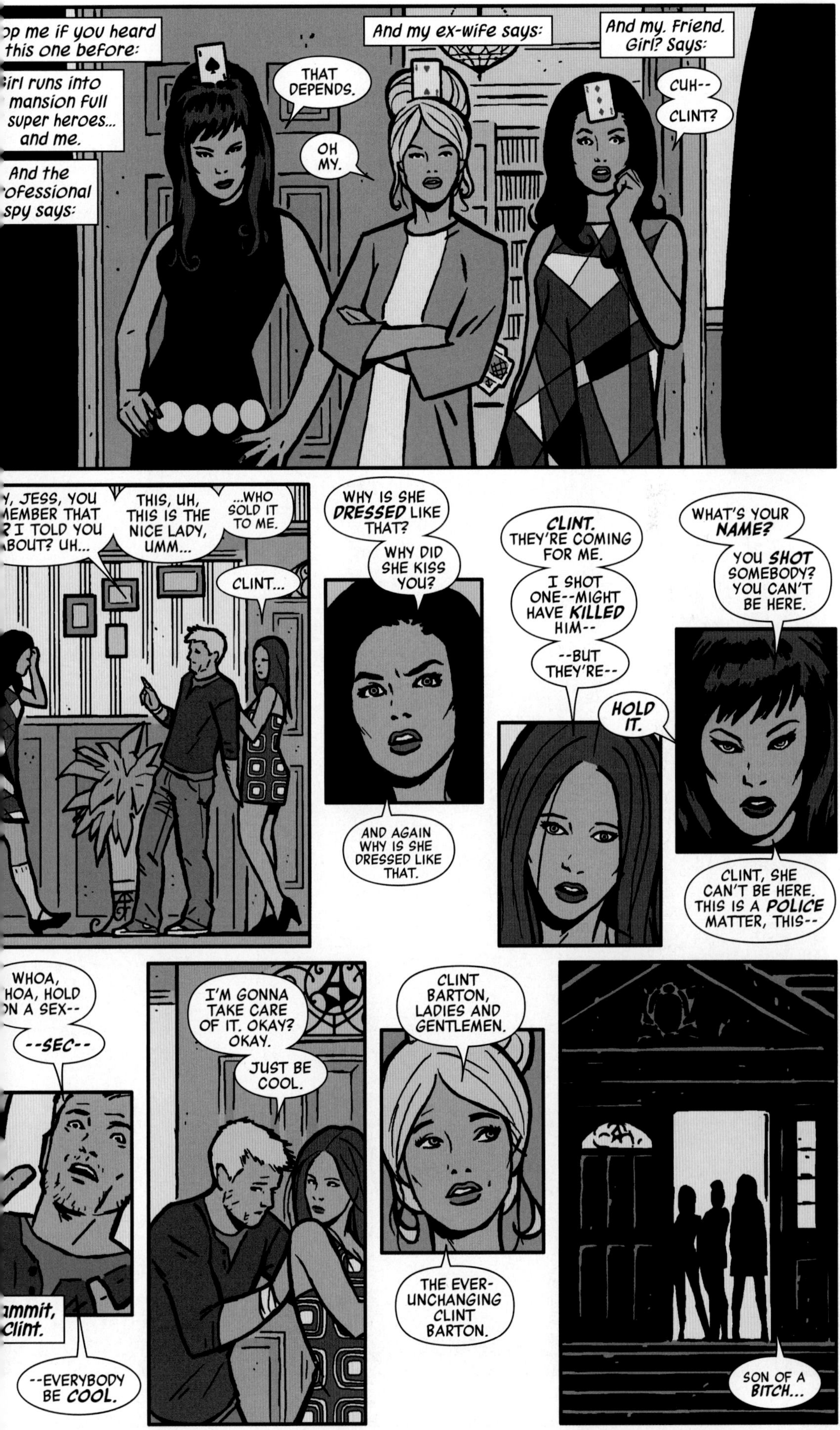

op me if you heard this one before:
irl runs into mansion full super heroes... and me.
And the ofessional spy says:
THAT DEPENDS.
OH MY.
And my ex-wife says:
And my. Friend. Girl? Says:
CUH--
CLINT?
, JESS, YOU EMBER THAT I TOLD YOU BOUT? UH...
THIS, UH, THIS IS THE NICE LADY, UMM...
...WHO SOLD IT TO ME.
CLINT...
WHY IS SHE DRESSED LIKE THAT?
WHY DID SHE KISS YOU?
AND AGAIN WHY IS SHE DRESSED LIKE THAT.
CLINT. THEY'RE COMING FOR ME.
I SHOT ONE--MIGHT HAVE KILLED HIM--
--BUT THEY'RE--
HOLD IT.
WHAT'S YOUR NAME?
YOU SHOT SOMEBODY? YOU CAN'T BE HERE.
CLINT, SHE CAN'T BE HERE. THIS IS A POLICE MATTER, THIS--
WHOA, HOA, HOLD N A SEX--
--SEC--
ammit, Clint.
--EVERYBODY BE COOL.
I'M GONNA TAKE CARE OF IT. OKAY? OKAY.
JUST BE COOL.
CLINT BARTON, LADIES AND GENTLEMEN.
THE EVER-UNCHANGING CLINT BARTON.
SON OF A BITCH...

15¢
MYSTERY GIRL
?
APRIL
NO 1
. . . AND I'M NEVER COMING BACK!
I WAS A REDHEAD CAR THIEF!
MY FATHER, MY FIEND!
DO YOU KNOW THE WAY TO... ANYWHERE?
TEEN RUNAWAY!

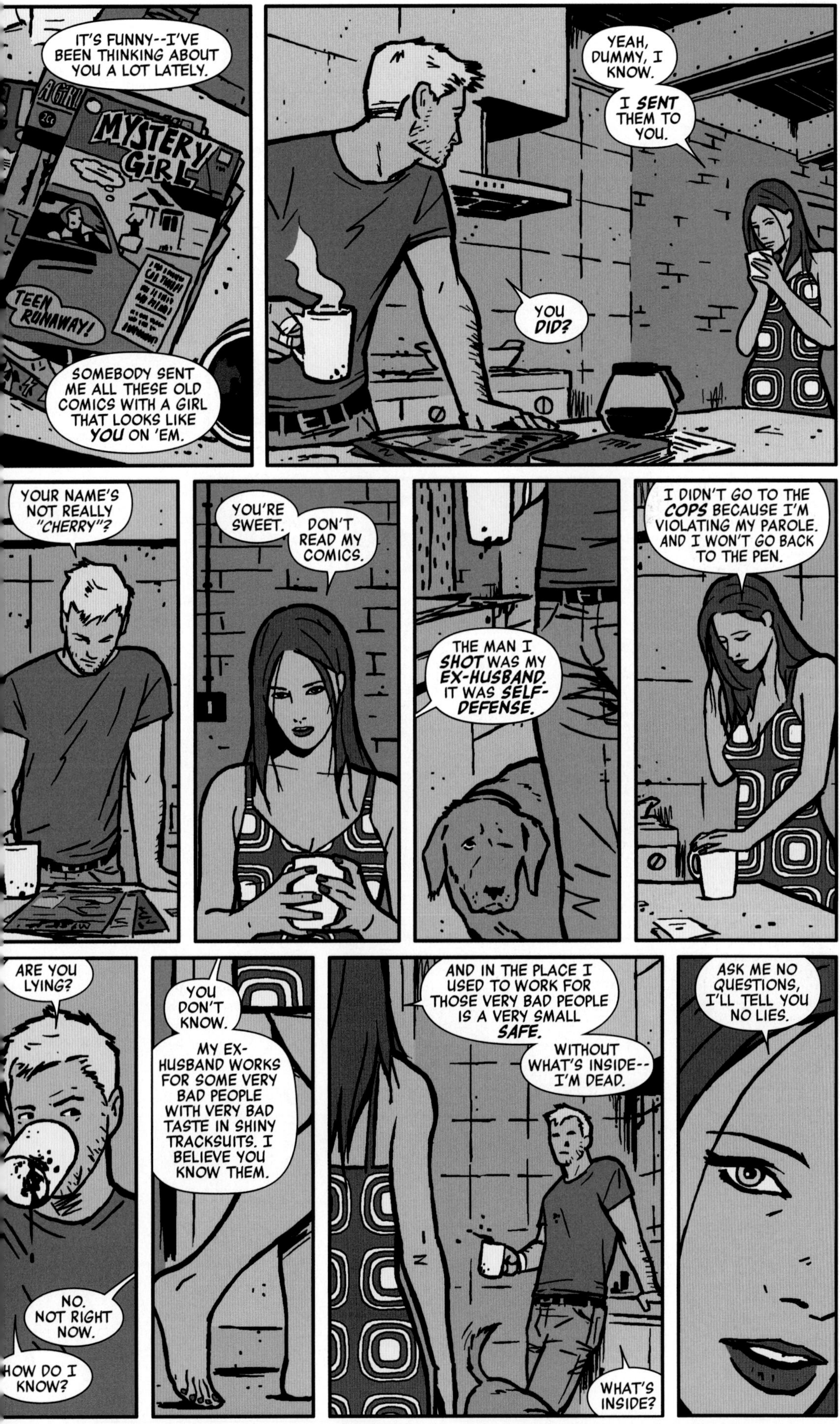
IT'S FUNNY--I'VE BEEN THINKING ABOUT YOU A LOT LATELY.
MYSTERY GIRL
TEEN RUNAWAY!
SOMEBODY SENT ME ALL THESE OLD COMICS WITH A GIRL THAT LOOKS LIKE YOU ON 'EM.
YEAH, DUMMY, I KNOW.
I SENT THEM TO YOU.
YOU DID?
YOUR NAME'S NOT REALLY "CHERRY"?
YOU'RE SWEET.
DON'T READ MY COMICS.
THE MAN I SHOT WAS MY EX-HUSBAND. IT WAS SELF-DEFENSE.
I DIDN'T GO TO THE COPS BECAUSE I'M VIOLATING MY PAROLE. AND I WON'T GO BACK TO THE PEN.
ARE YOU LYING?
YOU DON'T KNOW.
MY EX-HUSBAND WORKS FOR SOME VERY BAD PEOPLE WITH VERY BAD TASTE IN SHINY TRACKSUITS. I BELIEVE YOU KNOW THEM.
NO. NOT RIGHT NOW.
HOW DO I KNOW?
AND IN THE PLACE I USED TO WORK FOR THOSE VERY BAD PEOPLE IS A VERY SMALL SAFE.
WITHOUT WHAT'S INSIDE--I'M DEAD.
WHAT'S INSIDE?
ASK ME NO QUESTIONS, I'LL TELL YOU NO LIES.

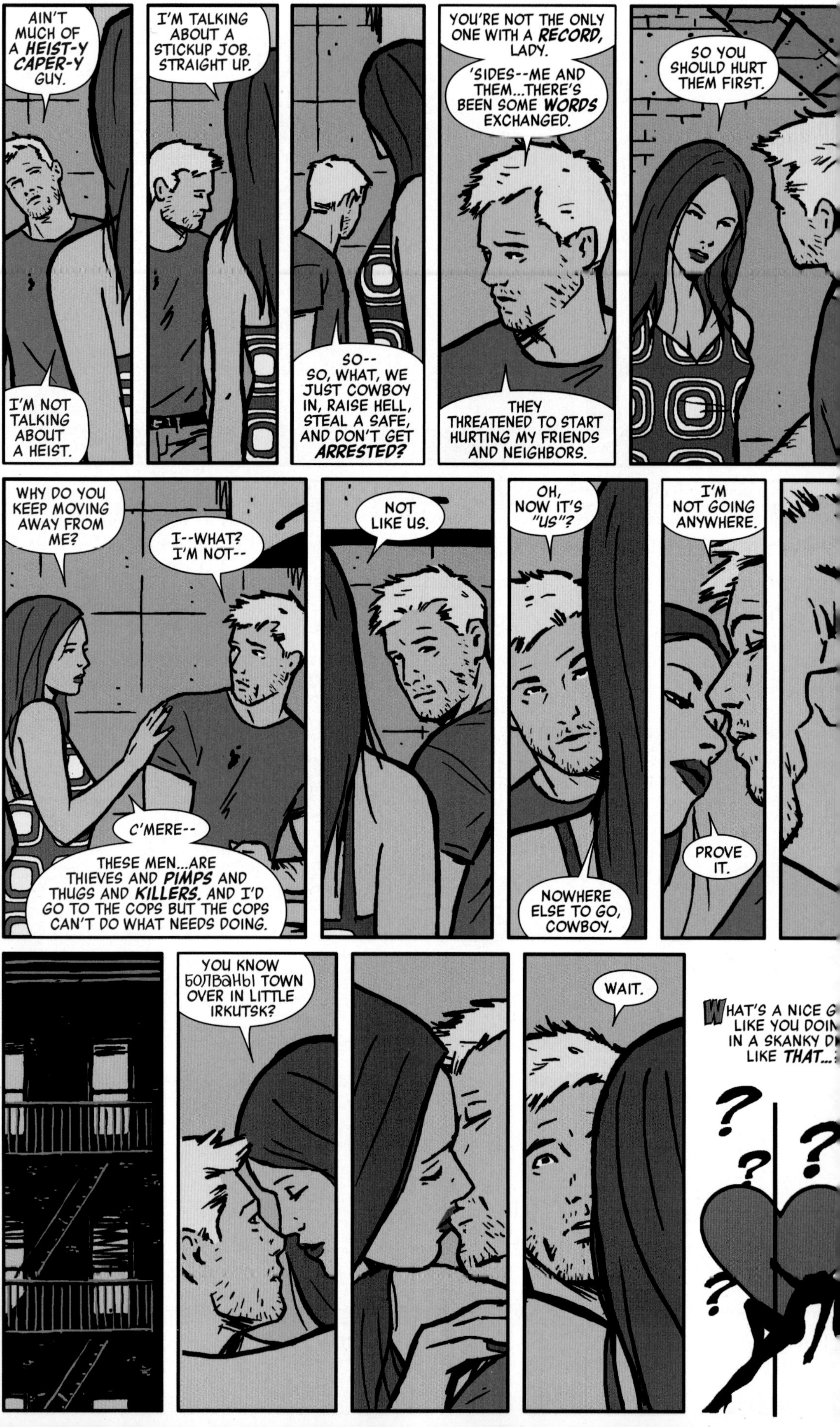
AIN'T MUCH OF A HEIST-Y CAPER-Y GUY.
I'M NOT TALKING ABOUT A HEIST.
I'M TALKING ABOUT A STICKUP JOB. STRAIGHT UP.
SO--
SO, WHAT, WE JUST COWBOY IN, RAISE HELL, STEAL A SAFE, AND DON'T GET ARRESTED?
YOU'RE NOT THE ONLY ONE WITH A RECORD, LADY.
'SIDES--ME AND THEM...THERE'S BEEN SOME WORDS EXCHANGED.
THEY THREATENED TO START HURTING MY FRIENDS AND NEIGHBORS.
SO YOU SHOULD HURT THEM FIRST.
WHY DO YOU KEEP MOVING AWAY FROM ME?
I--WHAT? I'M NOT--
C'MERE--
THESE MEN...ARE THIEVES AND PIMPS AND THUGS AND KILLERS. AND I'D GO TO THE COPS BUT THE COPS CAN'T DO WHAT NEEDS DOING.
NOT LIKE US.
OH, NOW IT'S "US"?
NOWHERE ELSE TO GO, COWBOY.
I'M NOT GOING ANYWHERE.
PROVE IT.
YOU KNOW БОЛВАНЫ TOWN OVER IN LITTLE IRKUTSK?
WAIT.
WHAT'S A NICE G
LIKE YOU DOIN
IN A SKANKY D
LIKE THAT...?

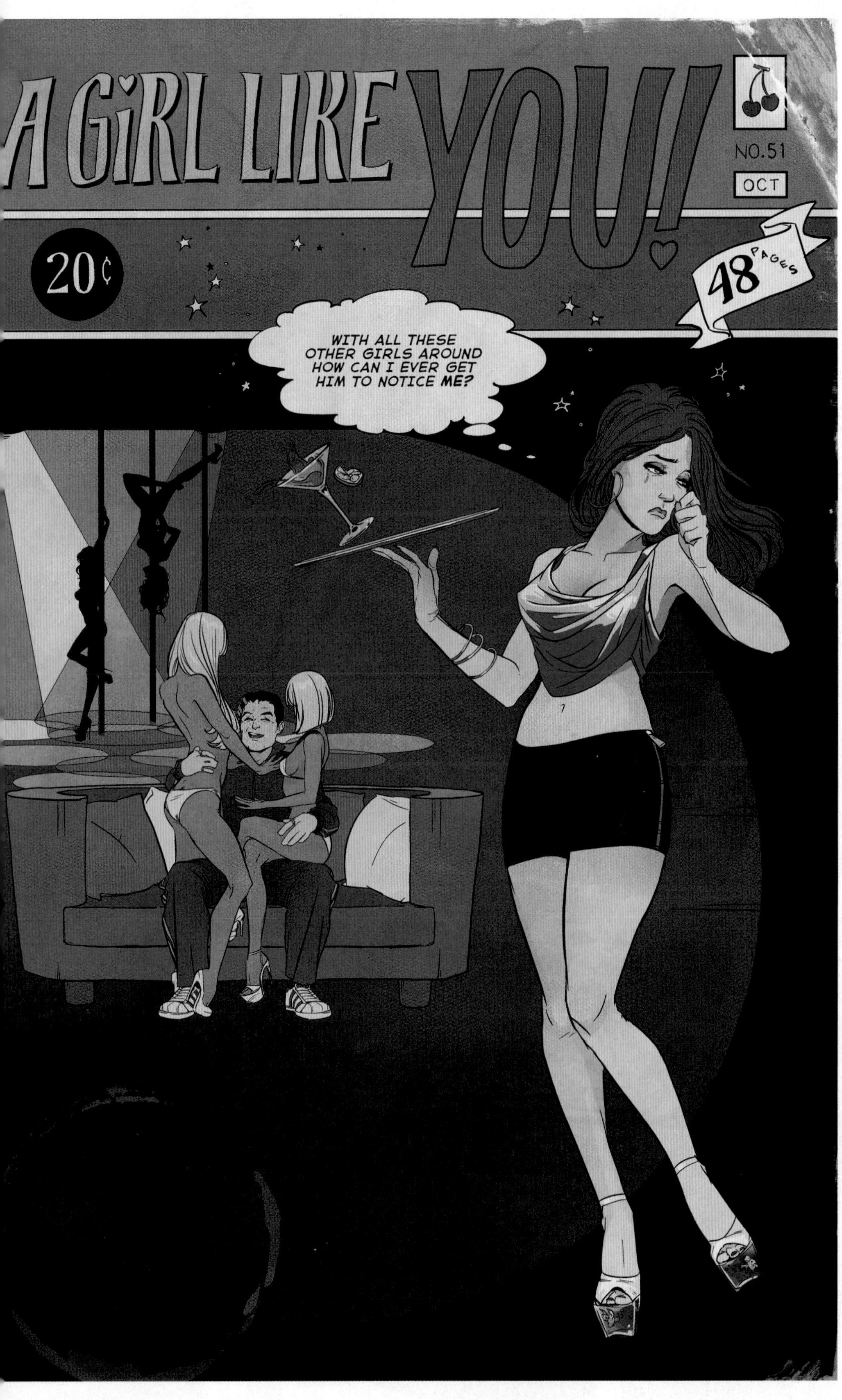
A GIRL LIKE YOU!
NO.51
OCT
20¢
48 PAGES
WITH ALL THESE OTHER GIRLS AROUND HOW CAN I EVER GET HIM TO NOTICE ME?

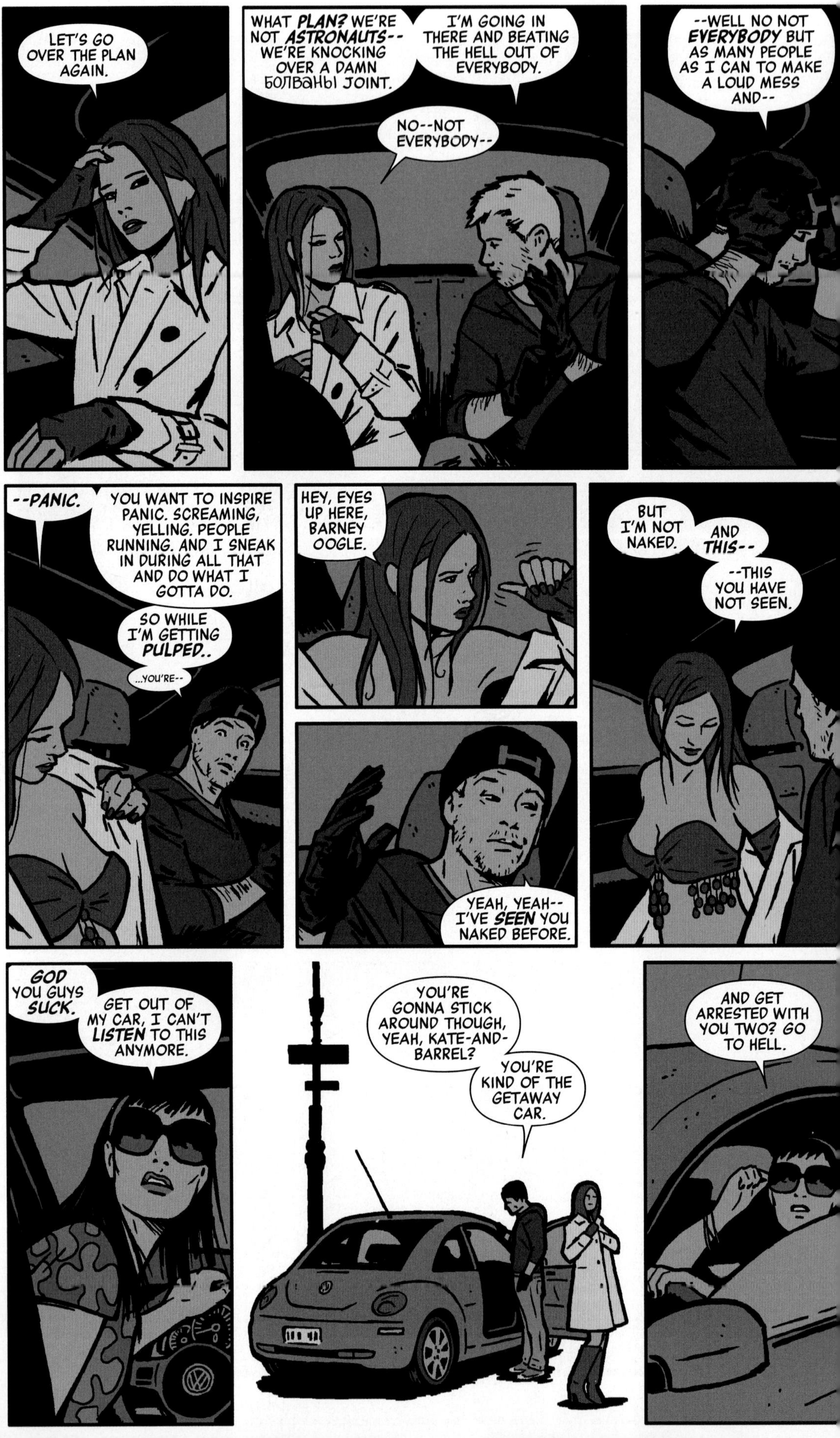
LET'S GO OVER THE PLAN AGAIN.
WHAT PLAN? WE'RE NOT ASTRONAUTS-- WE'RE KNOCKING OVER A DAMN БОЛВАНЫ JOINT.
I'M GOING IN THERE AND BEATING THE HELL OUT OF EVERYBODY.
NO--NOT EVERYBODY--
--WELL NO NOT EVERYBODY BUT AS MANY PEOPLE AS I CAN TO MAKE A LOUD MESS AND--
--PANIC.
YOU WANT TO INSPIRE PANIC. SCREAMING, YELLING. PEOPLE RUNNING. AND I SNEAK IN DURING ALL THAT AND DO WHAT I GOTTA DO.
SO WHILE I'M GETTING PULPED..
...YOU'RE--
HEY, EYES UP HERE, BARNEY OOGLE.
YEAH, YEAH-- I'VE SEEN YOU NAKED BEFORE.
BUT I'M NOT NAKED.
AND THIS--
--THIS YOU HAVE NOT SEEN.
GOD YOU GUYS SUCK.
GET OUT OF MY CAR, I CAN'T LISTEN TO THIS ANYMORE.
YOU'RE GONNA STICK AROUND THOUGH, YEAH, KATE-AND-BARREL?
YOU'RE KIND OF THE GETAWAY CAR.
AND GET ARRESTED WITH YOU TWO? GO TO HELL.

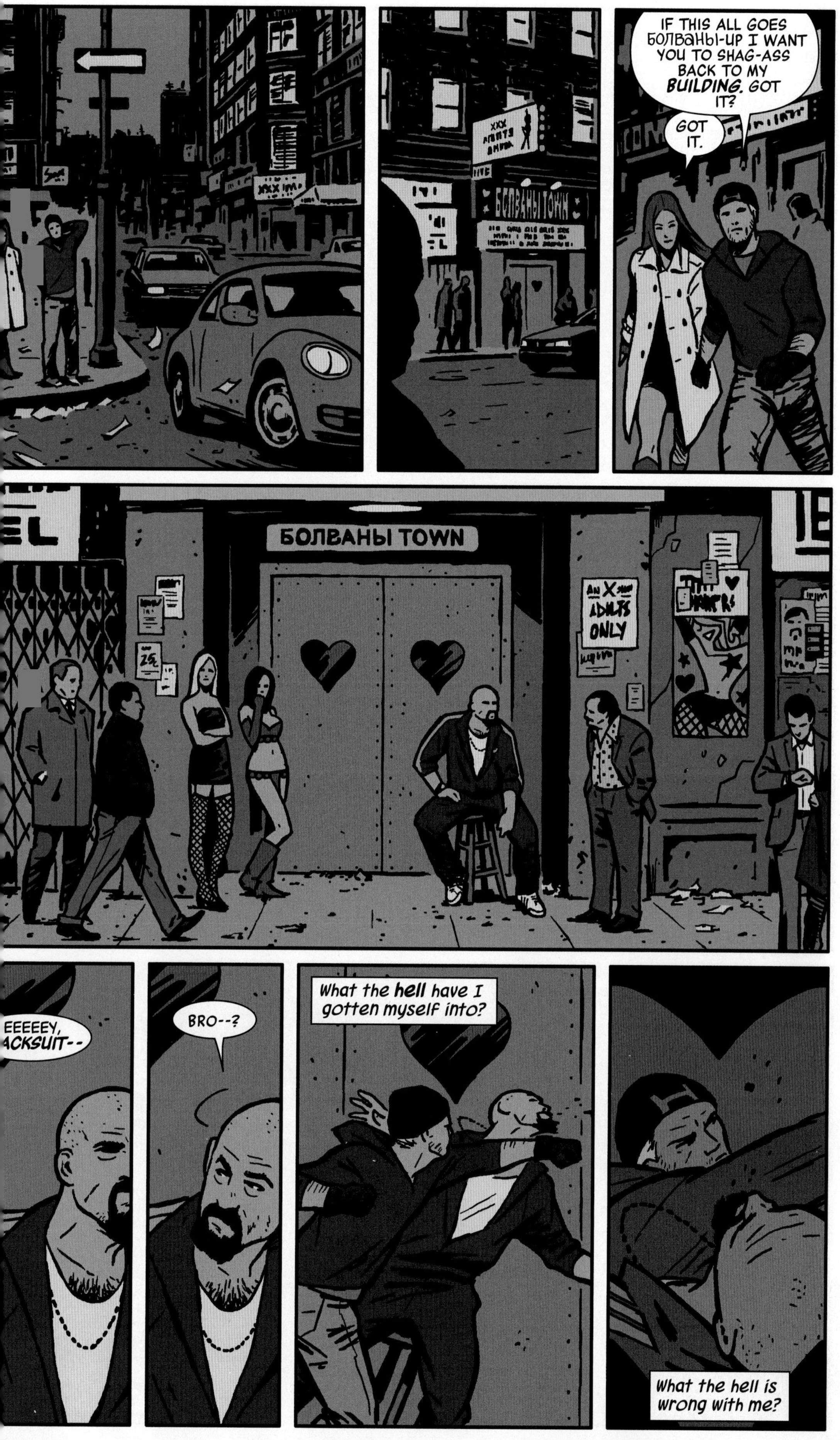

IF THIS ALL GOES БОЛВАНЫ-UP I WANT YOU TO SHAG-ASS BACK TO MY BUILDING. GOT IT?
GOT IT.
БОЛВАНЫ TOWN
ADULTS ONLY
EEEEEY, ACKSUIT--
BRO--?
What the hell have I gotten myself into?
What the hell is wrong with me?

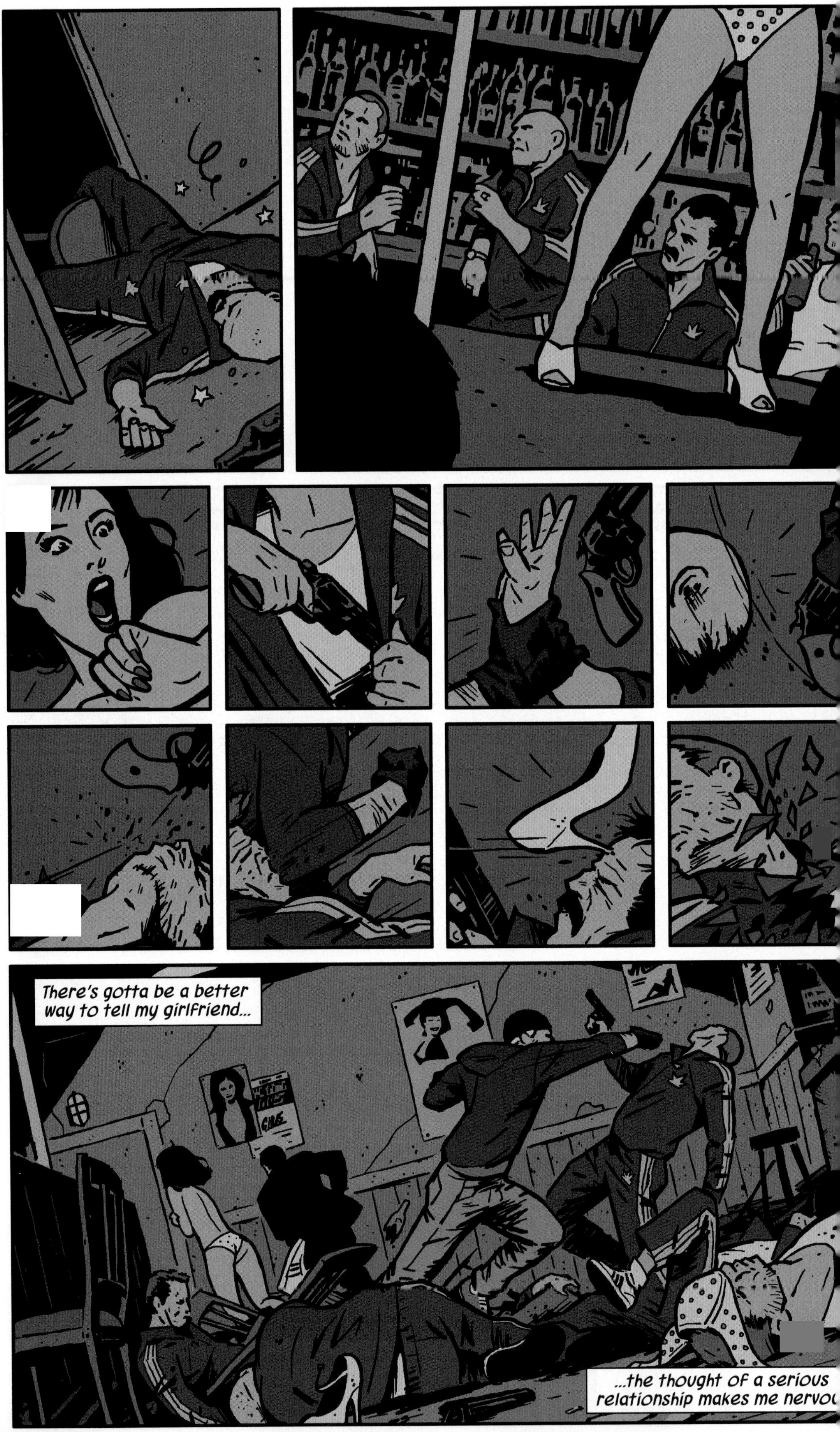
There's gotta be a better way to tell my girlfriend...
...the thought of a serious relationship makes me nervou

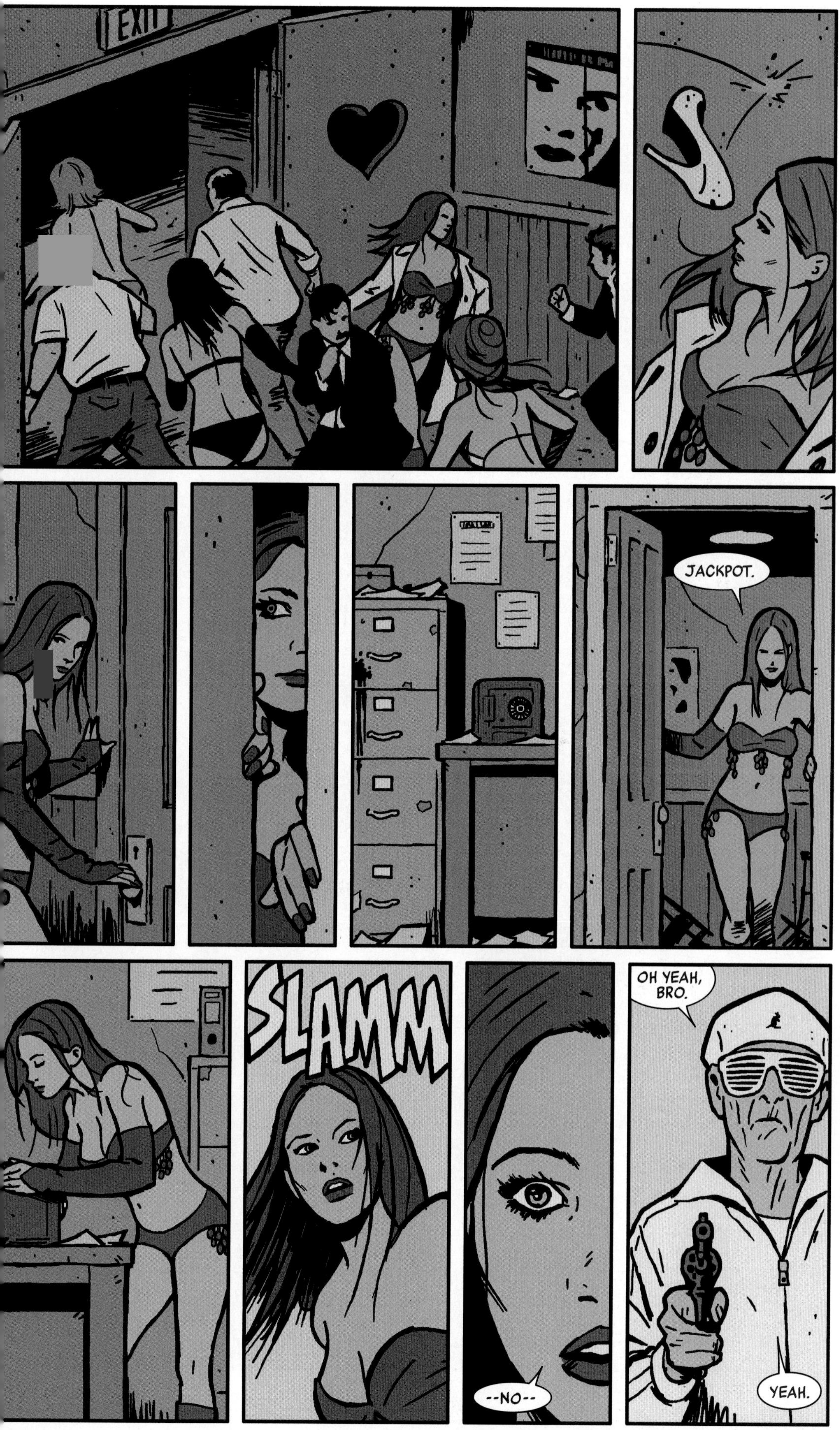
EXIT
JACKPOT.
SLAMM
--NO--
OH YEAH, BRO.
YEAH.

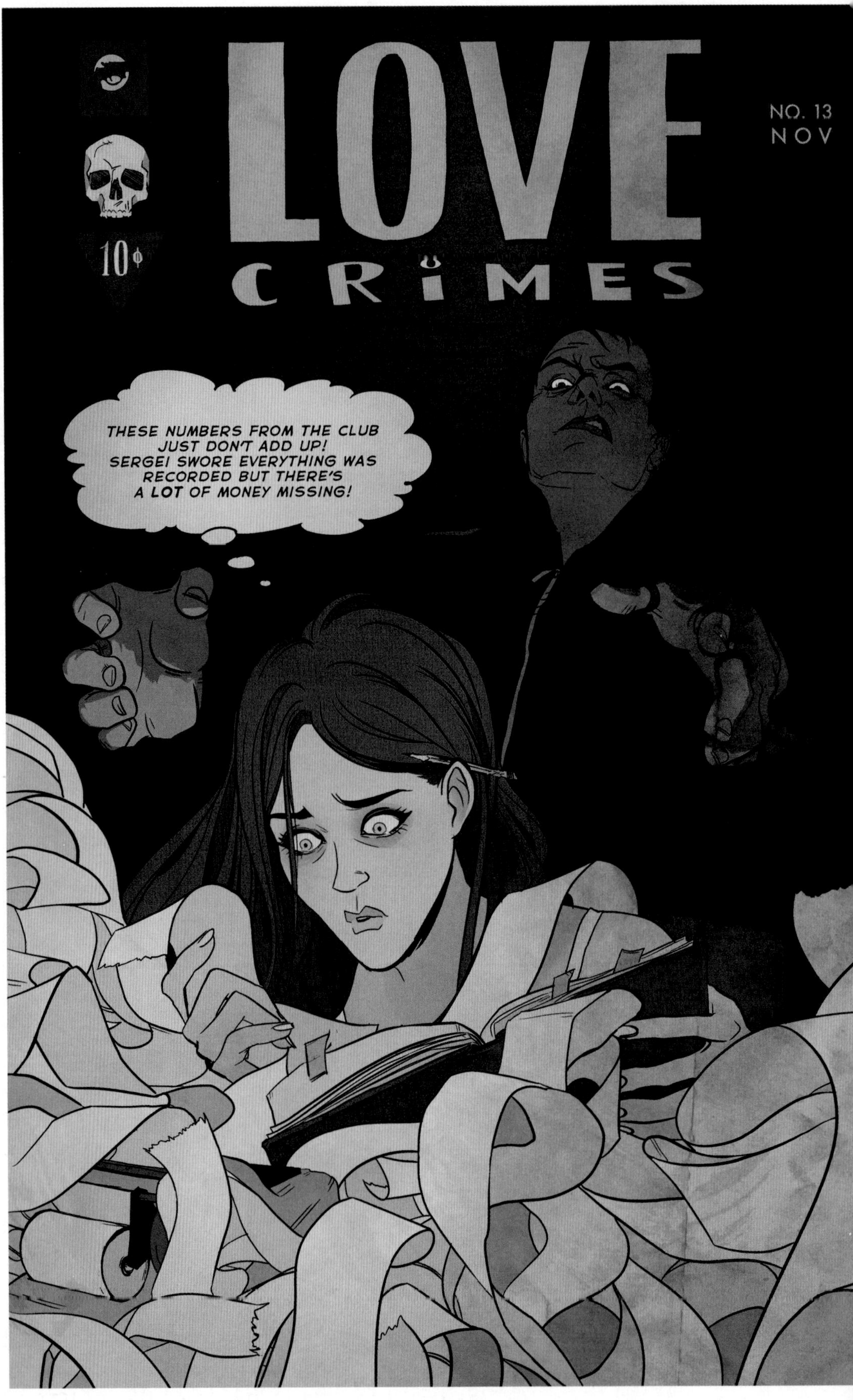
LOVE CRIMES
NO. 13
NOV
10¢
THESE NUMBERS FROM THE CLUB JUST DON'T ADD UP! SERGEI SWORE EVERYTHING WAS RECORDED BUT THERE'S A LOT OF MONEY MISSING!

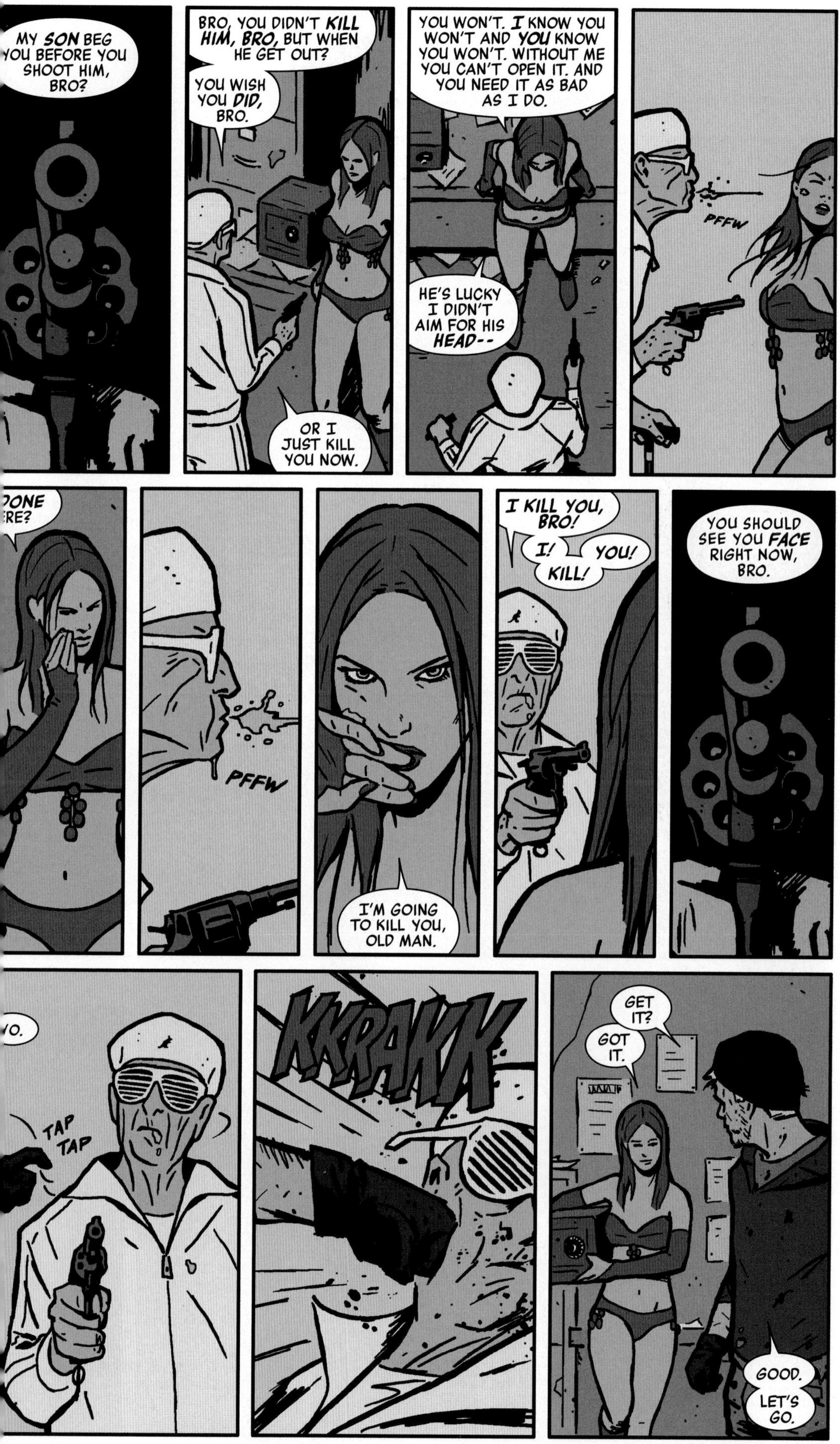
MY SON BEG YOU BEFORE YOU SHOOT HIM, BRO?
BRO, YOU DIDN'T KILL HIM, BRO, BUT WHEN HE GET OUT?
YOU WISH YOU DID, BRO.
OR I JUST KILL YOU NOW.
YOU WON'T. I KNOW YOU WON'T AND YOU KNOW YOU WON'T. WITHOUT ME YOU CAN'T OPEN IT. AND YOU NEED IT AS BAD AS I DO.
HE'S LUCKY I DIDN'T AIM FOR HIS HEAD--
PFFW
PFFW
I'M GOING TO KILL YOU, OLD MAN.
I KILL YOU, BRO!
I!
KILL!
YOU!
YOU SHOULD SEE YOU FACE RIGHT NOW, BRO.
TAP TAP
KKRAKK
GET IT?
GOT IT.
GOOD.
LET'S GO.

AHH, CRAP.

Now this.

DROP IT!

FREEZE!

HANDS UP!

EXIT

This looks b...

UM.

I'M AN AVENGER?

ARE YOU IRON FIST?

JEEZ WHY DOES EVERYBODY KEEP ASKING ME THAT--

GET DOWN!

OKAY, OKAY--

SERIOUSLY THOUGH I'M AN AVENGER.

I.D. AND EVERYTHING IS IN MY--

--WAAHHHH--

But it's okay.

It's all okay.

Good guys win.

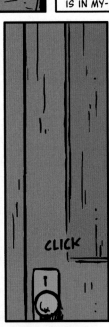

CLICK

...right?

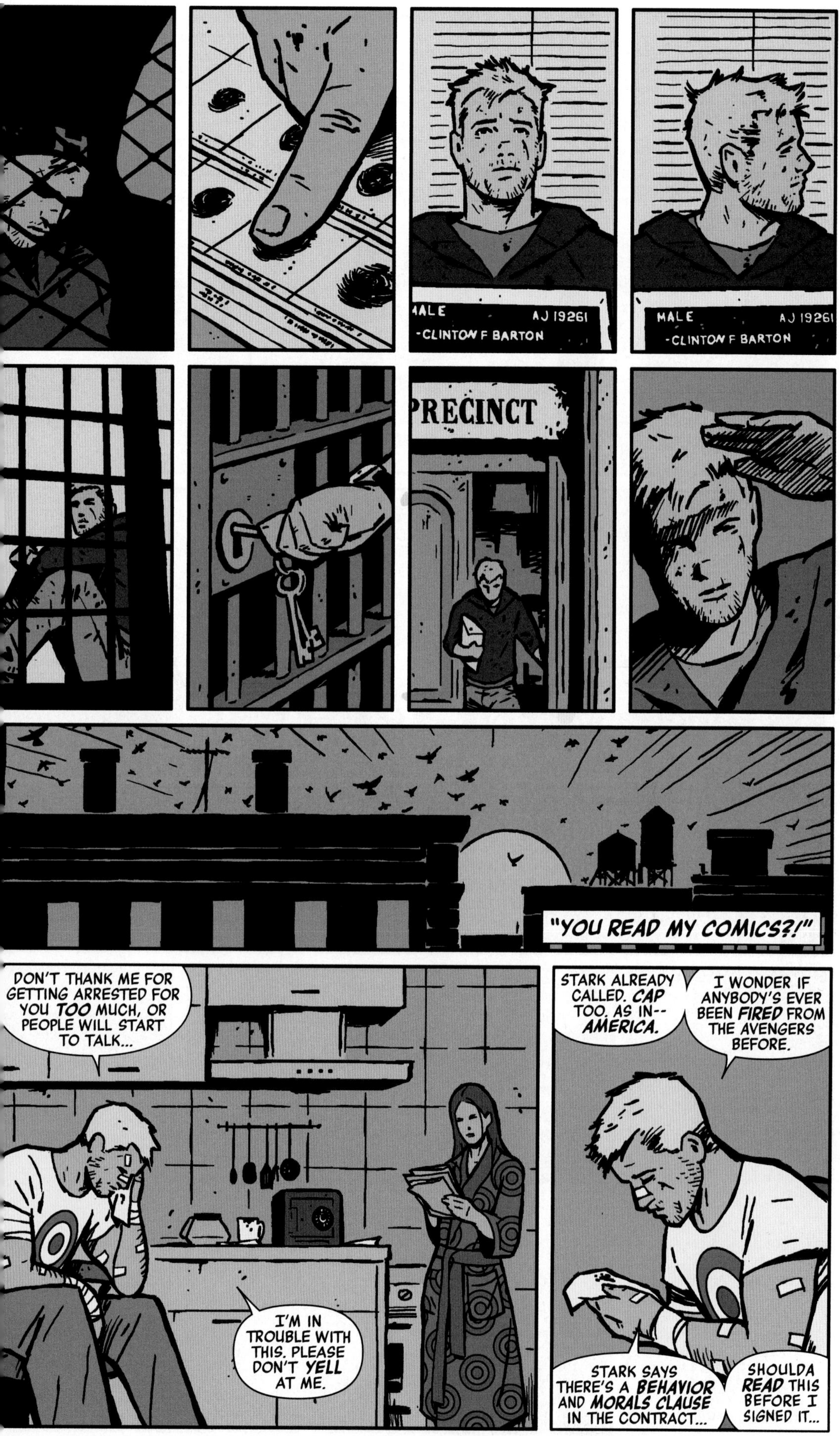
MALE AJ 19261
-CLINTON F BARTON
MALE AJ 19261
-CLINTON F BARTON
PRECINCT
"YOU READ MY COMICS?!"
DON'T THANK ME FOR GETTING ARRESTED FOR YOU TOO MUCH, OR PEOPLE WILL START TO TALK...
I'M IN TROUBLE WITH THIS. PLEASE DON'T YELL AT ME.
STARK ALREADY CALLED. CAP TOO. AS IN-- AMERICA.
I WONDER IF ANYBODY'S EVER BEEN FIRED FROM THE AVENGERS BEFORE.
STARK SAYS THERE'S A BEHAVIOR AND MORALS CLAUSE IN THE CONTRACT...
SHOULDA READ THIS BEFORE I SIGNED IT...

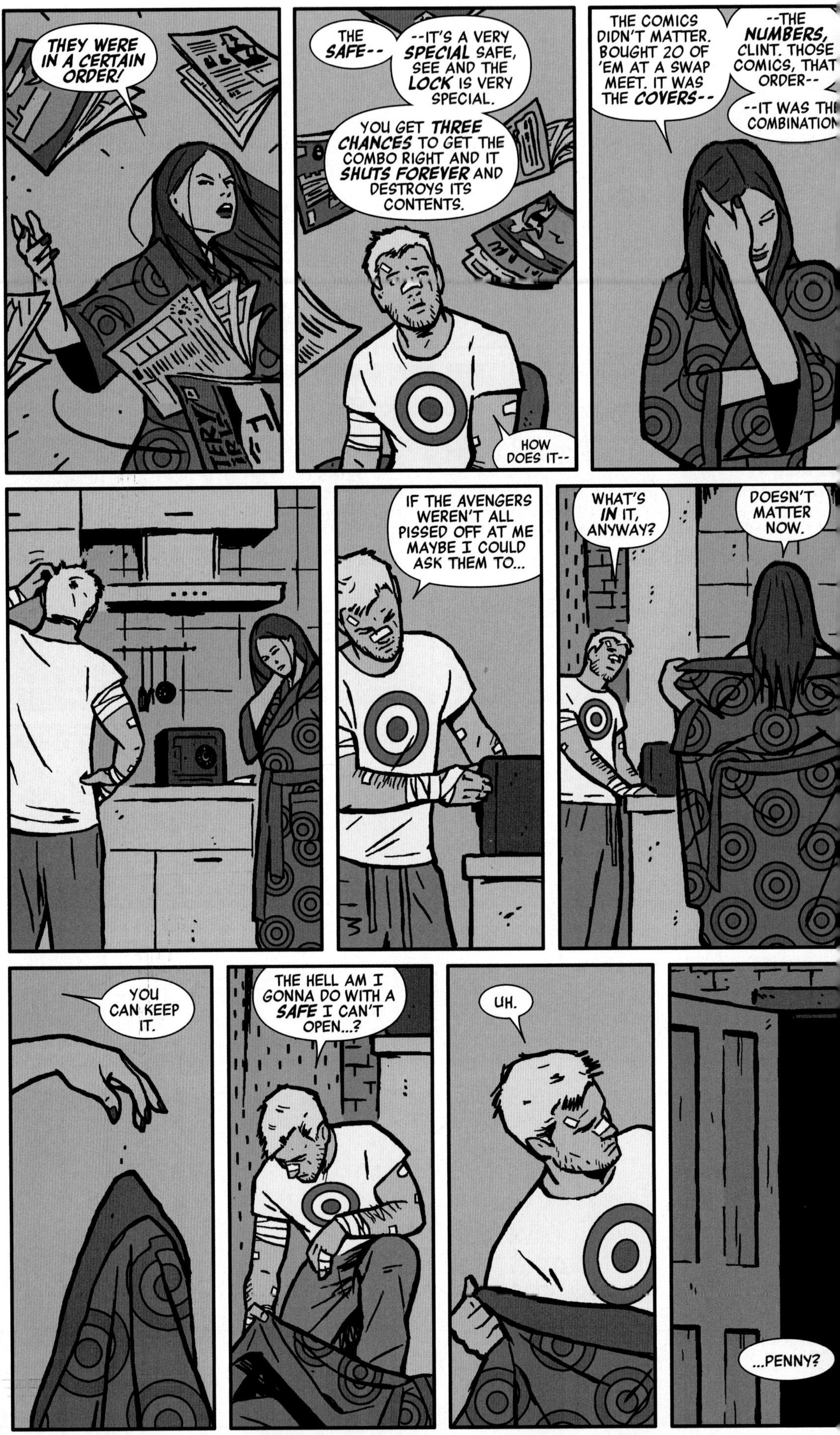
THEY WERE IN A CERTAIN ORDER!
THE SAFE--
--IT'S A VERY SPECIAL SAFE, SEE AND THE LOCK IS VERY SPECIAL.
YOU GET THREE CHANCES TO GET THE COMBO RIGHT AND IT SHUTS FOREVER AND DESTROYS ITS CONTENTS.
HOW DOES IT--
THE COMICS DIDN'T MATTER. BOUGHT 20 OF 'EM AT A SWAP MEET. IT WAS THE COVERS--
--THE NUMBERS, CLINT. THOSE COMICS, THAT ORDER--
--IT WAS TH COMBINATION
IF THE AVENGERS WEREN'T ALL PISSED OFF AT ME MAYBE I COULD ASK THEM TO...
WHAT'S IN IT, ANYWAY?
DOESN'T MATTER NOW.
YOU CAN KEEP IT.
THE HELL AM I GONNA DO WITH A SAFE I CAN'T OPEN...?
UH.
...PENNY?

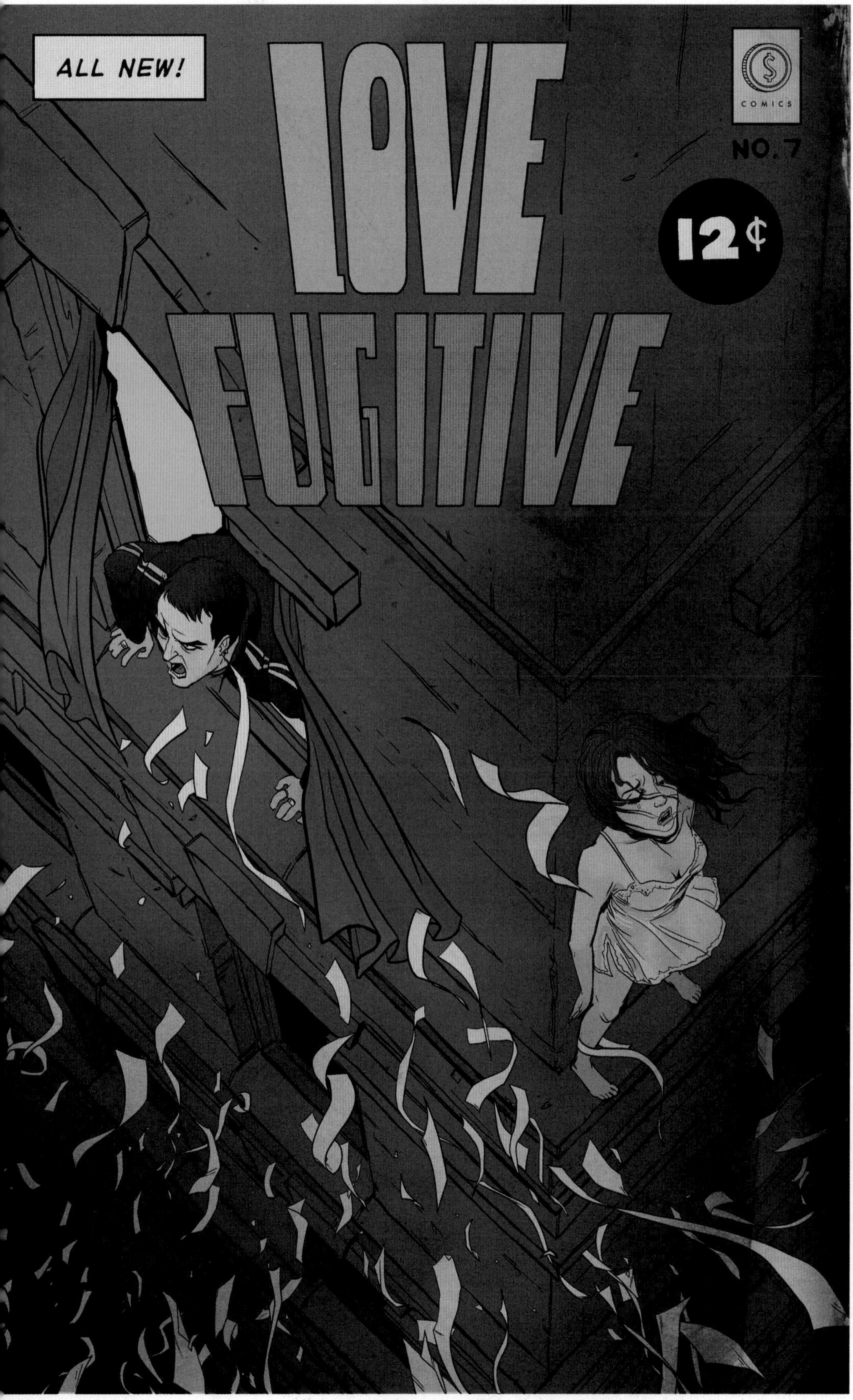
ALL NEW!
LOVE FUGITIVE
COMICS
NO. 7
12¢

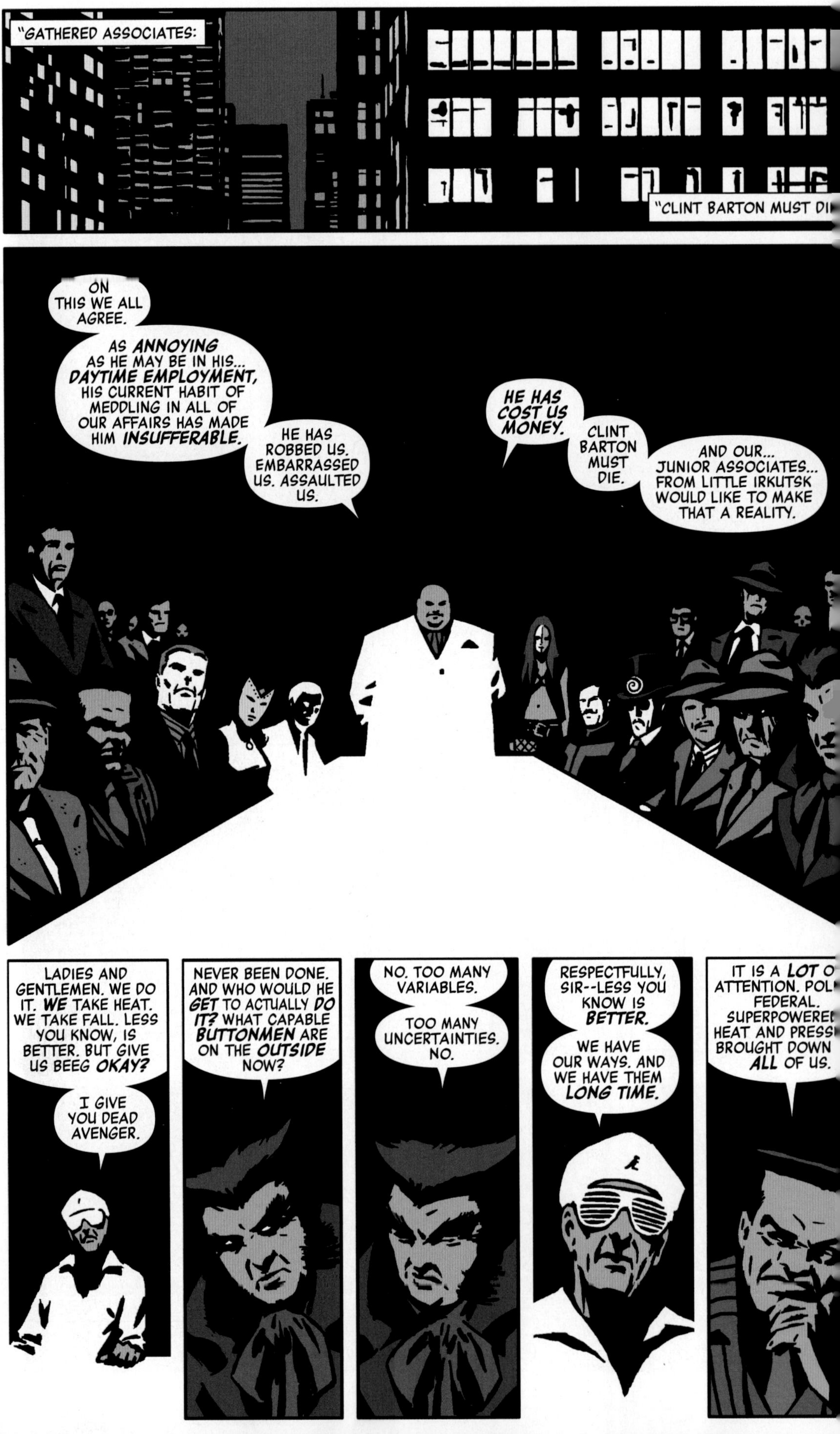
"GATHERED ASSOCIATES:
"CLINT BARTON MUST DI
ON THIS WE ALL AGREE.
AS ANNOYING AS HE MAY BE IN HIS... DAYTIME EMPLOYMENT, HIS CURRENT HABIT OF MEDDLING IN ALL OF OUR AFFAIRS HAS MADE HIM INSUFFERABLE.
HE HAS ROBBED US. EMBARRASSED US. ASSAULTED US.
HE HAS COST US MONEY.
CLINT BARTON MUST DIE.
AND OUR... JUNIOR ASSOCIATES... FROM LITTLE IRKUTSK WOULD LIKE TO MAKE THAT A REALITY.
LADIES AND GENTLEMEN. WE DO IT. WE TAKE HEAT. WE TAKE FALL. LESS YOU KNOW, IS BETTER. BUT GIVE US BEEG OKAY?
I GIVE YOU DEAD AVENGER.
NEVER BEEN DONE. AND WHO WOULD HE GET TO ACTUALLY DO IT? WHAT CAPABLE BUTTONMEN ARE ON THE OUTSIDE NOW?
NO. TOO MANY VARIABLES.
TOO MANY UNCERTAINTIES. NO.
RESPECTFULLY, SIR--LESS YOU KNOW IS BETTER.
WE HAVE OUR WAYS. AND WE HAVE THEM LONG TIME.
IT IS A LOT O ATTENTION. POL FEDERAL. SUPERPOWERE HEAT AND PRESS BROUGHT DOWN ALL OF US.

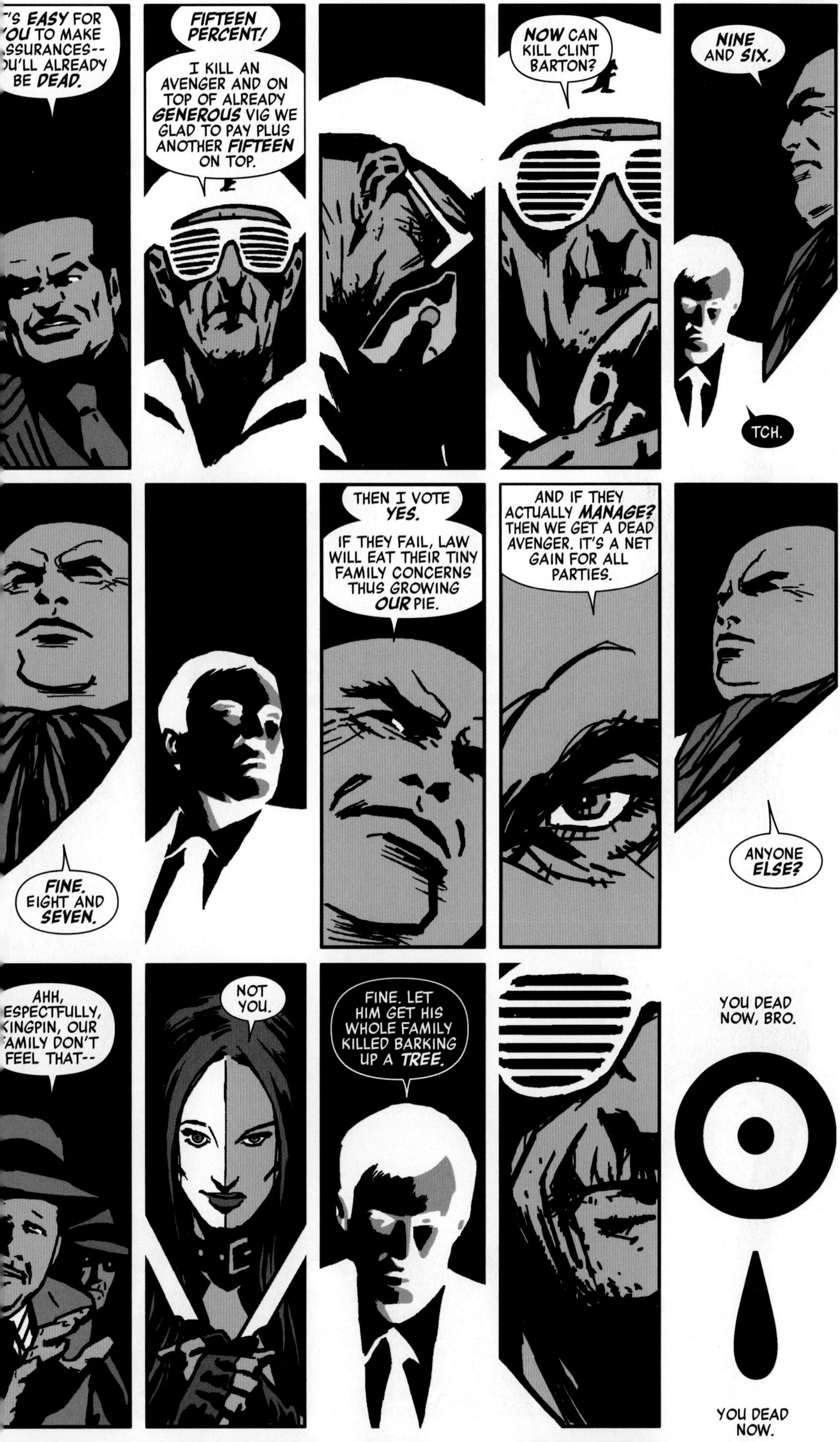
'S EASY FOR OU TO MAKE SSURANCES-- OU'LL ALREADY BE DEAD.
FIFTEEN PERCENT!
I KILL AN AVENGER AND ON TOP OF ALREADY GENEROUS VIG WE GLAD TO PAY PLUS ANOTHER FIFTEEN ON TOP.
NOW CAN KILL CLINT BARTON?
NINE AND SIX.
TCH.
FINE. EIGHT AND SEVEN.
THEN I VOTE YES.
IF THEY FAIL, LAW WILL EAT THEIR TINY FAMILY CONCERNS THUS GROWING OUR PIE.
AND IF THEY ACTUALLY MANAGE? THEN WE GET A DEAD AVENGER. IT'S A NET GAIN FOR ALL PARTIES.
ANYONE ELSE?
AHH, ESPECTFULLY, INGPIN, OUR AMILY DON'T FEEL THAT--
NOT YOU.
FINE. LET HIM GET HIS WHOLE FAMILY KILLED BARKING UP A TREE.
YOU DEAD NOW, BRO.
YOU DEAD NOW.

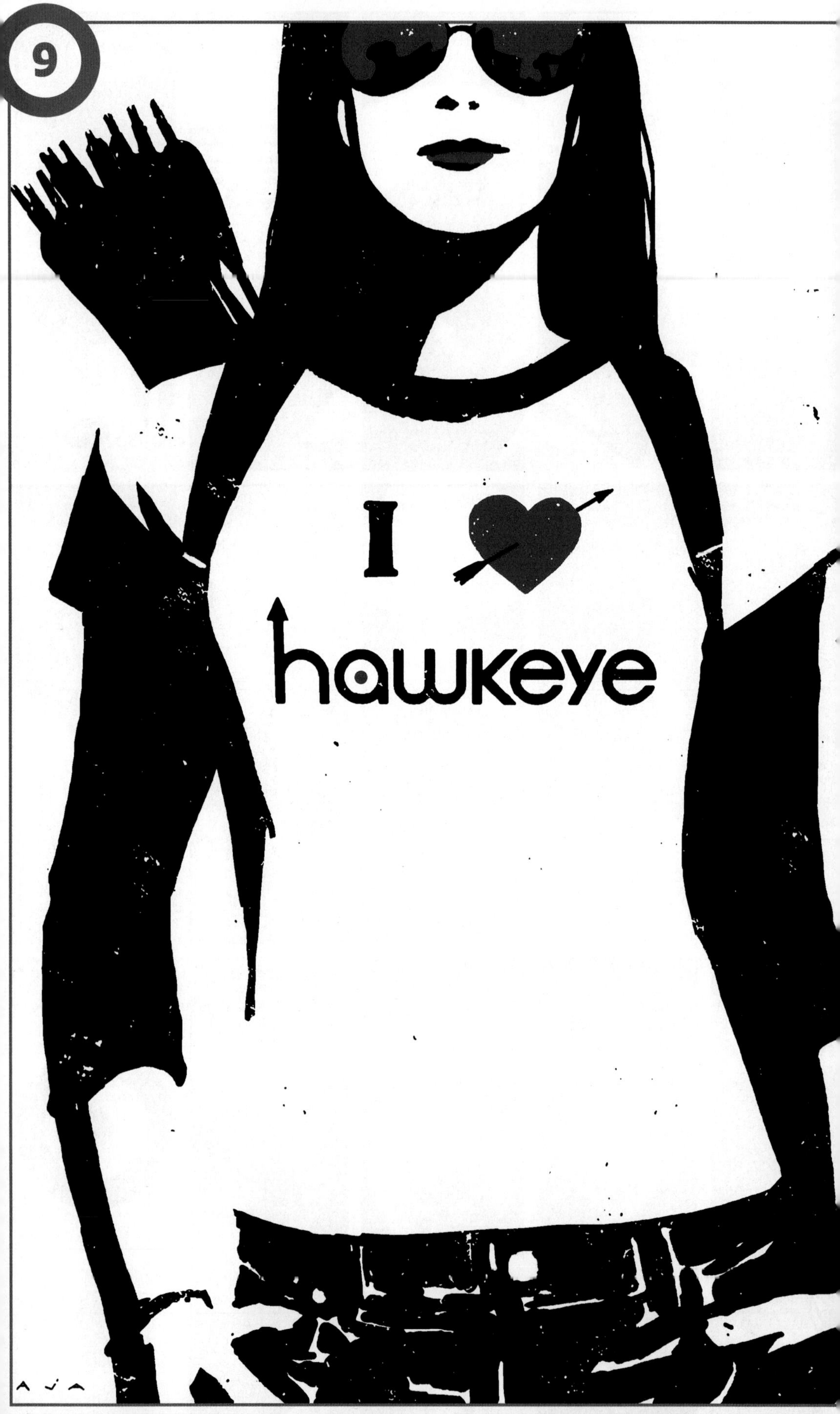
9
I ♥
hawkeye
AJA

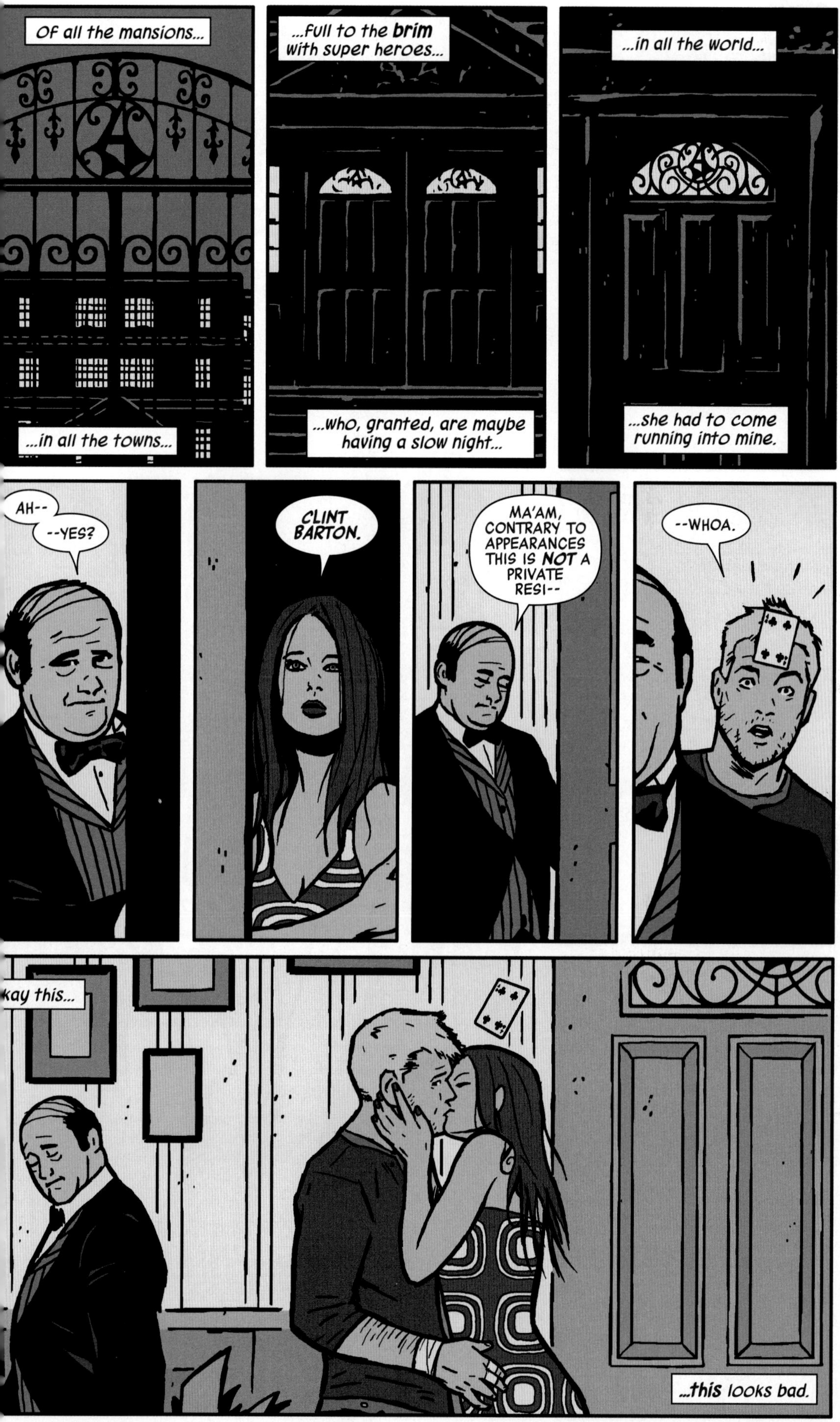
Of all the mansions...
...in all the towns...
...full to the **brim** with super heroes...
...who, granted, are maybe having a slow night...
...in all the world...
...she had to come running into mine.
AH--
--YES?
CLINT BARTON.
MA'AM, CONTRARY TO APPEARANCES THIS IS ***NOT*** A PRIVATE RESI--
--WHOA.
kay this...
...**this** looks bad.

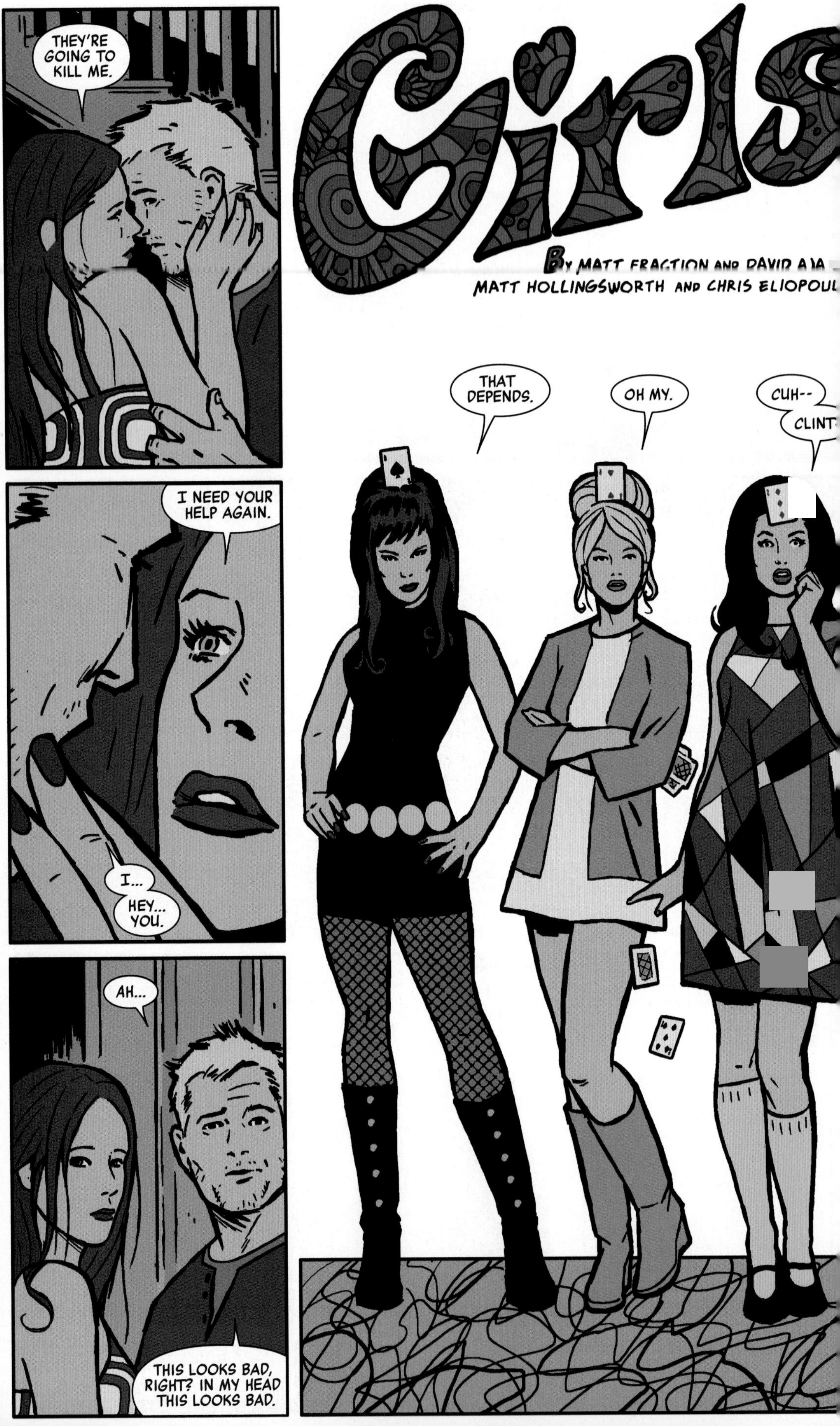
THEY'RE GOING TO KILL ME.
I NEED YOUR HELP AGAIN.
I... HEY... YOU.
AH...
THIS LOOKS BAD, RIGHT? IN MY HEAD THIS LOOKS BAD.
Girls
BY MATT FRACTION AND DAVID AJA
MATT HOLLINGSWORTH AND CHRIS ELIOPOUL
THAT DEPENDS.
OH MY.
CUH--
CLINT

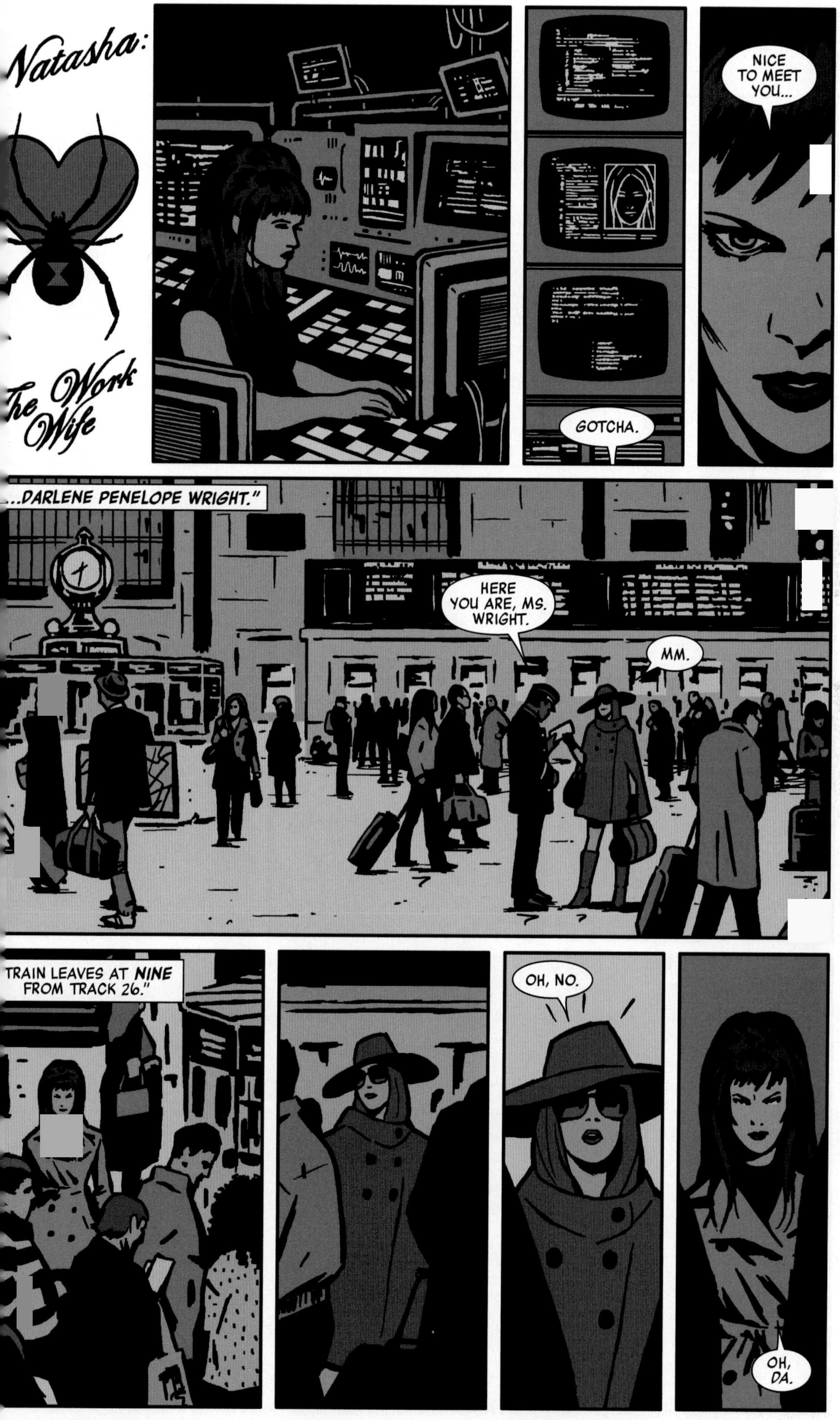
Natasha:
The Work Wife
GOTCHA.
NICE TO MEET YOU...
...DARLENE PENELOPE WRIGHT."
HERE YOU ARE, MS. WRIGHT.
MM.
TRAIN LEAVES AT NINE FROM TRACK 26."
OH, NO.
OH, DA.

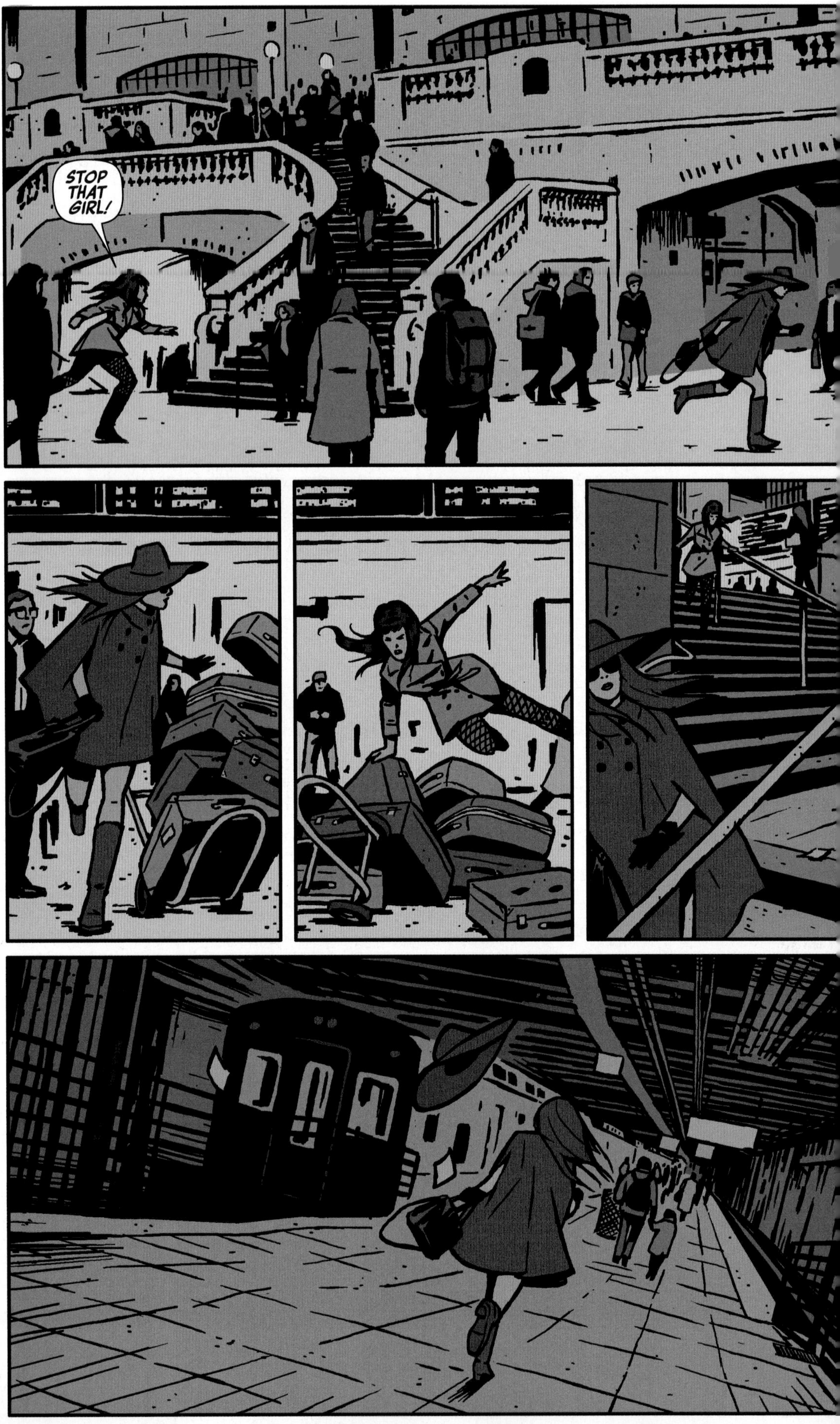
STOP THAT GIRL!

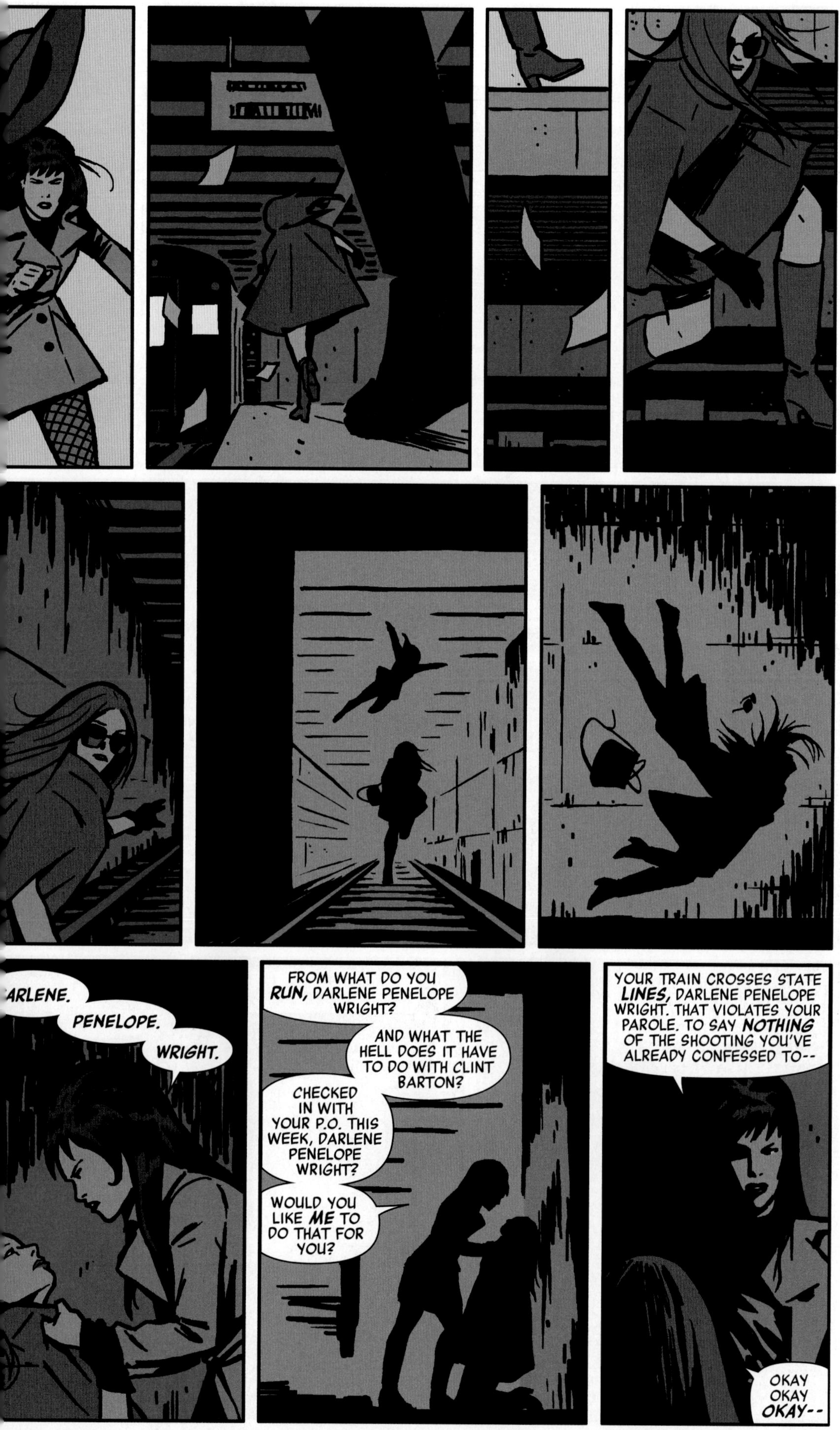

ARLENE.
PENELOPE.
WRIGHT.
FROM WHAT DO YOU RUN, DARLENE PENELOPE WRIGHT?
AND WHAT THE HELL DOES IT HAVE TO DO WITH CLINT BARTON?
CHECKED IN WITH YOUR P.O. THIS WEEK, DARLENE PENELOPE WRIGHT?
WOULD YOU LIKE ME TO DO THAT FOR YOU?
YOUR TRAIN CROSSES STATE LINES, DARLENE PENELOPE WRIGHT. THAT VIOLATES YOUR PAROLE. TO SAY NOTHING OF THE SHOOTING YOU'VE ALREADY CONFESSED TO--
OKAY OKAY OKAY--

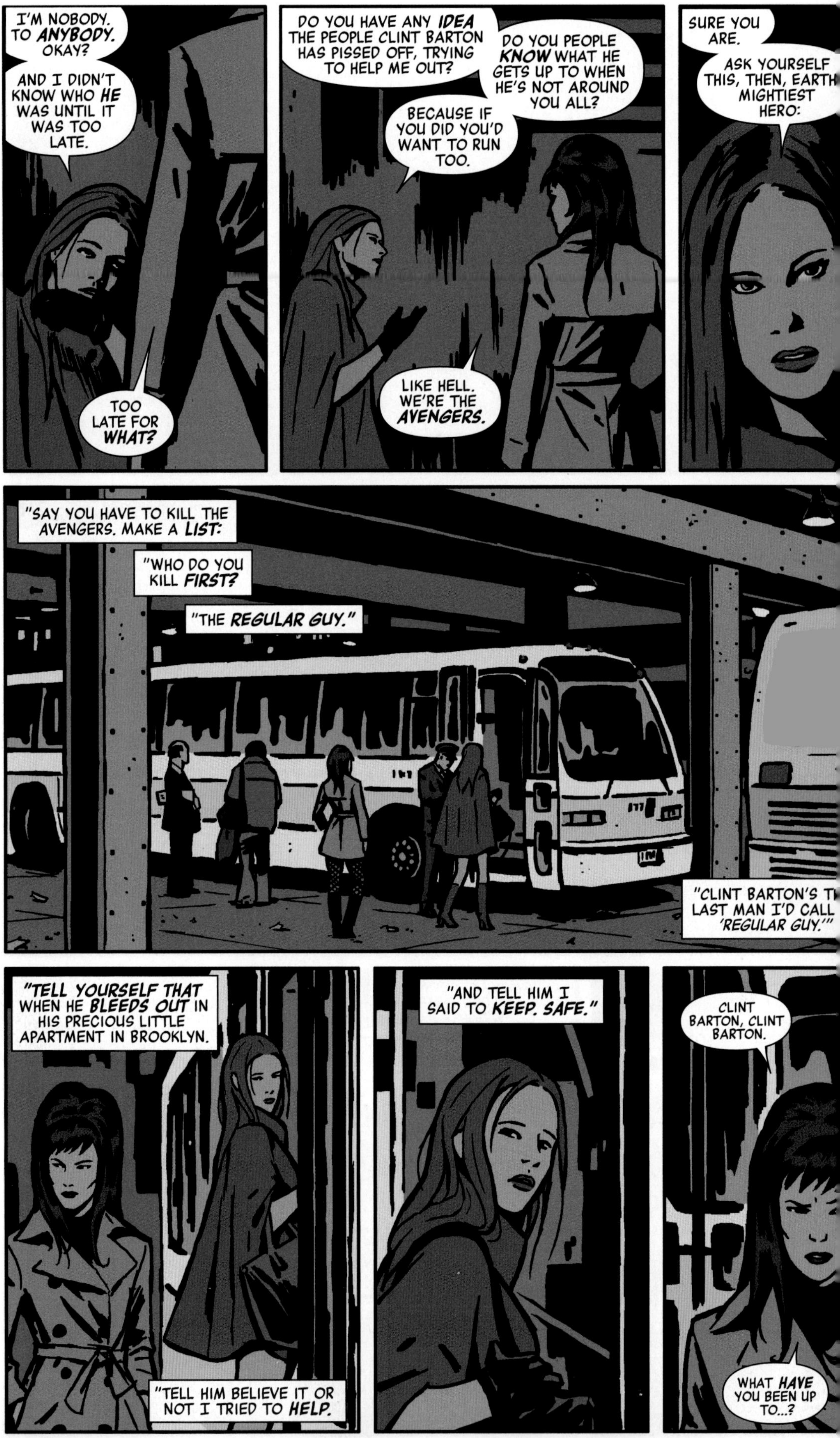

I'M NOBODY. TO ANYBODY. OKAY?
AND I DIDN'T KNOW WHO HE WAS UNTIL IT WAS TOO LATE.
TOO LATE FOR WHAT?
DO YOU HAVE ANY IDEA THE PEOPLE CLINT BARTON HAS PISSED OFF, TRYING TO HELP ME OUT?
DO YOU PEOPLE KNOW WHAT HE GETS UP TO WHEN HE'S NOT AROUND YOU ALL?
BECAUSE IF YOU DID YOU'D WANT TO RUN TOO.
LIKE HELL. WE'RE THE AVENGERS.
SURE YOU ARE.
ASK YOURSELF THIS, THEN, EARTH MIGHTIEST HERO:
"SAY YOU HAVE TO KILL THE AVENGERS. MAKE A LIST:
"WHO DO YOU KILL FIRST?
"THE REGULAR GUY."
"CLINT BARTON'S T LAST MAN I'D CALL 'REGULAR GUY.'"
"TELL YOURSELF THAT WHEN HE BLEEDS OUT IN HIS PRECIOUS LITTLE APARTMENT IN BROOKLYN.
"TELL HIM BELIEVE IT OR NOT I TRIED TO HELP.
"AND TELL HIM I SAID TO KEEP. SAFE."
CLINT BARTON, CLINT BARTON.
WHAT HAVE YOU BEEN UP TO...?

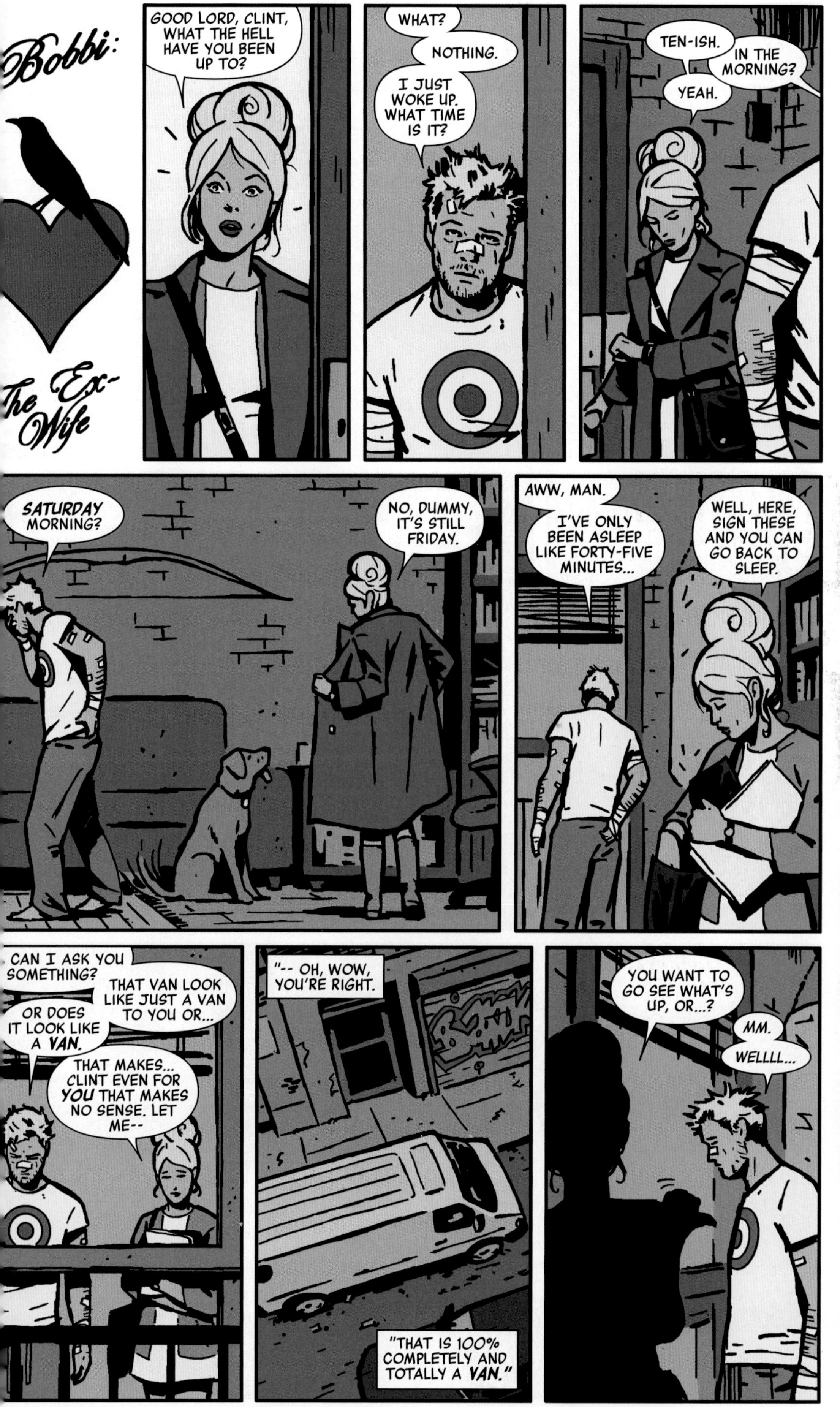
Bobbi:
The Ex-Wife
GOOD LORD, CLINT, WHAT THE HELL HAVE YOU BEEN UP TO?
WHAT?
NOTHING.
I JUST WOKE UP. WHAT TIME IS IT?
TEN-ISH.
IN THE MORNING?
YEAH.
SATURDAY MORNING?
NO, DUMMY, IT'S STILL FRIDAY.
AWW, MAN.
I'VE ONLY BEEN ASLEEP LIKE FORTY-FIVE MINUTES...
WELL, HERE, SIGN THESE AND YOU CAN GO BACK TO SLEEP.
CAN I ASK YOU SOMETHING?
THAT VAN LOOK LIKE JUST A VAN TO YOU OR...
OR DOES IT LOOK LIKE A VAN.
THAT MAKES... CLINT EVEN FOR YOU THAT MAKES NO SENSE. LET ME--
"-- OH, WOW, YOU'RE RIGHT.
"THAT IS 100% COMPLETELY AND TOTALLY A VAN."
YOU WANT TO GO SEE WHAT'S UP, OR...?
MM.
WELLLL...

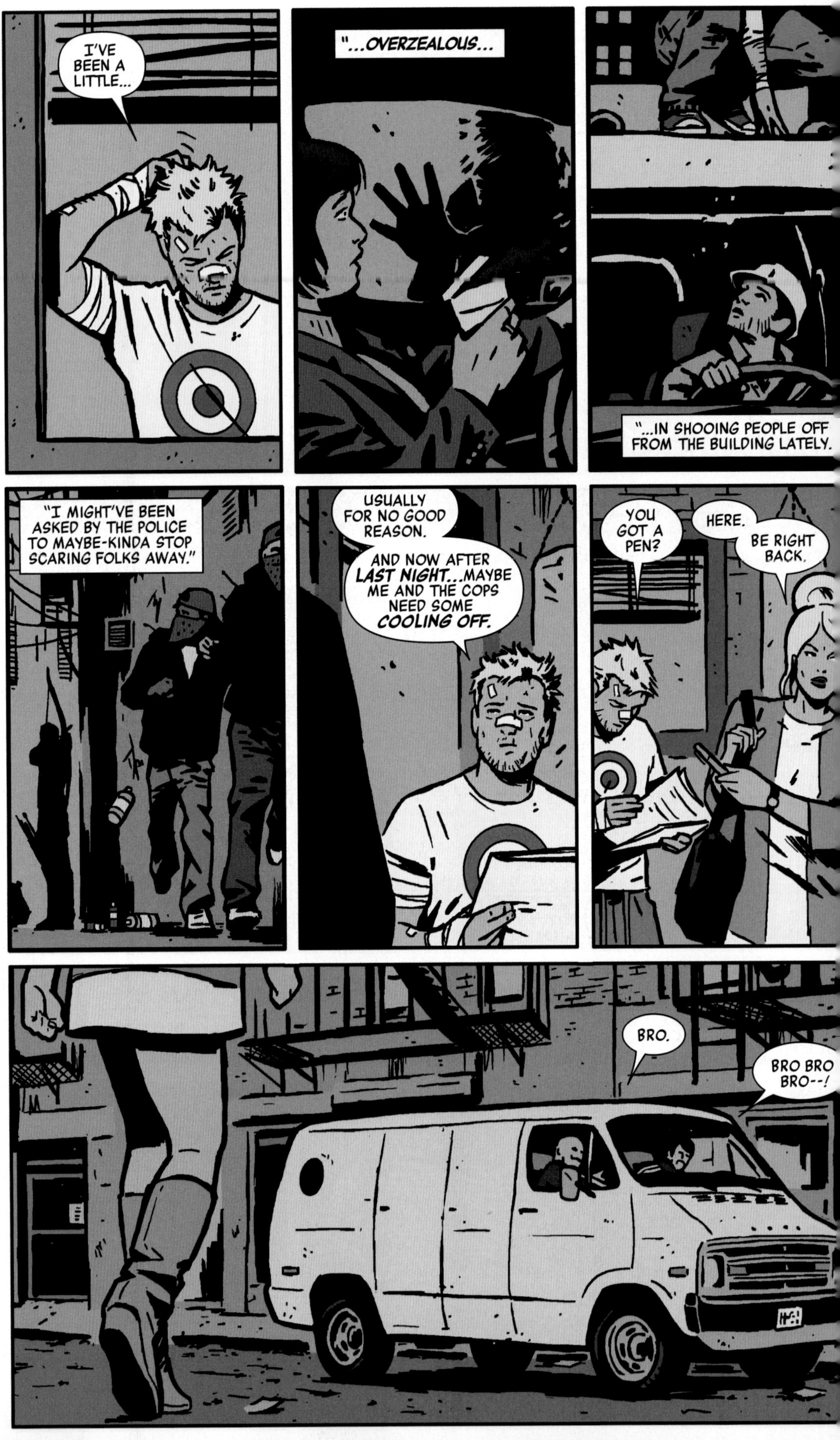
I'VE BEEN A LITTLE...
"...OVERZEALOUS...
"...IN SHOOING PEOPLE OFF FROM THE BUILDING LATELY.
"I MIGHT'VE BEEN ASKED BY THE POLICE TO MAYBE-KINDA STOP SCARING FOLKS AWAY."
USUALLY FOR NO GOOD REASON.
AND NOW AFTER LAST NIGHT...MAYBE ME AND THE COPS NEED SOME COOLING OFF.
YOU GOT A PEN?
HERE.
BE RIGHT BACK.
BRO.
BRO BRO BRO--!

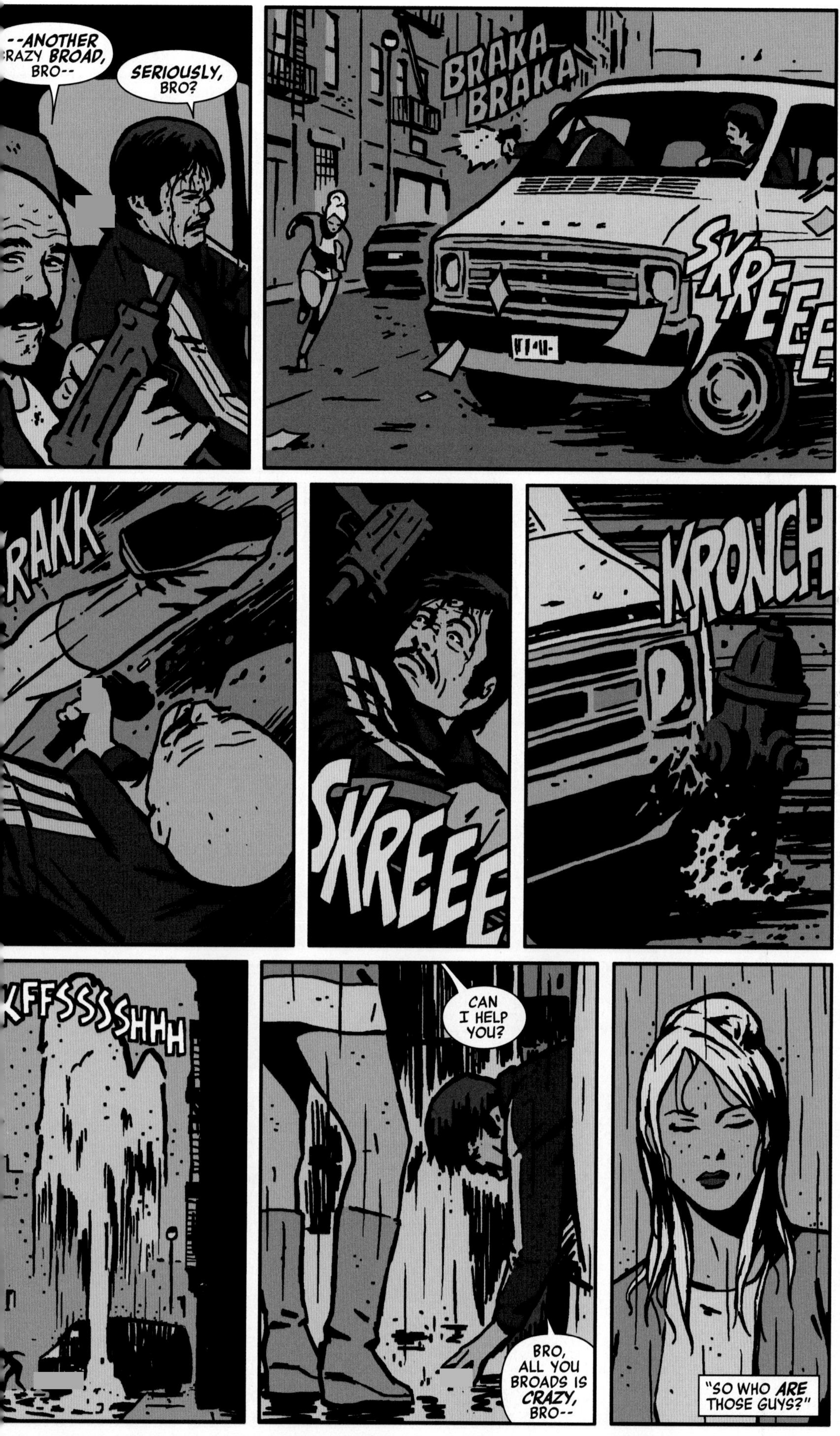
--ANOTHER RAZY BROAD, BRO--
SERIOUSLY, BRO?
BRAKA BRAKA
SKREEEE
RAKK
SKREEE
KRONCH
KFFSSSSHHH
CAN I HELP YOU?
BRO, ALL YOU BROADS IS CRAZY, BRO--
"SO WHO ARE THOSE GUYS?"

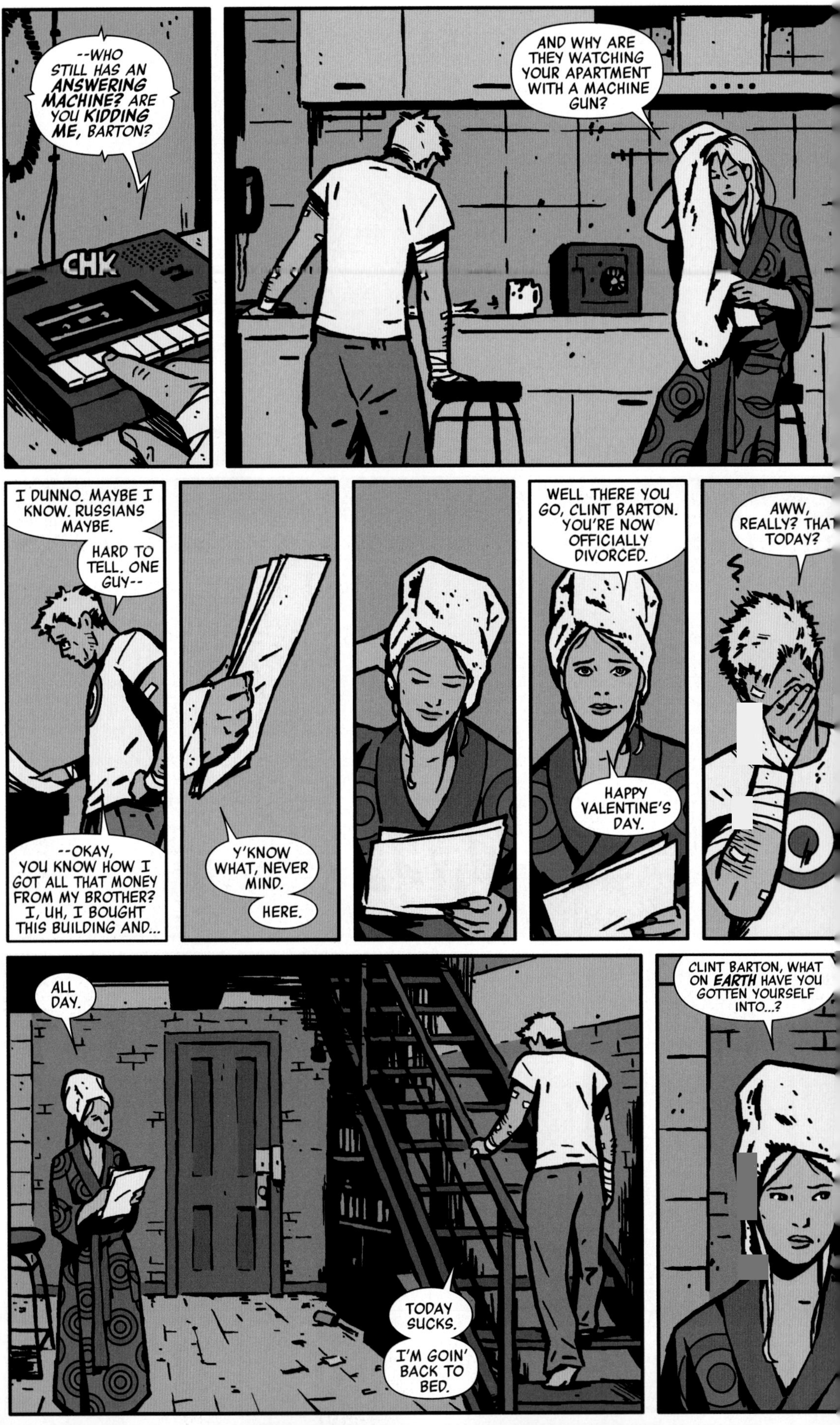
--WHO STILL HAS AN ANSWERING MACHINE? ARE YOU KIDDING ME, BARTON?
CHK
AND WHY ARE THEY WATCHING YOUR APARTMENT WITH A MACHINE GUN?
I DUNNO. MAYBE I KNOW. RUSSIANS MAYBE.
HARD TO TELL. ONE GUY--
--OKAY, YOU KNOW HOW I GOT ALL THAT MONEY FROM MY BROTHER? I, UH, I BOUGHT THIS BUILDING AND...
Y'KNOW WHAT, NEVER MIND.
HERE.
WELL THERE YOU GO, CLINT BARTON. YOU'RE NOW OFFICIALLY DIVORCED.
HAPPY VALENTINE'S DAY.
AWW, REALLY? THAT TODAY?
ALL DAY.
TODAY SUCKS.
I'M GOIN' BACK TO BED.
CLINT BARTON, WHAT ON EARTH HAVE YOU GOTTEN YOURSELF INTO...?

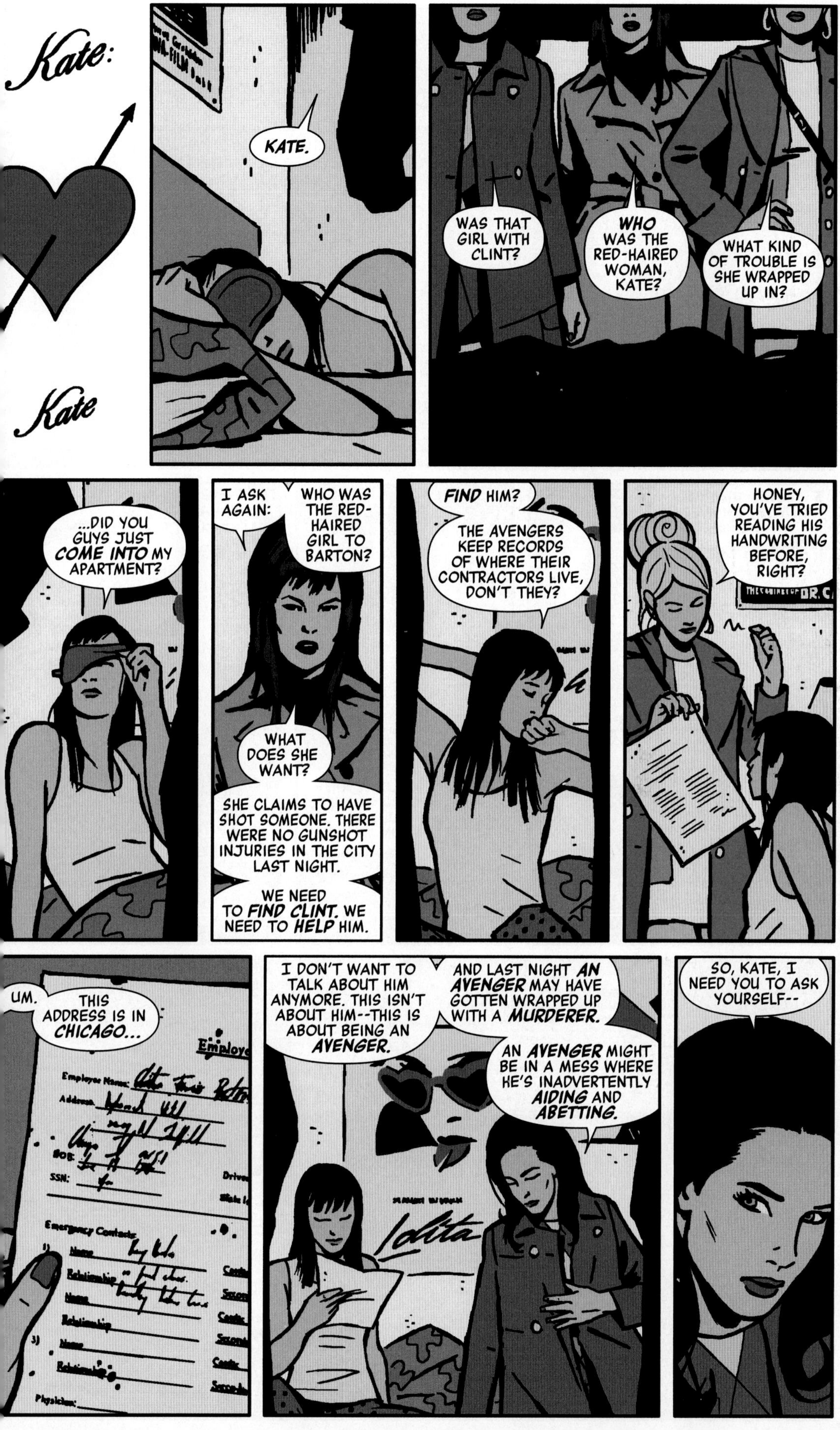
Kate:
Kate
KATE.
WAS THAT GIRL WITH CLINT?
WHO WAS THE RED-HAIRED WOMAN, KATE?
WHAT KIND OF TROUBLE IS SHE WRAPPED UP IN?
...DID YOU GUYS JUST COME INTO MY APARTMENT?
I ASK AGAIN:
WHO WAS THE RED-HAIRED GIRL TO BARTON?
WHAT DOES SHE WANT?
SHE CLAIMS TO HAVE SHOT SOMEONE. THERE WERE NO GUNSHOT INJURIES IN THE CITY LAST NIGHT.
WE NEED TO FIND CLINT. WE NEED TO HELP HIM.
FIND HIM?
THE AVENGERS KEEP RECORDS OF WHERE THEIR CONTRACTORS LIVE, DON'T THEY?
HONEY, YOU'VE TRIED READING HIS HANDWRITING BEFORE, RIGHT?
UM.
THIS ADDRESS IS IN CHICAGO...
Employee Name:
Address:
DOB:
SSN:
Emergency Contacts:
Name
Relationship
Name
Relationship
Name
Relationship
Physician:
I DON'T WANT TO TALK ABOUT HIM ANYMORE. THIS ISN'T ABOUT HIM--THIS IS ABOUT BEING AN AVENGER.
AND LAST NIGHT AN AVENGER MAY HAVE GOTTEN WRAPPED UP WITH A MURDERER.
AN AVENGER MIGHT BE IN A MESS WHERE HE'S INADVERTENTLY AIDING AND ABETTING.
Lolita
SO, KATE, I NEED YOU TO ASK YOURSELF--

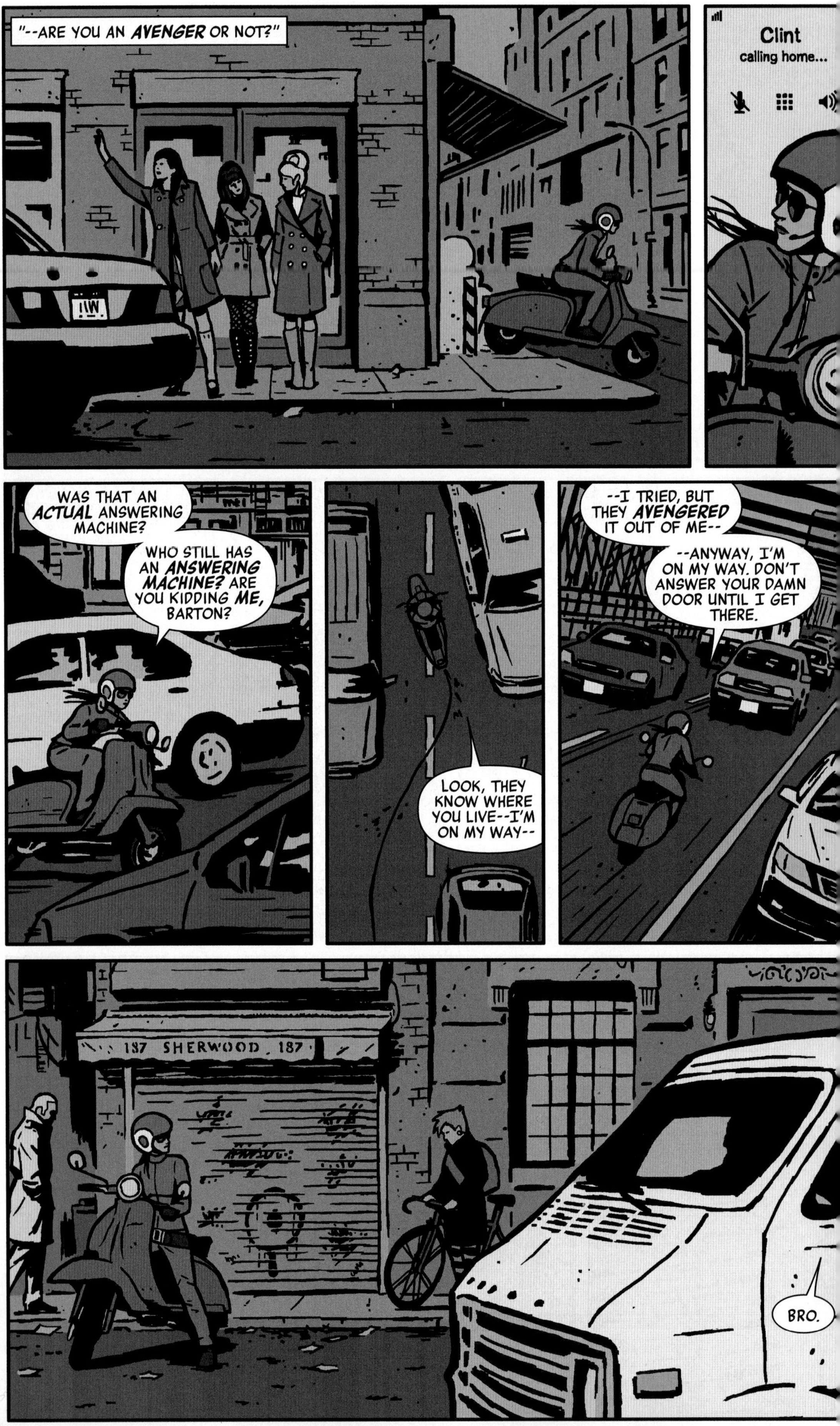
"--ARE YOU AN AVENGER OR NOT?"
Clint
calling home...
!IW
WAS THAT AN ACTUAL ANSWERING MACHINE?
WHO STILL HAS AN ANSWERING MACHINE? ARE YOU KIDDING ME, BARTON?
LOOK, THEY KNOW WHERE YOU LIVE--I'M ON MY WAY--
--I TRIED, BUT THEY AVENGERED IT OUT OF ME--
--ANYWAY, I'M ON MY WAY. DON'T ANSWER YOUR DAMN DOOR UNTIL I GET THERE.
187 SHERWOOD 187
BRO.

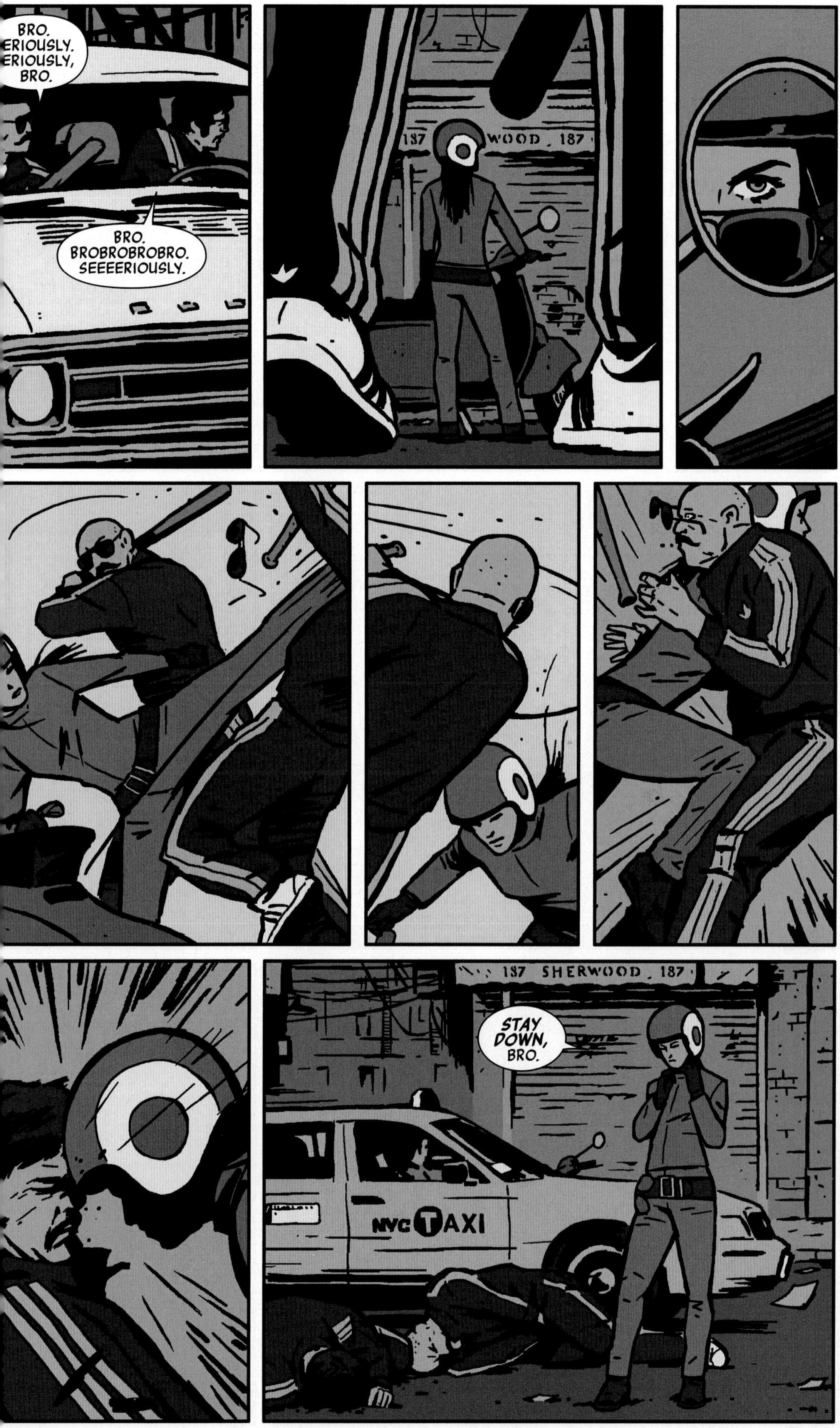
BRO.
ERIOUSLY.
ERIOUSLY,
BRO.
BRO.
BROBROBROBRO.
SEEEERIOUSLY.
187 WOOD 187
187 SHERWOOD 187
STAY DOWN, BRO.
NYC TAXI

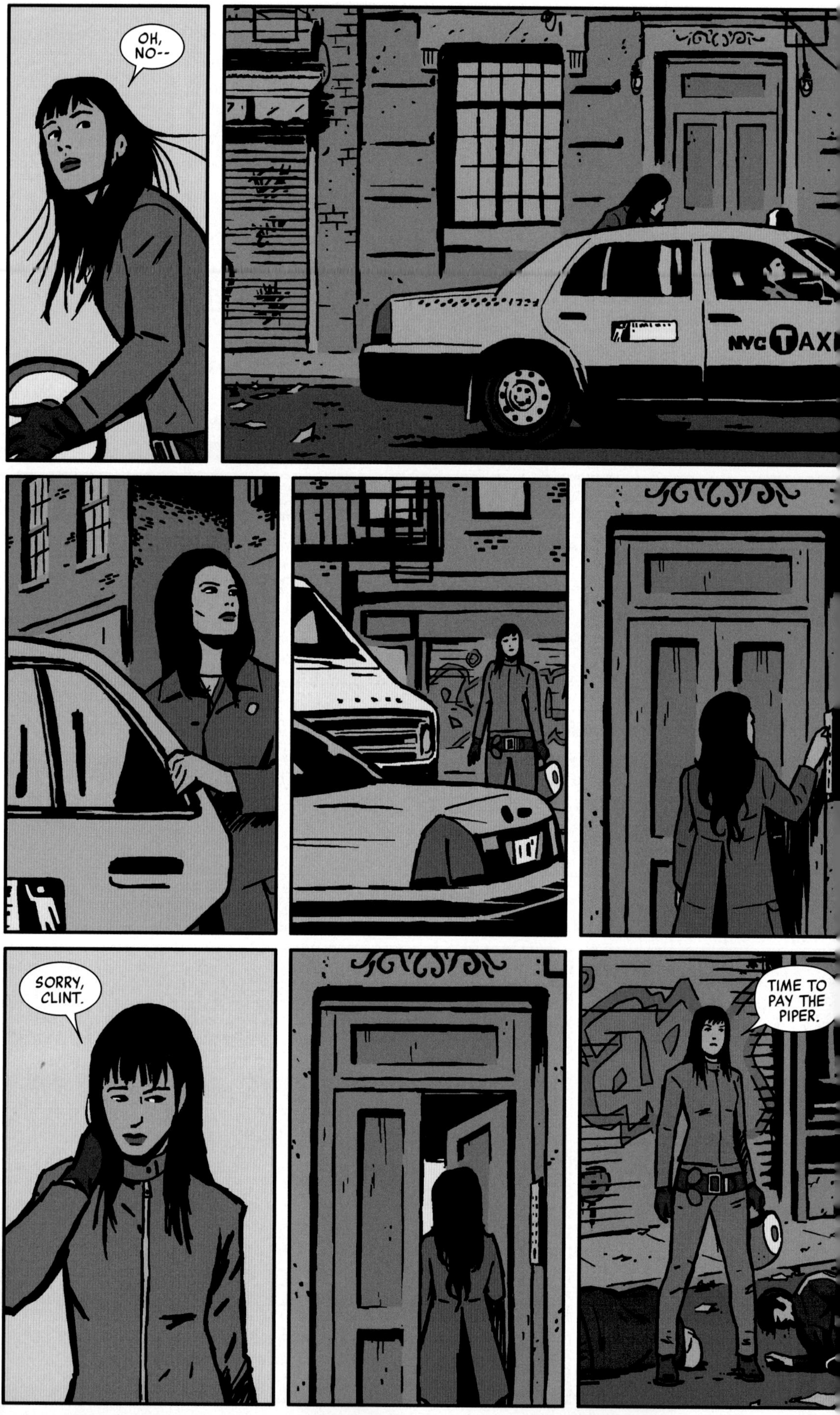
OH, NO--
NYC TAXI
SORRY, CLINT.
TIME TO PAY THE PIPER.

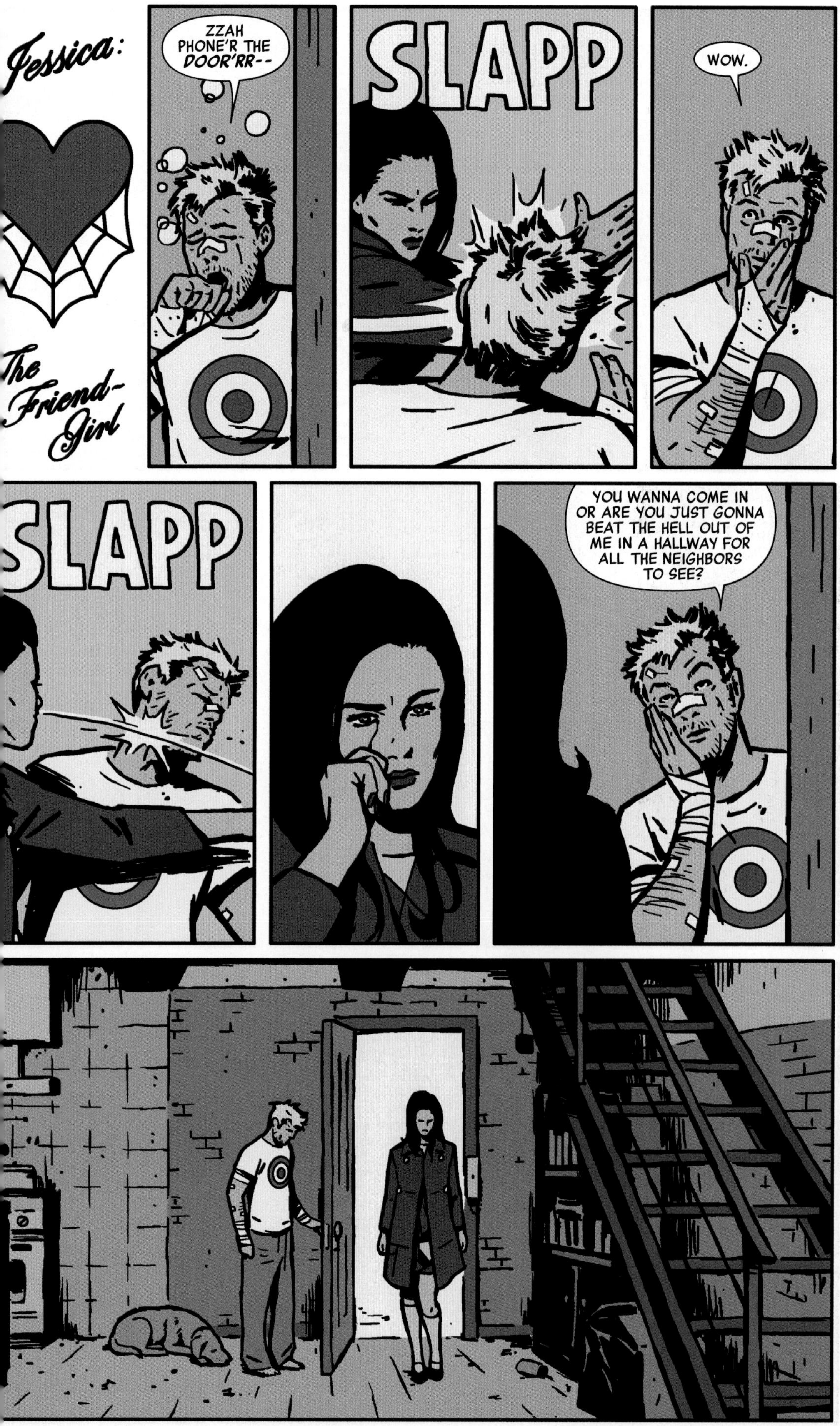
Jessica:
The Friend-Girl
ZZAH PHONE'R THE DOOR'RR--
SLAPP
WOW.
SLAPP
YOU WANNA COME IN OR ARE YOU JUST GONNA BEAT THE HELL OUT OF ME IN A HALLWAY FOR ALL THE NEIGHBORS TO SEE?

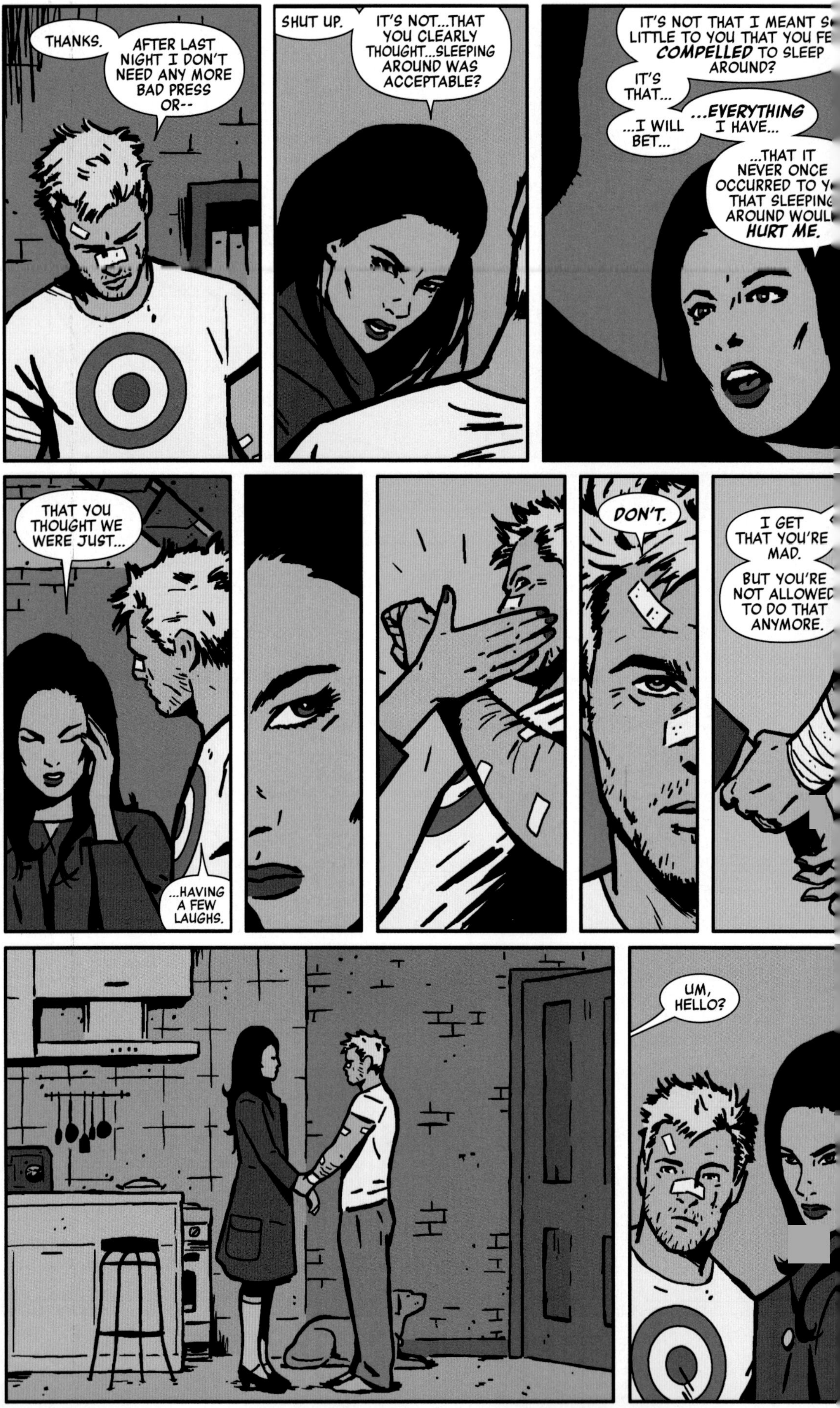
THANKS.
AFTER LAST NIGHT I DON'T NEED ANY MORE BAD PRESS OR--
SHUT UP.
IT'S NOT...THAT YOU CLEARLY THOUGHT...SLEEPING AROUND WAS ACCEPTABLE?
IT'S NOT THAT I MEANT S LITTLE TO YOU THAT YOU FE COMPELLED TO SLEEP AROUND?
IT'S THAT...
...I WILL BET...
...EVERYTHING I HAVE...
...THAT IT NEVER ONCE OCCURRED TO Y THAT SLEEPING AROUND WOUL HURT ME.
THAT YOU THOUGHT WE WERE JUST...
...HAVING A FEW LAUGHS.
DON'T.
I GET THAT YOU'RE MAD.
BUT YOU'RE NOT ALLOWED TO DO THAT ANYMORE.
UM, HELLO?

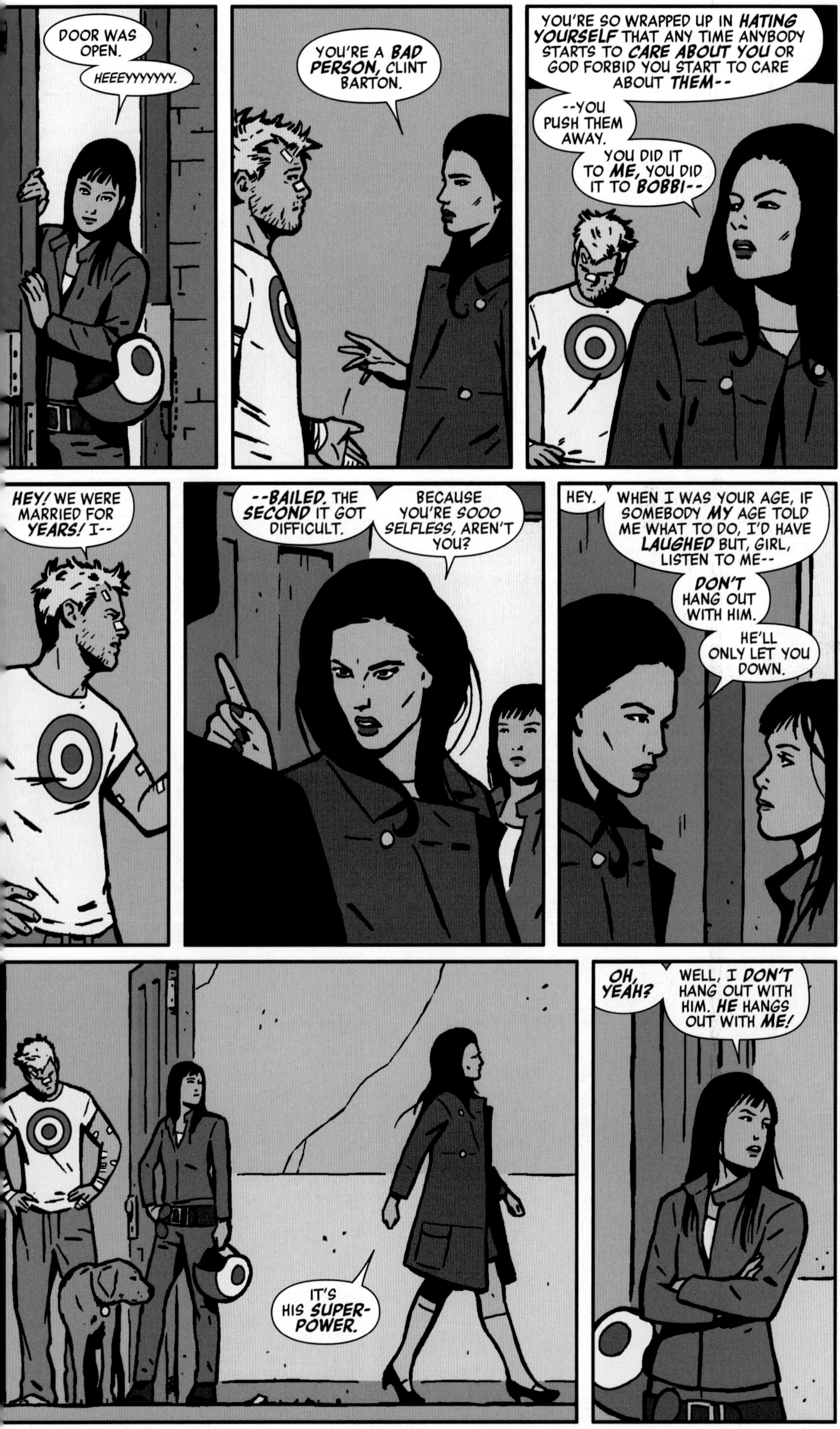
DOOR WAS OPEN.
HEEEYYYYYYY.
YOU'RE A BAD PERSON, CLINT BARTON.
YOU'RE SO WRAPPED UP IN HATING YOURSELF THAT ANY TIME ANYBODY STARTS TO CARE ABOUT YOU OR GOD FORBID YOU START TO CARE ABOUT THEM--
--YOU PUSH THEM AWAY.
YOU DID IT TO ME, YOU DID IT TO BOBBI--
HEY! WE WERE MARRIED FOR YEARS! I--
--BAILED. THE SECOND IT GOT DIFFICULT.
BECAUSE YOU'RE SOOO SELFLESS, AREN'T YOU?
HEY.
WHEN I WAS YOUR AGE, IF SOMEBODY MY AGE TOLD ME WHAT TO DO, I'D HAVE LAUGHED BUT, GIRL, LISTEN TO ME--
DON'T HANG OUT WITH HIM.
HE'LL ONLY LET YOU DOWN.
IT'S HIS SUPER-POWER.
OH, YEAH?
WELL, I DON'T HANG OUT WITH HIM. HE HANGS OUT WITH ME!

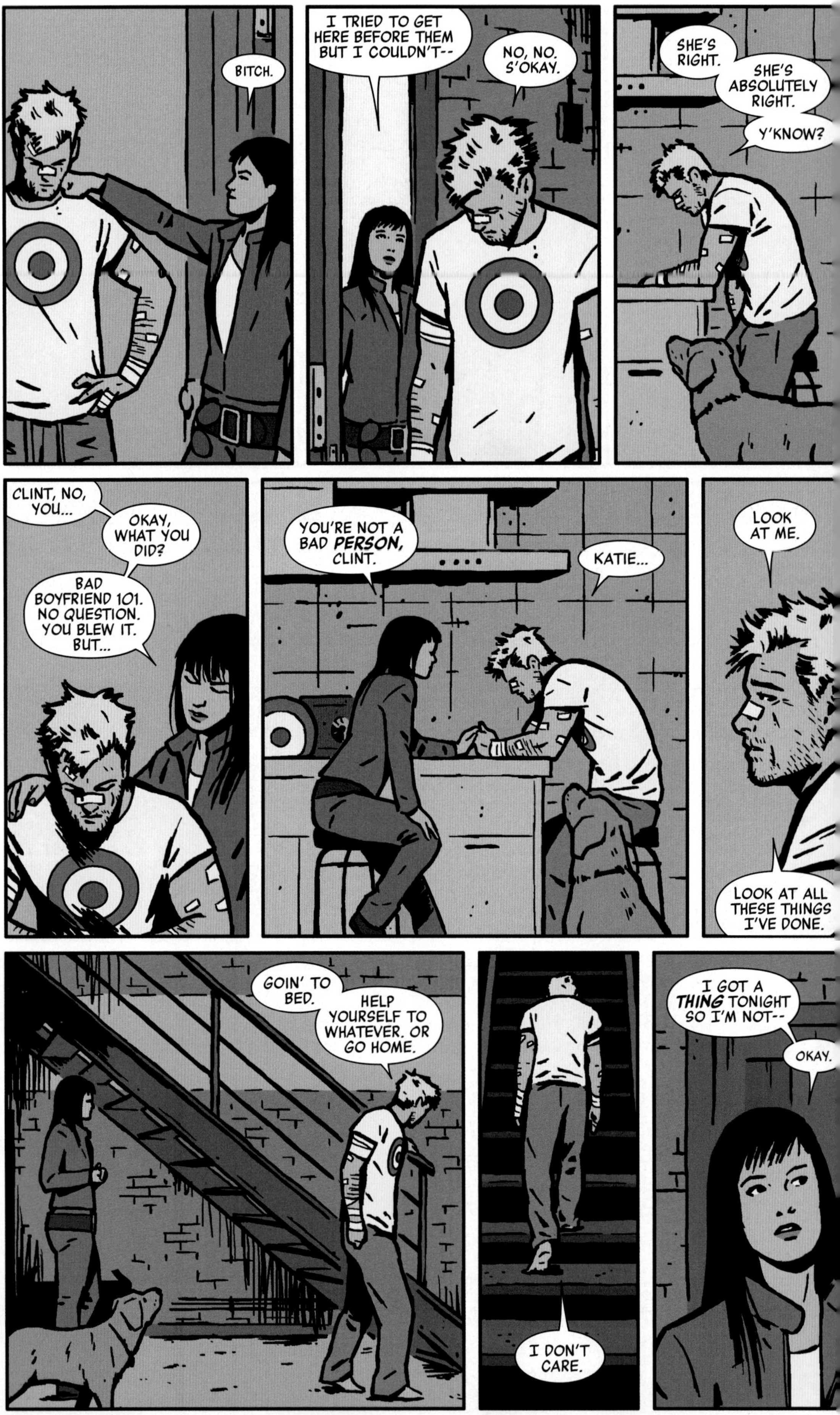
BITCH.
I TRIED TO GET HERE BEFORE THEM BUT I COULDN'T--
NO, NO. S'OKAY.
SHE'S RIGHT.
SHE'S ABSOLUTELY RIGHT.
Y'KNOW?
CLINT, NO, YOU...
OKAY, WHAT YOU DID?
BAD BOYFRIEND 101. NO QUESTION. YOU BLEW IT. BUT...
YOU'RE NOT A BAD *PERSON,* CLINT.
KATIE...
LOOK AT ME.
LOOK AT ALL THESE THINGS I'VE DONE.
GOIN' TO BED.
HELP YOURSELF TO WHATEVER. OR GO HOME.
I DON'T CARE.
I GOT A *THING* TONIGHT SO I'M NOT--
OKAY.

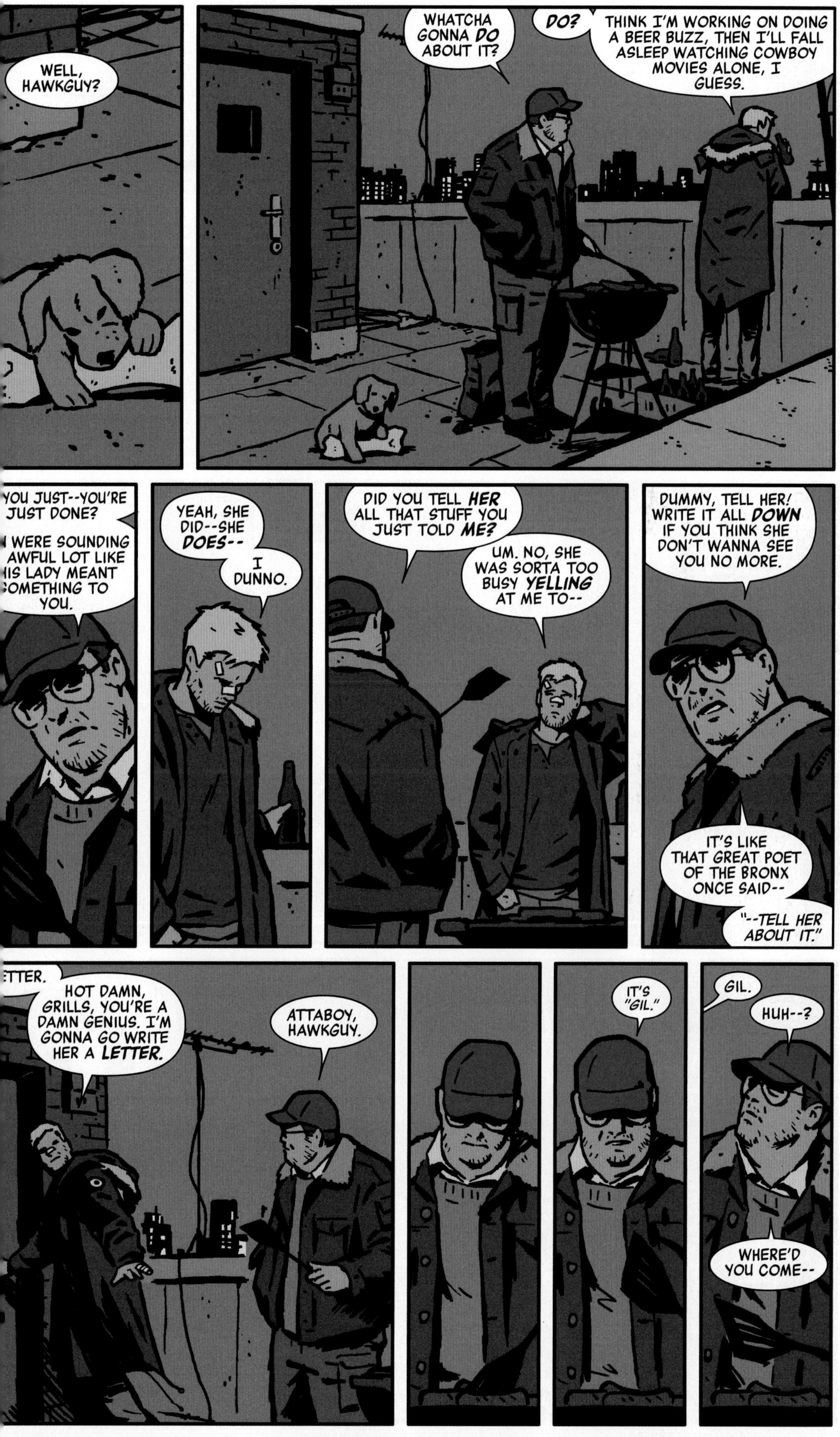
WELL, HAWKGUY?
WHATCHA GONNA DO ABOUT IT?
DO?
THINK I'M WORKING ON DOING A BEER BUZZ, THEN I'LL FALL ASLEEP WATCHING COWBOY MOVIES ALONE, I GUESS.
YOU JUST--YOU'RE JUST DONE?
WERE SOUNDING AWFUL LOT LIKE IS LADY MEANT OMETHING TO YOU.
YEAH, SHE DID--SHE DOES--
I DUNNO.
DID YOU TELL HER ALL THAT STUFF YOU JUST TOLD ME?
UM. NO, SHE WAS SORTA TOO BUSY YELLING AT ME TO--
DUMMY, TELL HER! WRITE IT ALL DOWN IF YOU THINK SHE DON'T WANNA SEE YOU NO MORE.
IT'S LIKE THAT GREAT POET OF THE BRONX ONCE SAID--
"--TELL HER ABOUT IT."
TTER.
HOT DAMN, GRILLS, YOU'RE A DAMN GENIUS. I'M GONNA GO WRITE HER A LETTER.
ATTABOY, HAWKGUY.
IT'S "GIL."
GIL.
HUH--?
WHERE'D YOU COME--

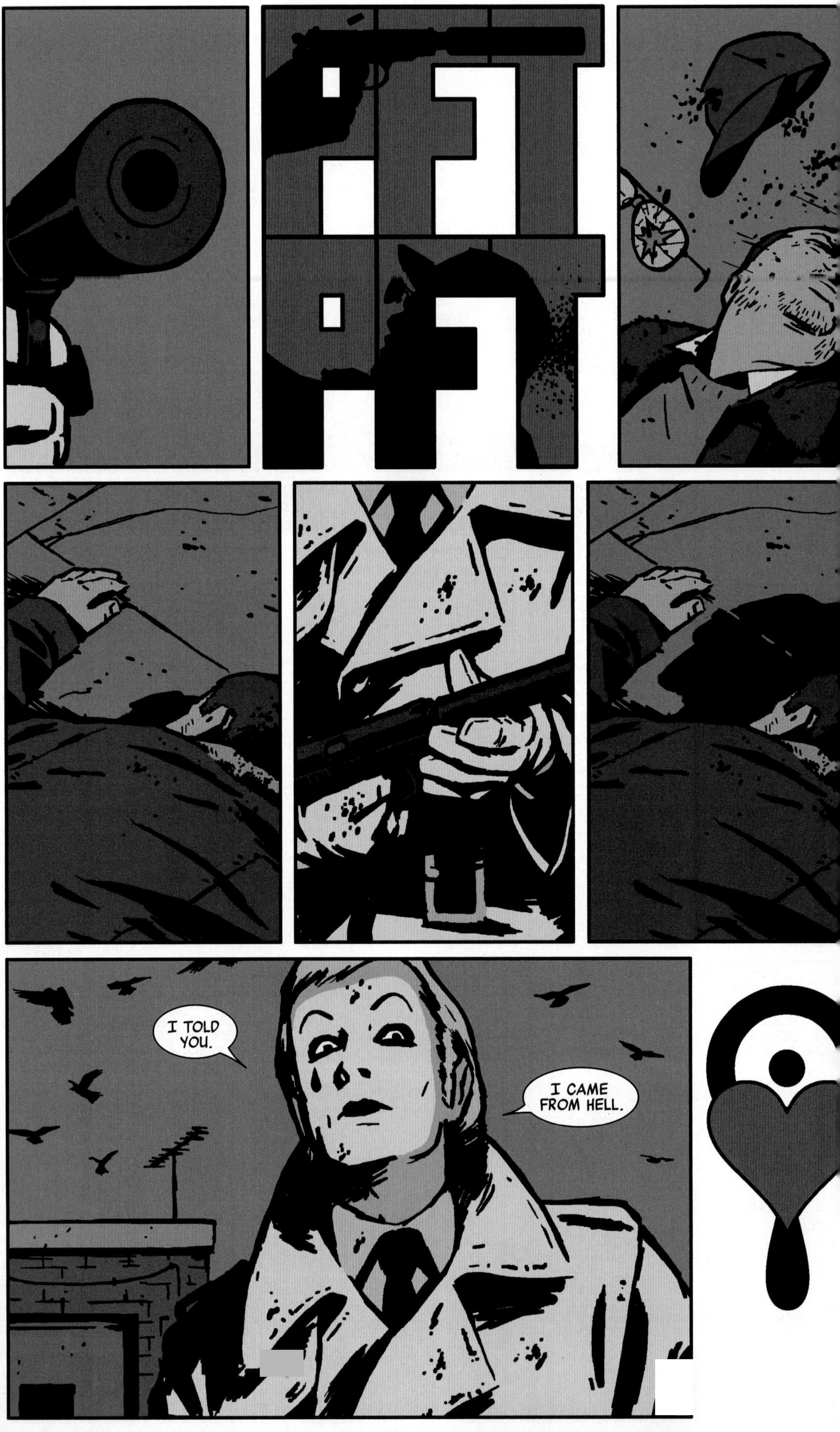
PFT
PFT
I TOLD YOU.
I CAME FROM HELL.

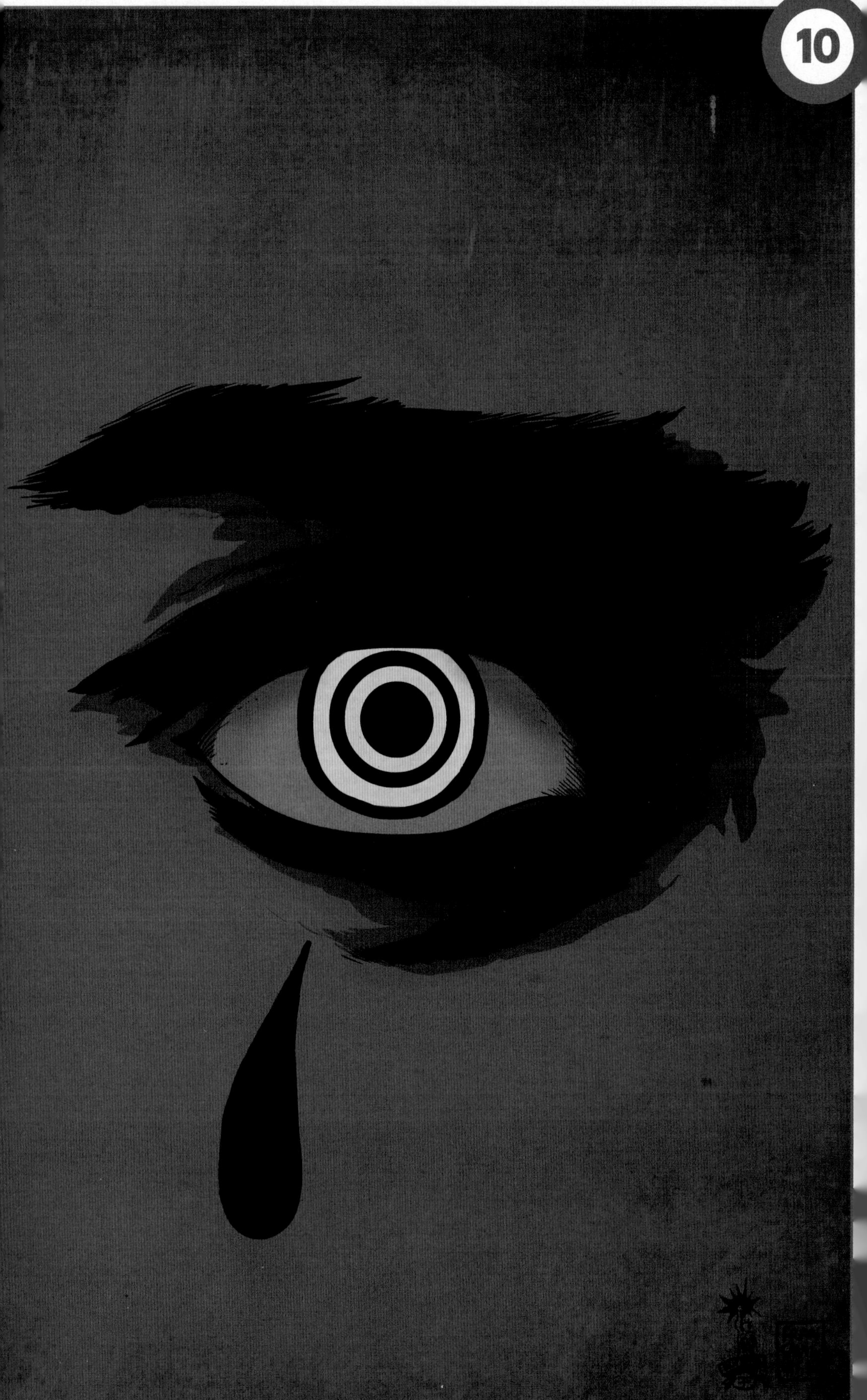
10

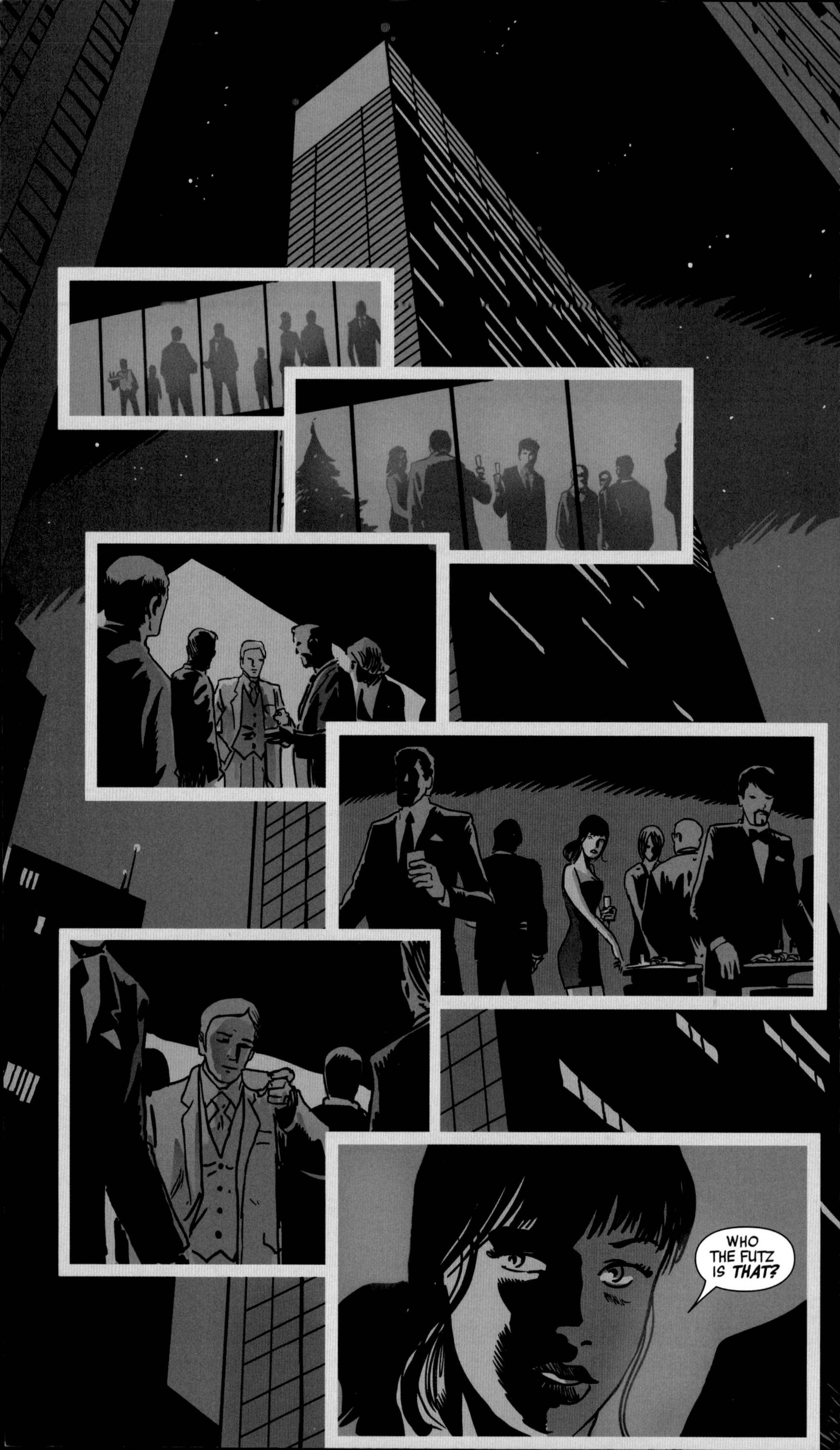
WHO THE FUTZ IS *THAT?*

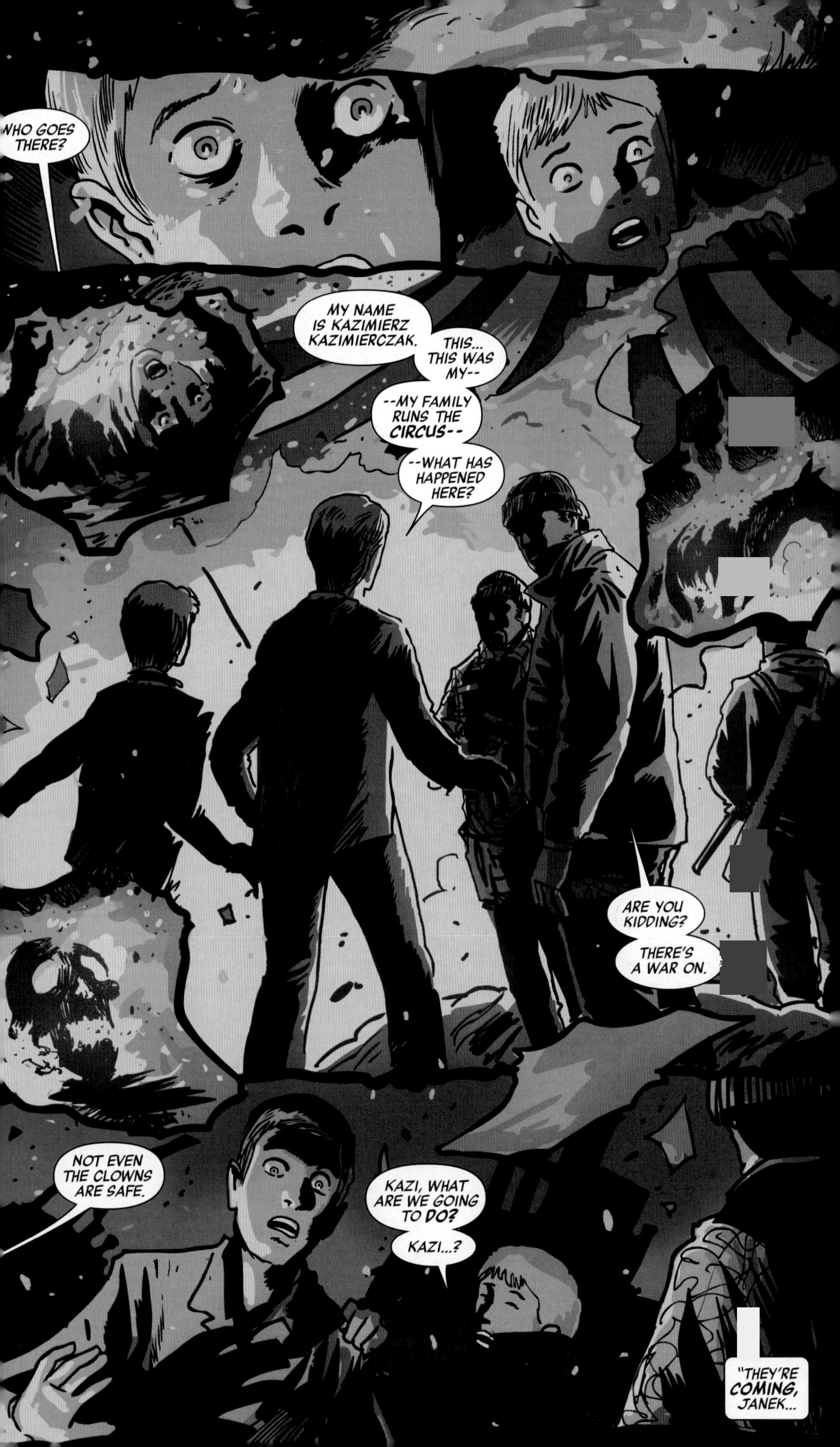
WHO GOES THERE?
MY NAME IS KAZIMIERZ KAZIMIERCZAK.
THIS... THIS WAS MY--
--MY FAMILY RUNS THE **CIRCUS**--
--WHAT HAS HAPPENED HERE?
ARE YOU KIDDING?
THERE'S A WAR ON.
NOT EVEN THE CLOWNS ARE SAFE.
KAZI, WHAT ARE WE GOING TO **DO?**
KAZI...?
"THEY'RE **COMING,** JANEK...

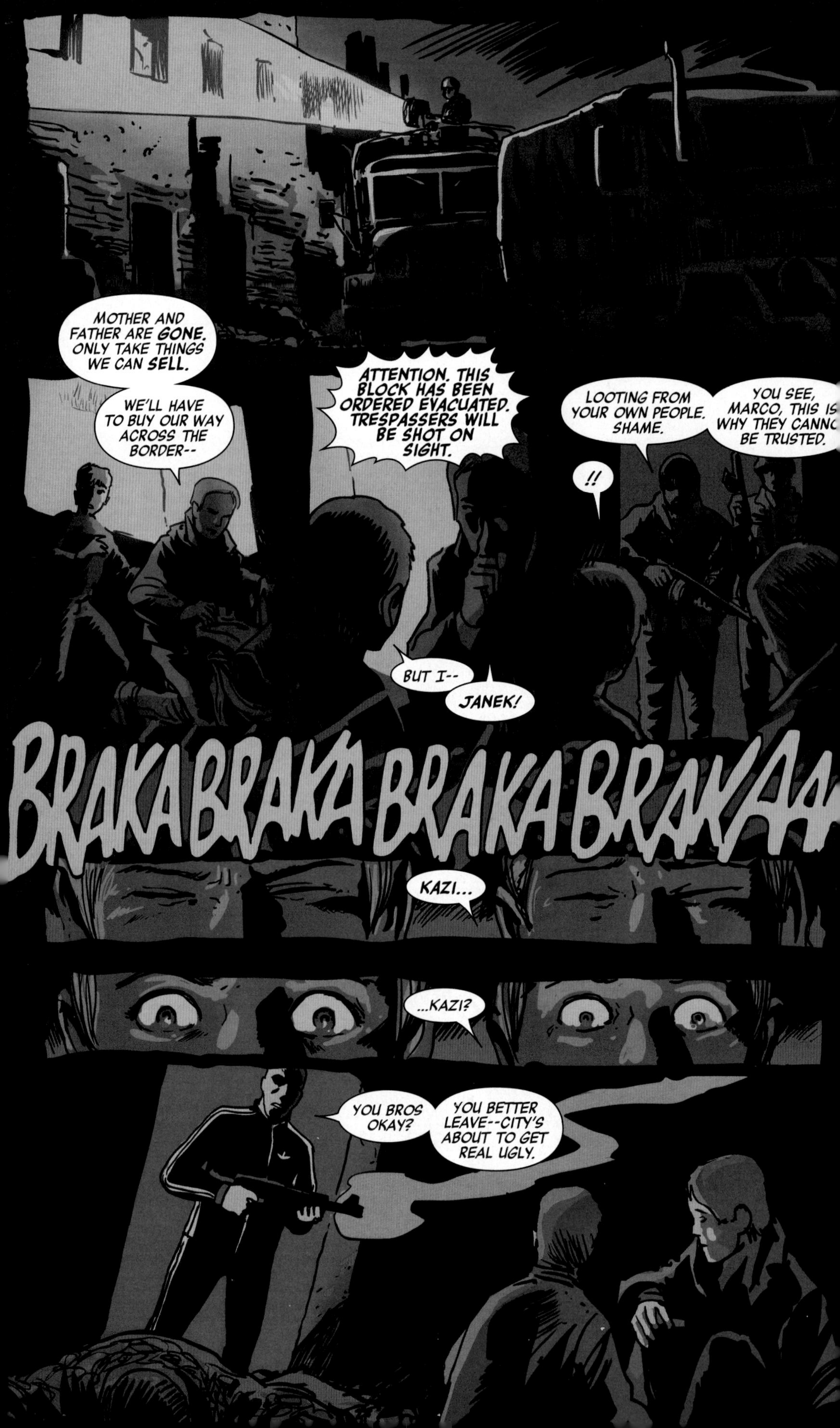
MOTHER AND FATHER ARE GONE. ONLY TAKE THINGS WE CAN SELL.
WE'LL HAVE TO BUY OUR WAY ACROSS THE BORDER--
ATTENTION. THIS BLOCK HAS BEEN ORDERED EVACUATED. TRESPASSERS WILL BE SHOT ON SIGHT.
LOOTING FROM YOUR OWN PEOPLE. SHAME.
YOU SEE, MARCO, THIS IS WHY THEY CANNO BE TRUSTED.
!!
BUT I--
JANEK!
BRAKA BRAKA BRAKA BRAKAA
KAZI...
...KAZI?
YOU BROS OKAY?
YOU BETTER LEAVE--CITY'S ABOUT TO GET REAL UGLY.

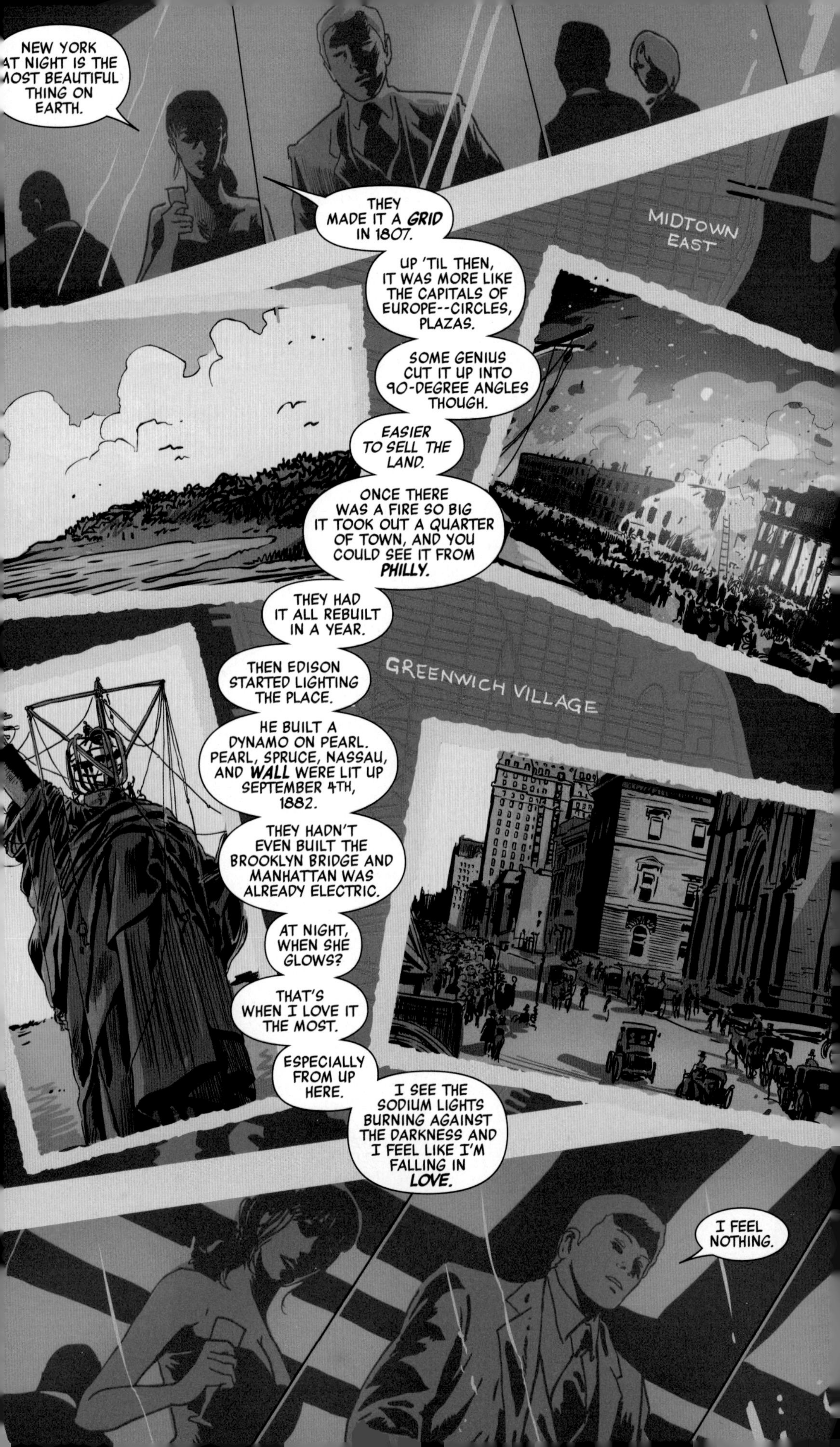

NEW YORK AT NIGHT IS THE MOST BEAUTIFUL THING ON EARTH.
THEY MADE IT A GRID IN 1807.
MIDTOWN EAST
UP 'TIL THEN, IT WAS MORE LIKE THE CAPITALS OF EUROPE--CIRCLES, PLAZAS.
SOME GENIUS CUT IT UP INTO 90-DEGREE ANGLES THOUGH.
EASIER TO SELL THE LAND.
ONCE THERE WAS A FIRE SO BIG IT TOOK OUT A QUARTER OF TOWN, AND YOU COULD SEE IT FROM PHILLY.
THEY HAD IT ALL REBUILT IN A YEAR.
THEN EDISON STARTED LIGHTING THE PLACE.
GREENWICH VILLAGE
HE BUILT A DYNAMO ON PEARL. PEARL, SPRUCE, NASSAU, AND WALL WERE LIT UP SEPTEMBER 4TH, 1882.
THEY HADN'T EVEN BUILT THE BROOKLYN BRIDGE AND MANHATTAN WAS ALREADY ELECTRIC.
AT NIGHT, WHEN SHE GLOWS?
THAT'S WHEN I LOVE IT THE MOST.
ESPECIALLY FROM UP HERE.
I SEE THE SODIUM LIGHTS BURNING AGAINST THE DARKNESS AND I FEEL LIKE I'M FALLING IN LOVE.
I FEEL NOTHING.

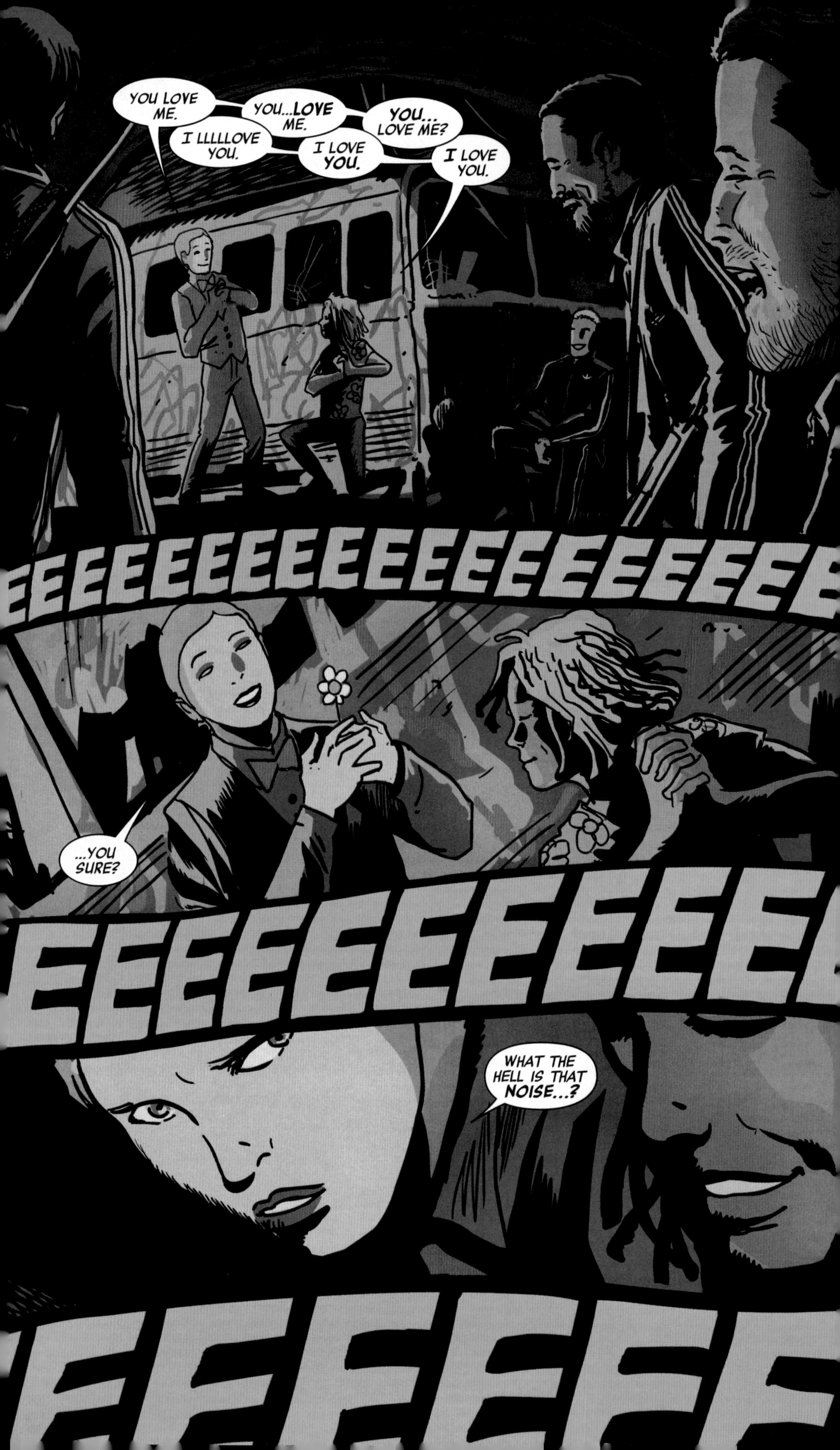
YOU LOVE ME.
I LLLLLOVE YOU.
YOU...LOVE ME.
I LOVE YOU.
YOU... LOVE ME?
I LOVE YOU.
EEEEEEEEEEEEEEEEEEEE
...YOU SURE?
EEEEEEEEEEEEEE
WHAT THE HELL IS THAT NOISE...?
EEEEEE

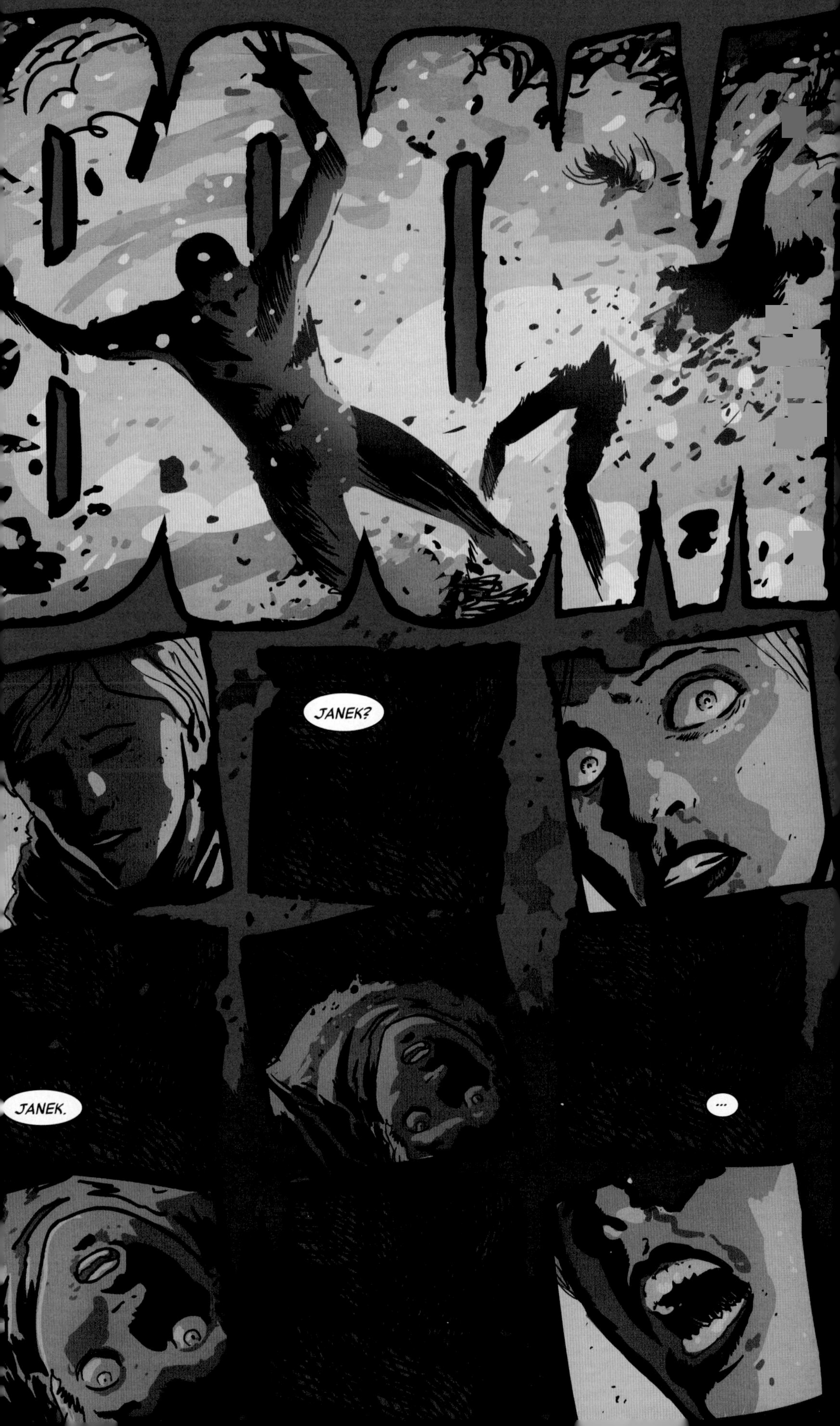
JANEK?
JANEK.
...

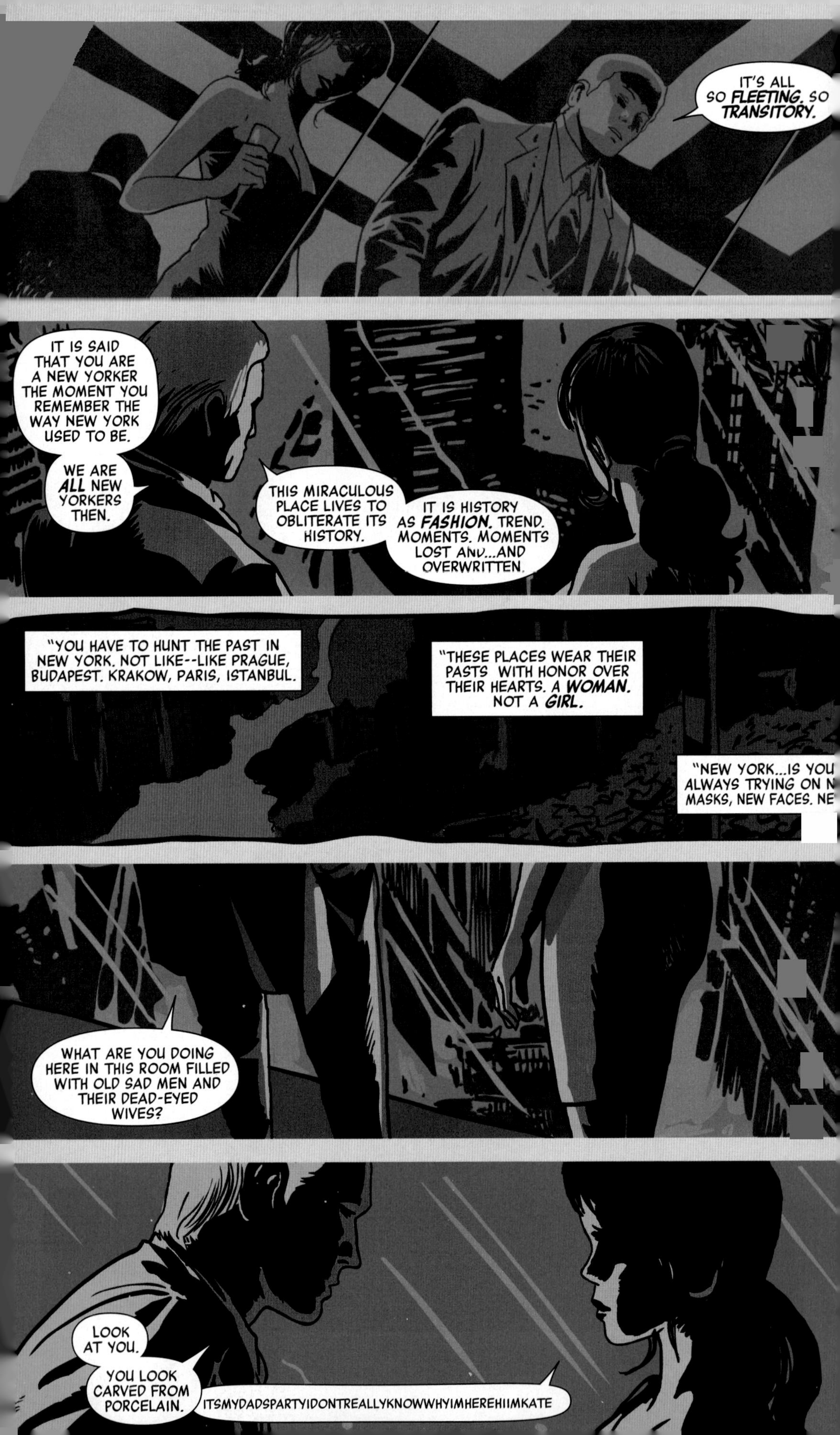

IT'S ALL SO FLEETING. SO TRANSITORY.
IT IS SAID THAT YOU ARE A NEW YORKER THE MOMENT YOU REMEMBER THE WAY NEW YORK USED TO BE.
WE ARE ALL NEW YORKERS THEN.
THIS MIRACULOUS PLACE LIVES TO OBLITERATE ITS HISTORY.
IT IS HISTORY AS FASHION. TREND. MOMENTS. MOMENTS LOST AND...AND OVERWRITTEN.
"YOU HAVE TO HUNT THE PAST IN NEW YORK. NOT LIKE--LIKE PRAGUE, BUDAPEST. KRAKOW, PARIS, ISTANBUL.
"THESE PLACES WEAR THEIR PASTS WITH HONOR OVER THEIR HEARTS. A WOMAN. NOT A GIRL.
"NEW YORK...IS YOU ALWAYS TRYING ON N MASKS, NEW FACES. NE
WHAT ARE YOU DOING HERE IN THIS ROOM FILLED WITH OLD SAD MEN AND THEIR DEAD-EYED WIVES?
LOOK AT YOU.
YOU LOOK CARVED FROM PORCELAIN.
ITSMYDADSPARTYIDONTREALLYKNOWWHYIMHEREHIIMKATE

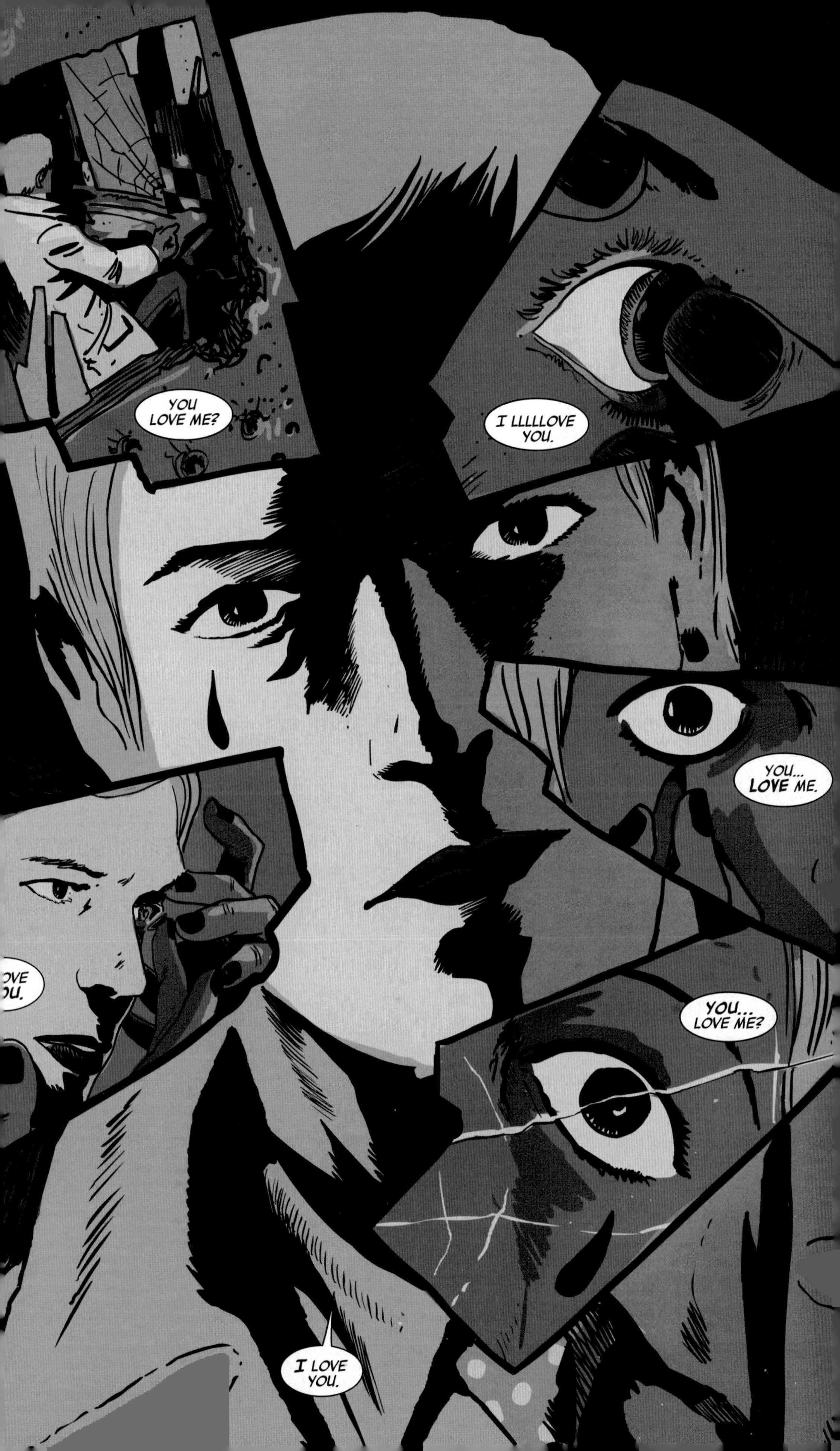
YOU LOVE ME?
I LLLLLOVE YOU.
YOU... LOVE ME.
YOU... LOVE ME?
I LOVE YOU.

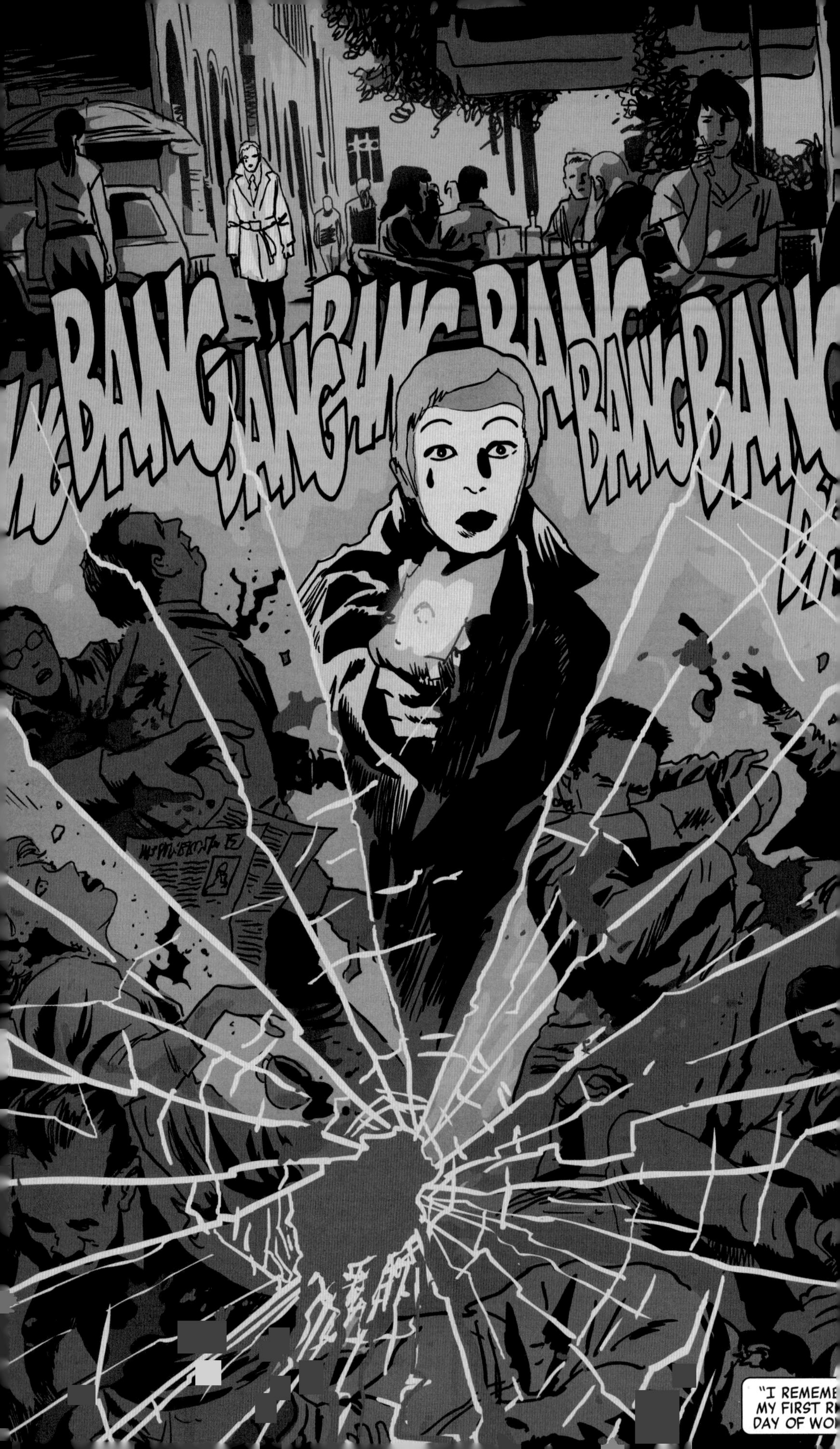
BANG
BANG
BANG
BANG
BANG
BANG
"I REMEME
MY FIRST R
DAY OF WO

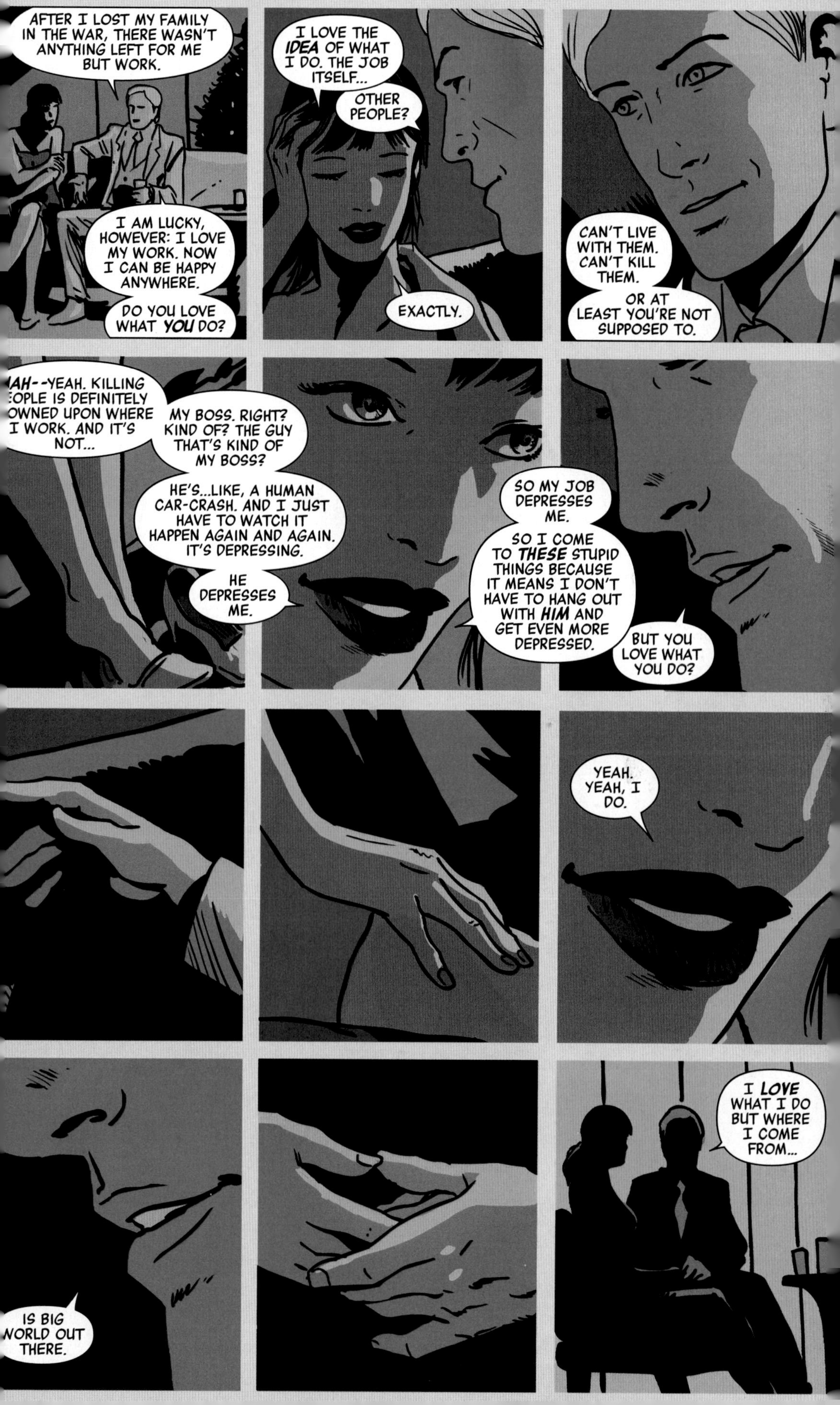
AFTER I LOST MY FAMILY IN THE WAR, THERE WASN'T ANYTHING LEFT FOR ME BUT WORK.
I AM LUCKY, HOWEVER: I LOVE MY WORK. NOW I CAN BE HAPPY ANYWHERE.
DO YOU LOVE WHAT YOU DO?
I LOVE THE IDEA OF WHAT I DO. THE JOB ITSELF...
OTHER PEOPLE?
EXACTLY.
CAN'T LIVE WITH THEM. CAN'T KILL THEM.
OR AT LEAST YOU'RE NOT SUPPOSED TO.
AH--YEAH. KILLING EOPLE IS DEFINITELY OWNED UPON WHERE I WORK. AND IT'S NOT...
MY BOSS. RIGHT? KIND OF? THE GUY THAT'S KIND OF MY BOSS?
HE'S...LIKE, A HUMAN CAR-CRASH. AND I JUST HAVE TO WATCH IT HAPPEN AGAIN AND AGAIN. IT'S DEPRESSING.
HE DEPRESSES ME.
SO MY JOB DEPRESSES ME.
SO I COME TO THESE STUPID THINGS BECAUSE IT MEANS I DON'T HAVE TO HANG OUT WITH HIM AND GET EVEN MORE DEPRESSED.
BUT YOU LOVE WHAT YOU DO?
YEAH. YEAH, I DO.
IS BIG VORLD OUT THERE.
I LOVE WHAT I DO BUT WHERE I COME FROM...

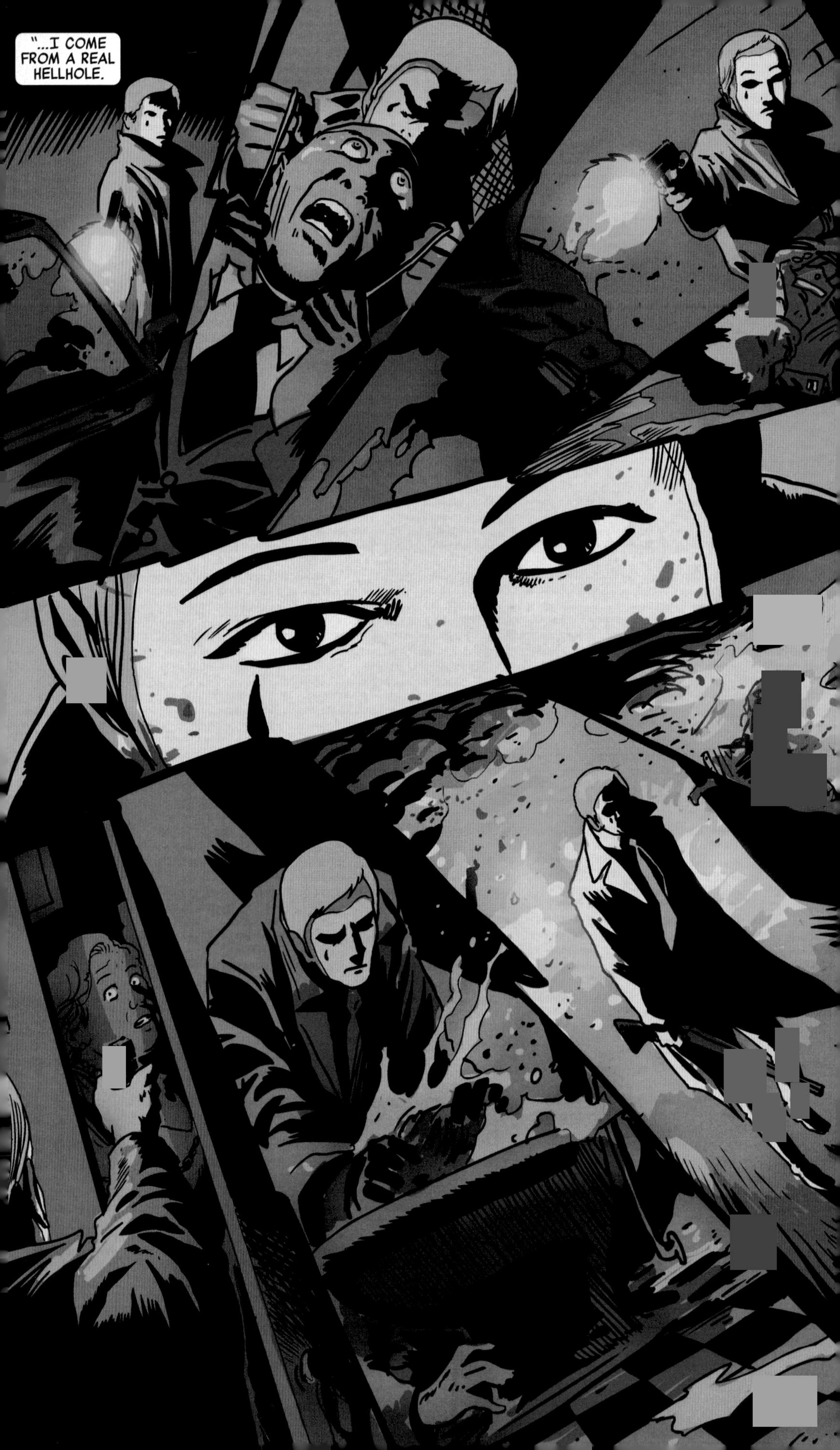
"...I COME FROM A REAL HELLHOLE.

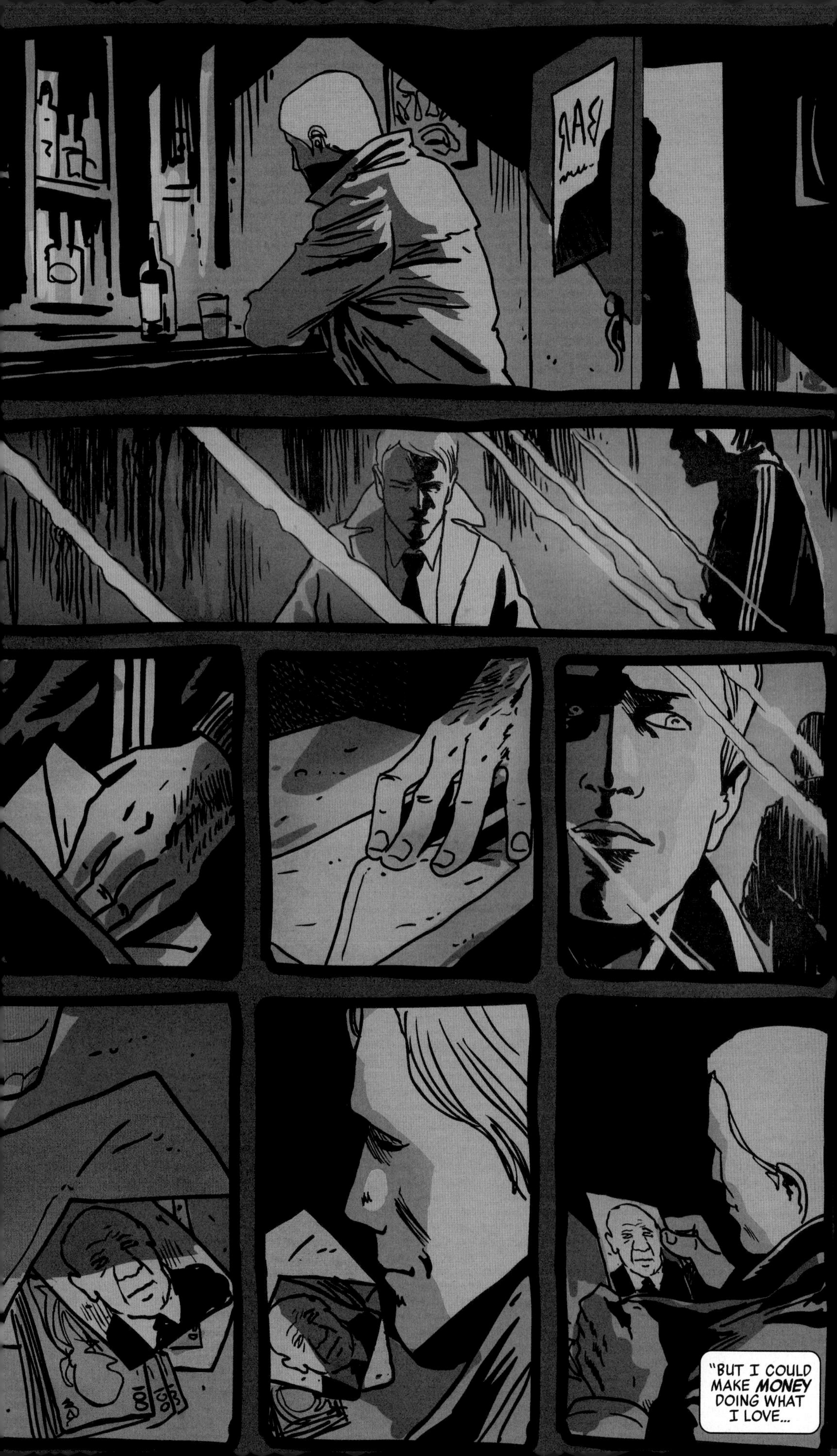
"BUT I COULD MAKE *MONEY* DOING WHAT I LOVE...

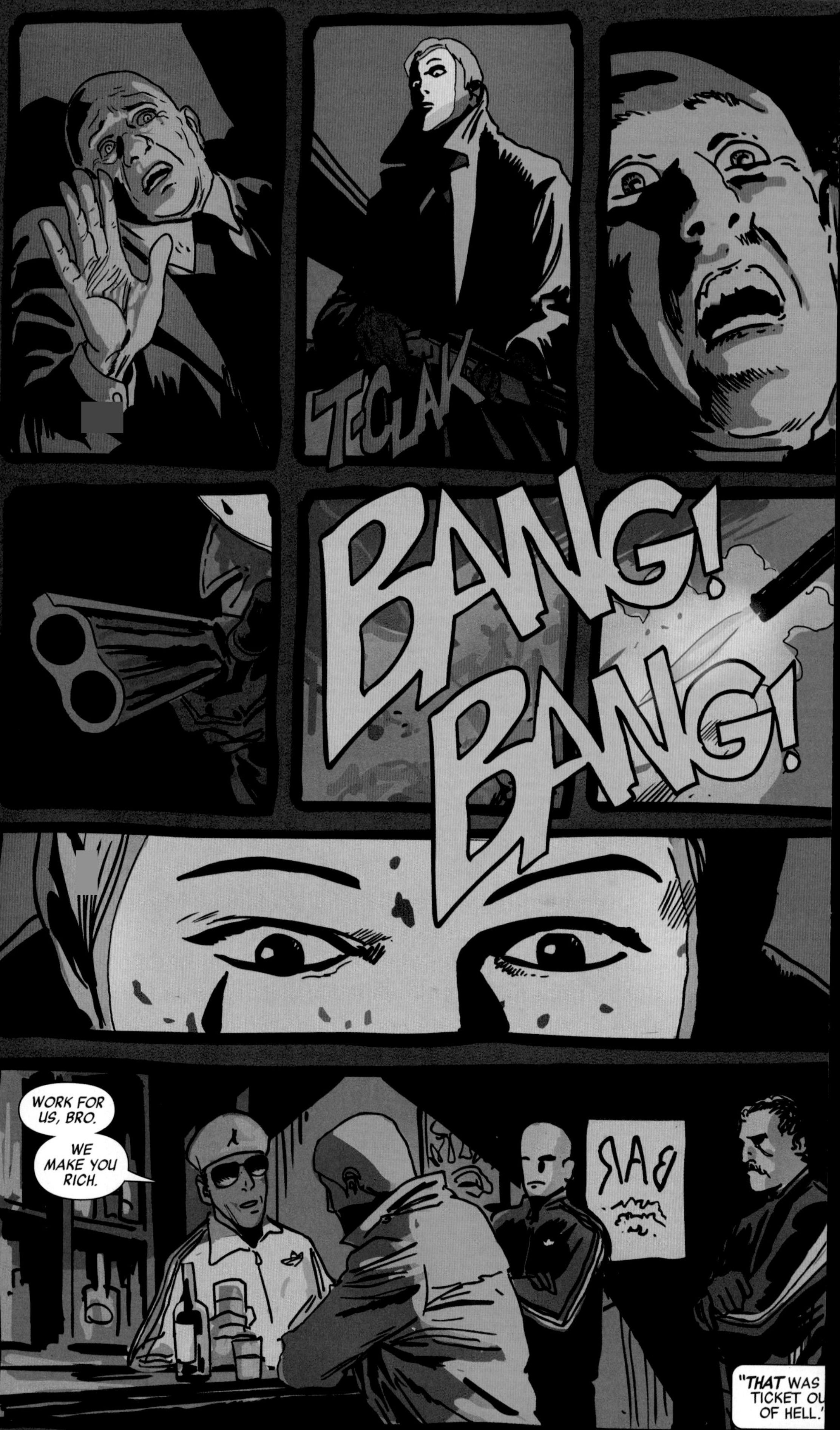
T-CLAK
BANG!
BANG!
WORK FOR US, BRO.
WE MAKE YOU RICH.
"THAT WAS
TICKET OU
OF HELL."

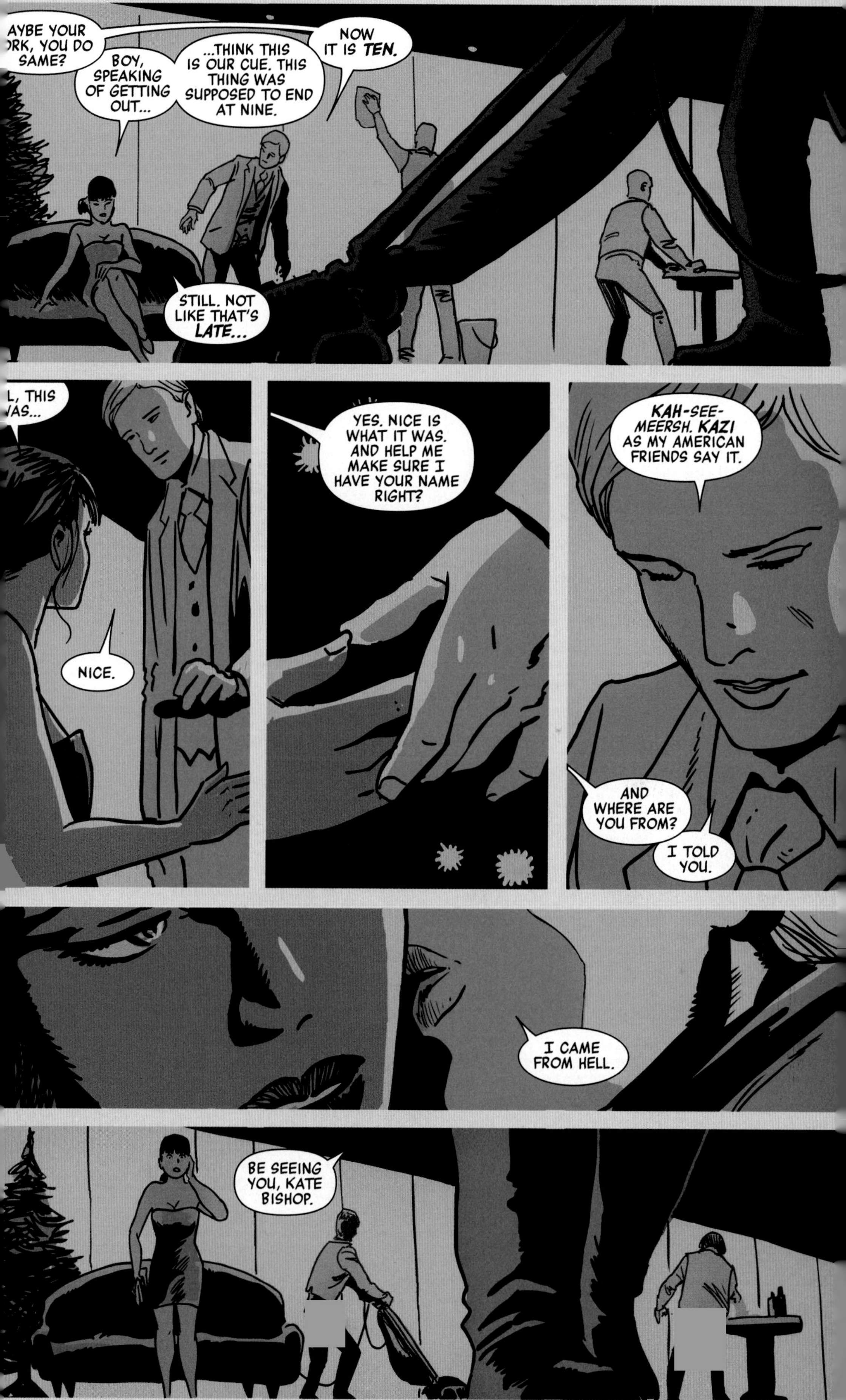
AYBE YOUR RK, YOU DO SAME?
BOY, SPEAKING OF GETTING OUT...
...THINK THIS IS OUR CUE. THIS THING WAS SUPPOSED TO END AT NINE.
NOW IT IS TEN.
STILL. NOT LIKE THAT'S LATE...
L, THIS AS...
NICE.
YES. NICE IS WHAT IT WAS. AND HELP ME MAKE SURE I HAVE YOUR NAME RIGHT?
KAH-SEE-MEERSH. KAZI AS MY AMERICAN FRIENDS SAY IT.
AND WHERE ARE YOU FROM?
I TOLD YOU.
I CAME FROM HELL.
BE SEEING YOU, KATE BISHOP.

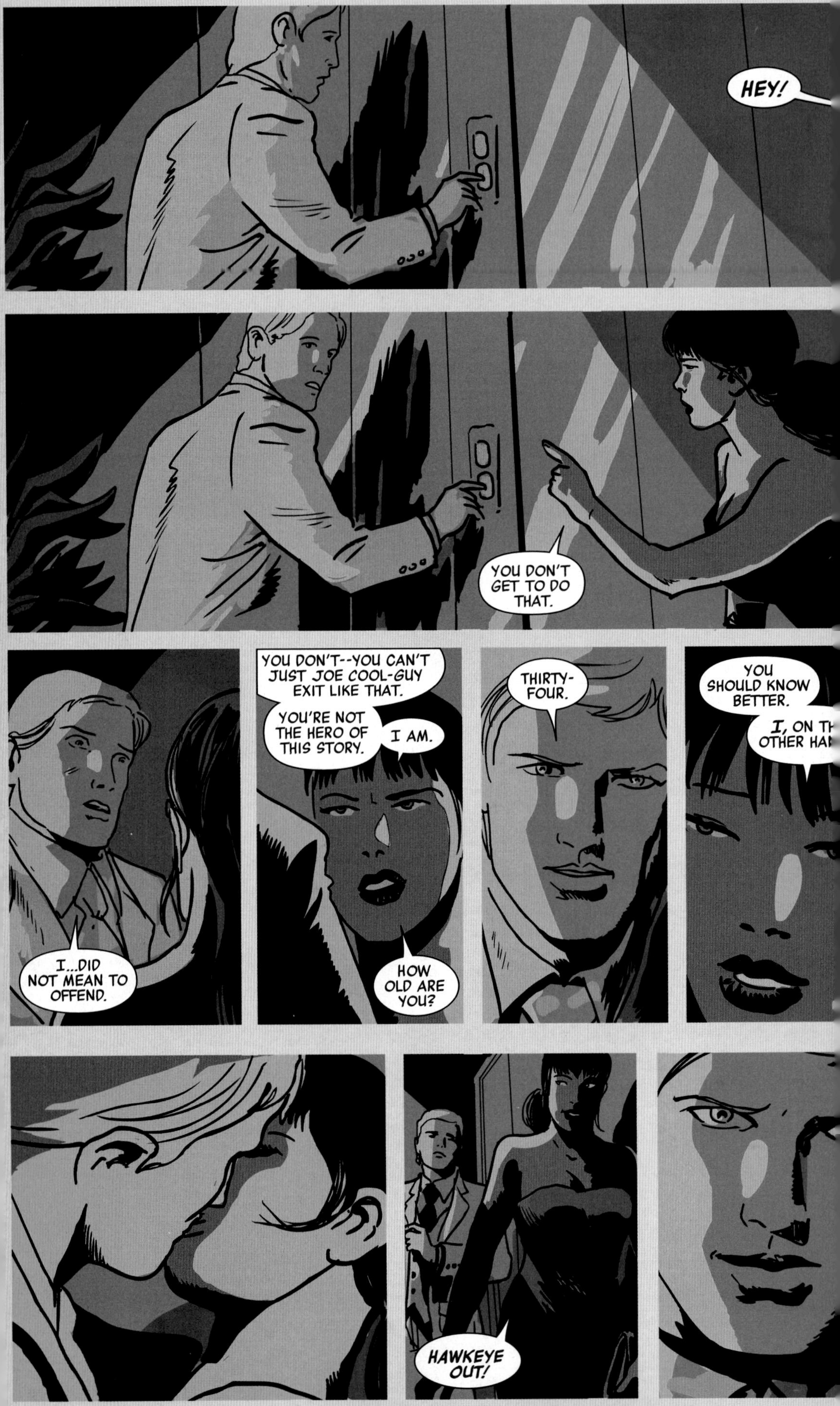
HEY!
YOU DON'T GET TO DO THAT.
I...DID NOT MEAN TO OFFEND.
YOU DON'T--YOU CAN'T JUST JOE COOL-GUY EXIT LIKE THAT.
YOU'RE NOT THE HERO OF THIS STORY.
I AM.
HOW OLD ARE YOU?
THIRTY-FOUR.
YOU SHOULD KNOW BETTER.
HAWKEYE OUT!

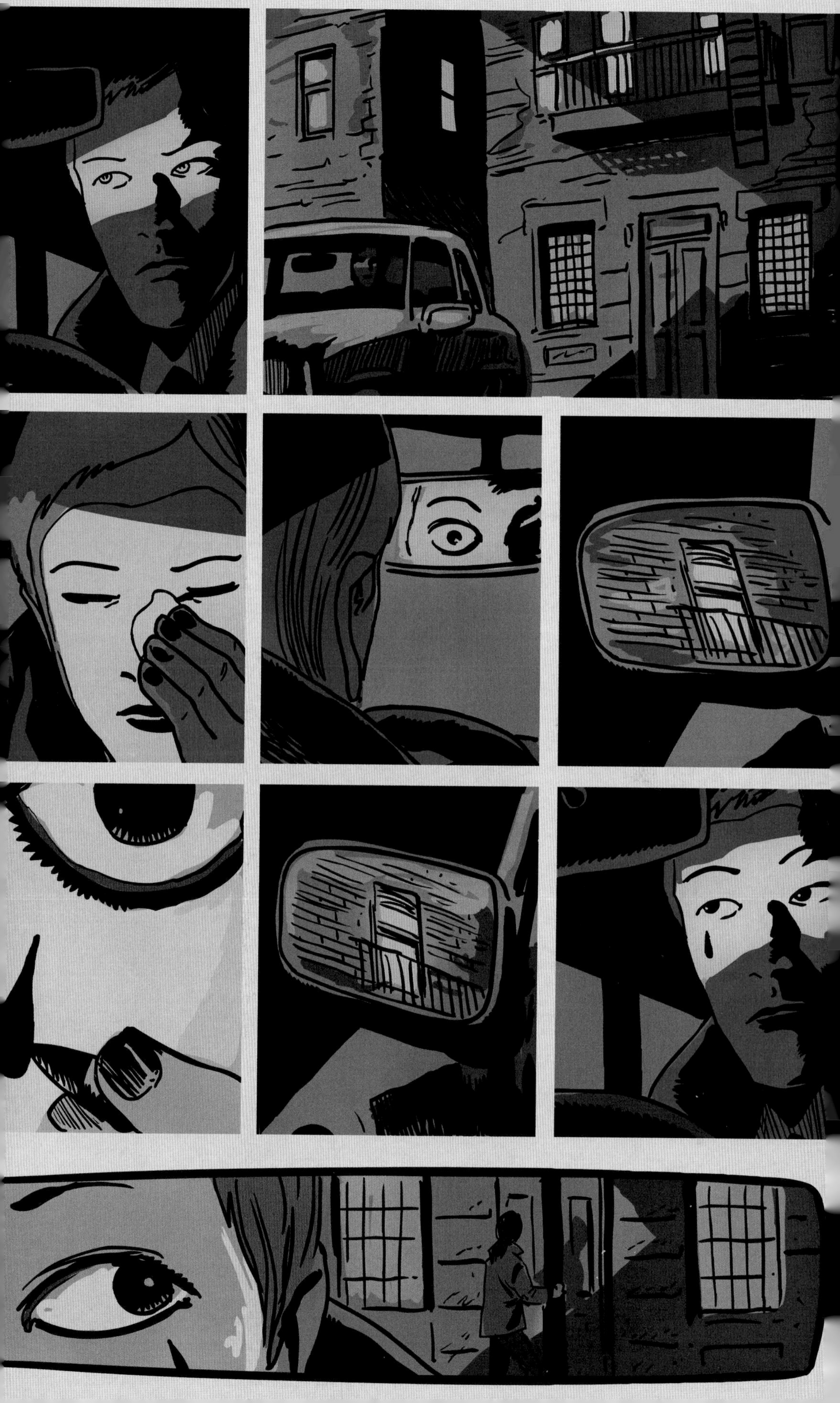

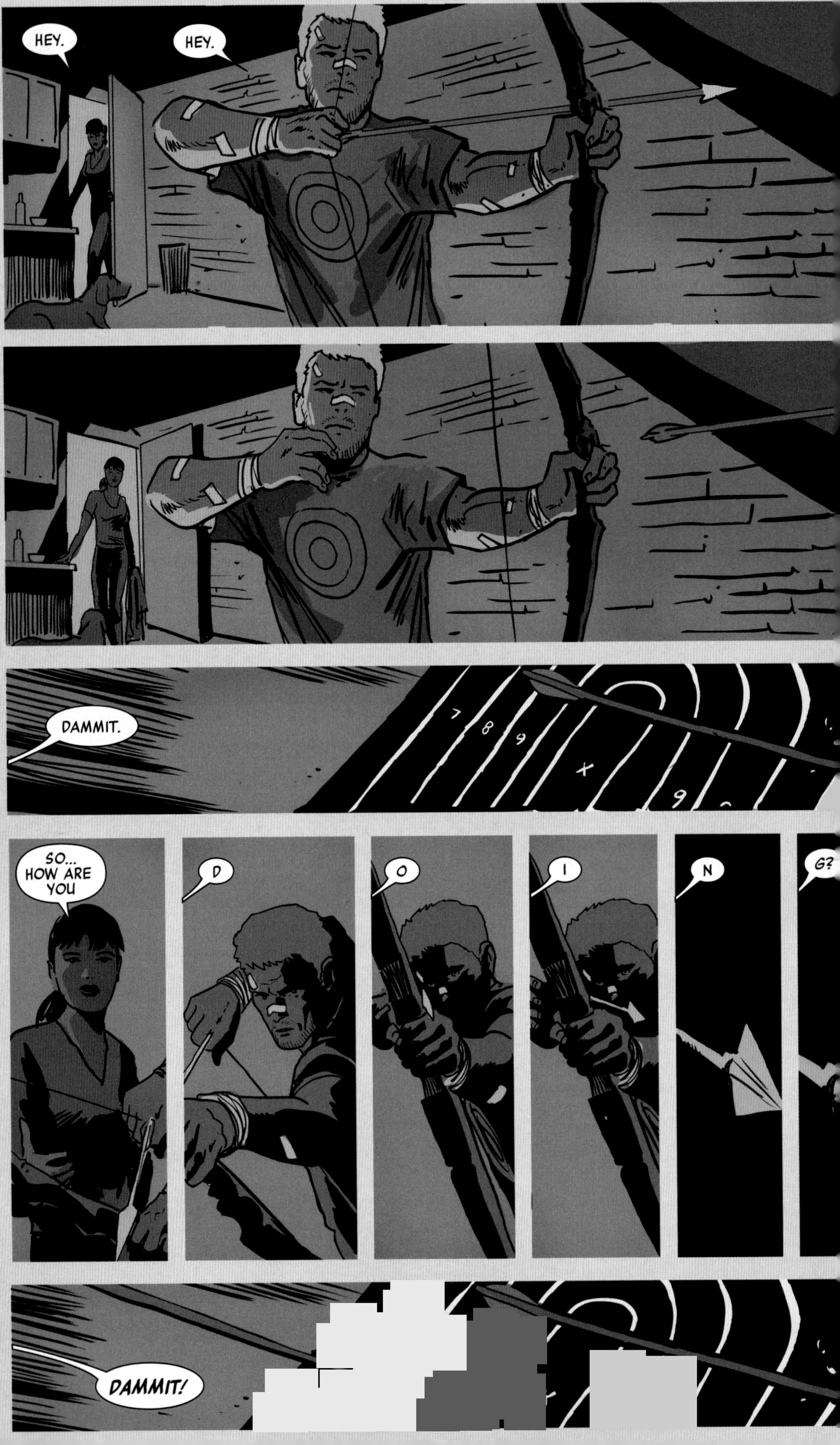
HEY.
HEY.
DAMMIT.
SO... HOW ARE YOU
D
O
I
N
G?
DAMMIT!

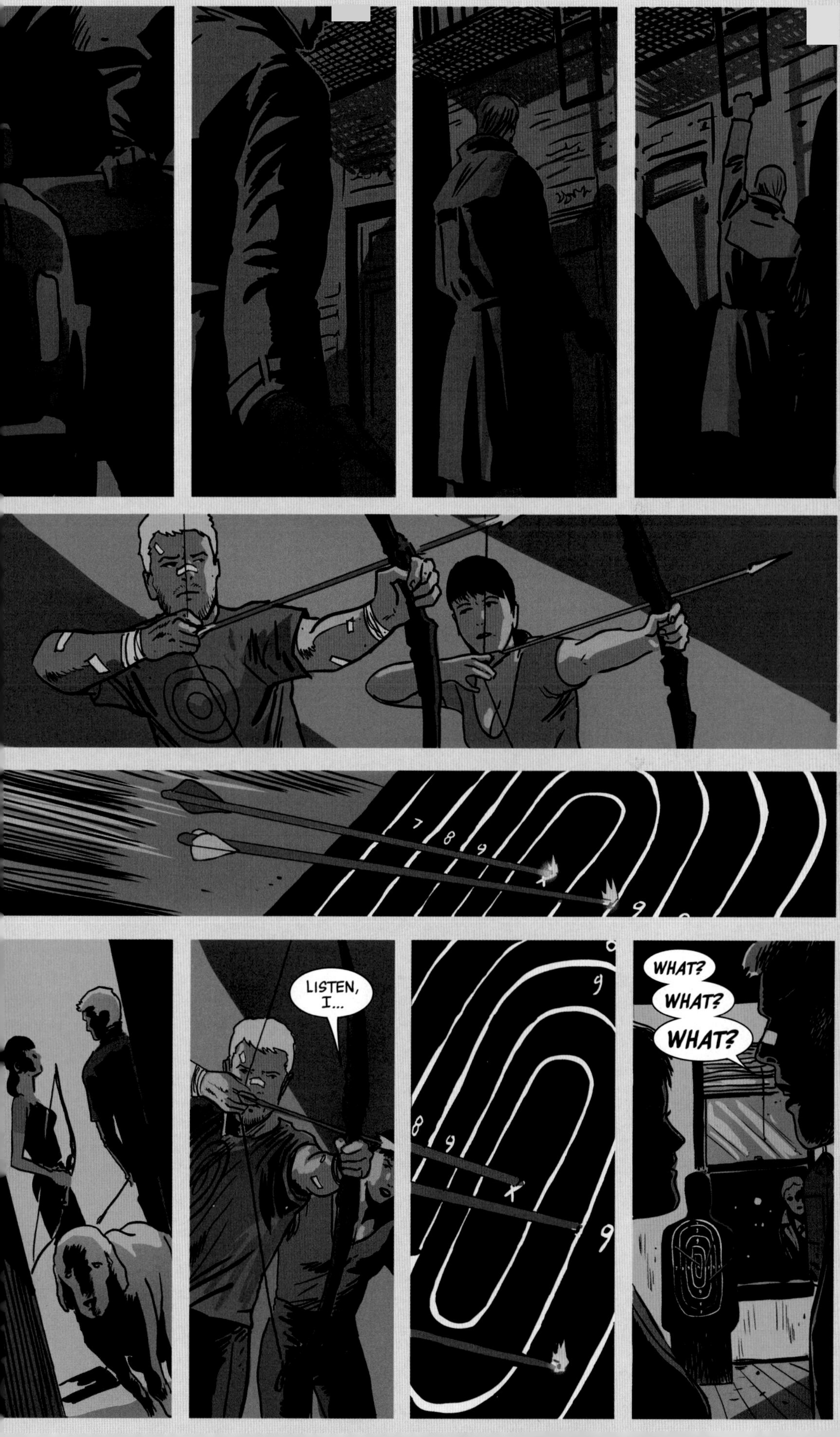
7
8
9
X
9
LISTEN, I...
9
8
9
X
9
WHAT?
WHAT?
WHAT?

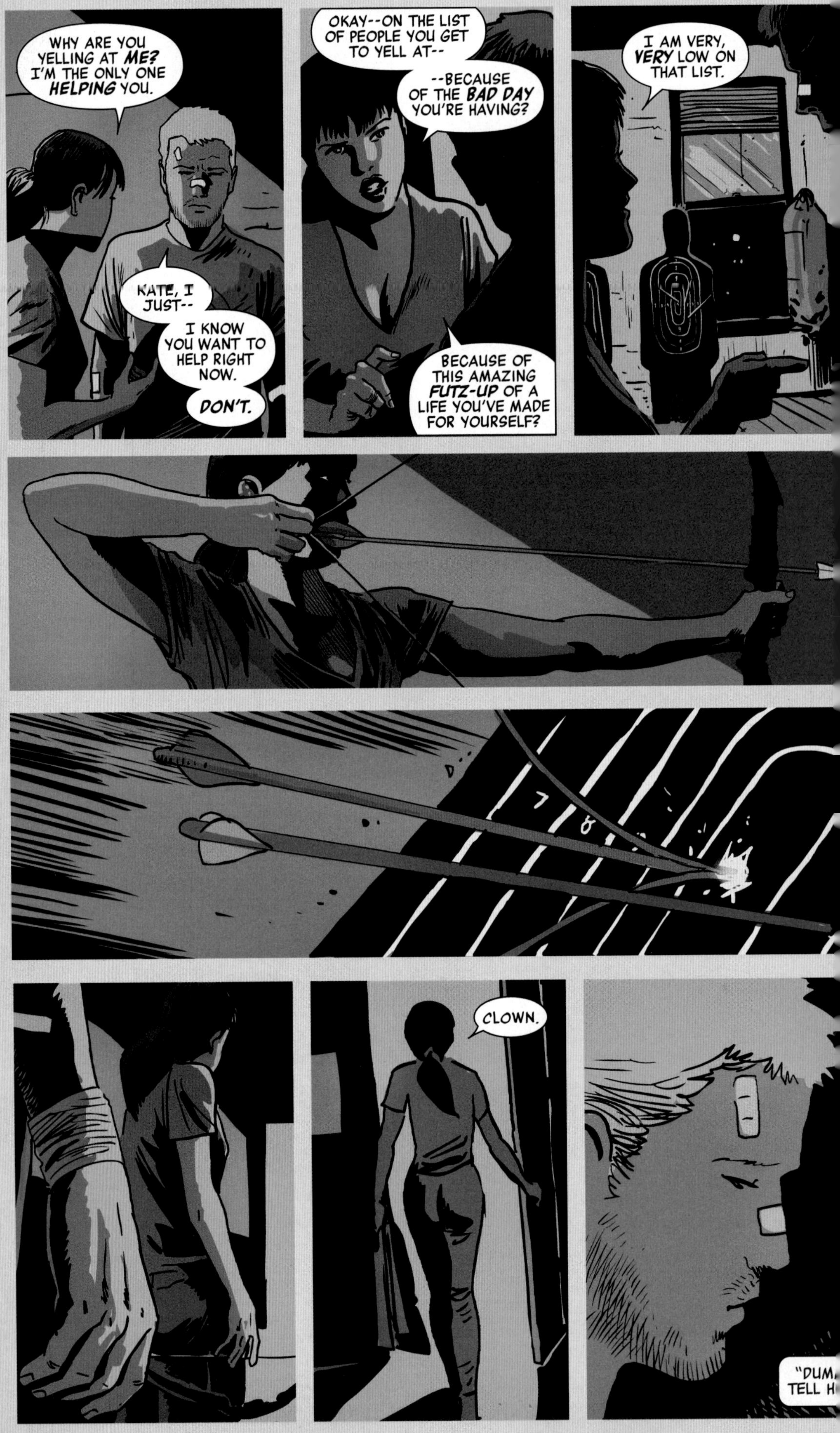
WHY ARE YOU YELLING AT ME? I'M THE ONLY ONE HELPING YOU.
KATE, I JUST--
I KNOW YOU WANT TO HELP RIGHT NOW.
DON'T.
OKAY--ON THE LIST OF PEOPLE YOU GET TO YELL AT--
--BECAUSE OF THE BAD DAY YOU'RE HAVING?
BECAUSE OF THIS AMAZING FUTZ-UP OF A LIFE YOU'VE MADE FOR YOURSELF?
I AM VERY, VERY LOW ON THAT LIST.
CLOWN.

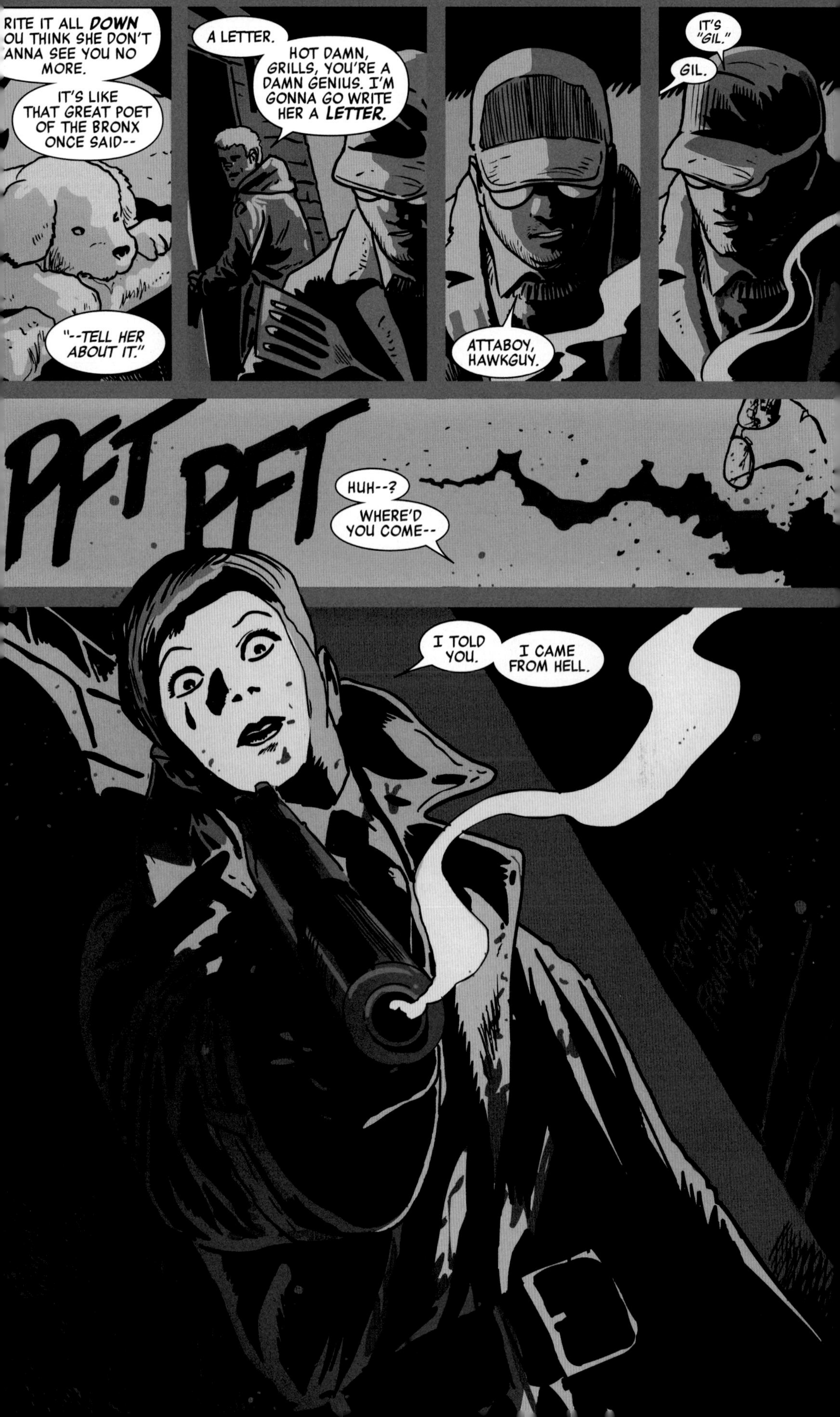

RITE IT ALL DOWN
OU THINK SHE DON'T ANNA SEE YOU NO MORE.
IT'S LIKE THAT GREAT POET OF THE BRONX ONCE SAID--
"--TELL HER ABOUT IT."
A LETTER.
HOT DAMN, GRILLS, YOU'RE A DAMN GENIUS. I'M GONNA GO WRITE HER A LETTER.
ATTABOY, HAWKGUY.
IT'S "GIL."
GIL.
PFT PFT
HUH--?
WHERE'D YOU COME--
I TOLD YOU.
I CAME FROM HELL.

11

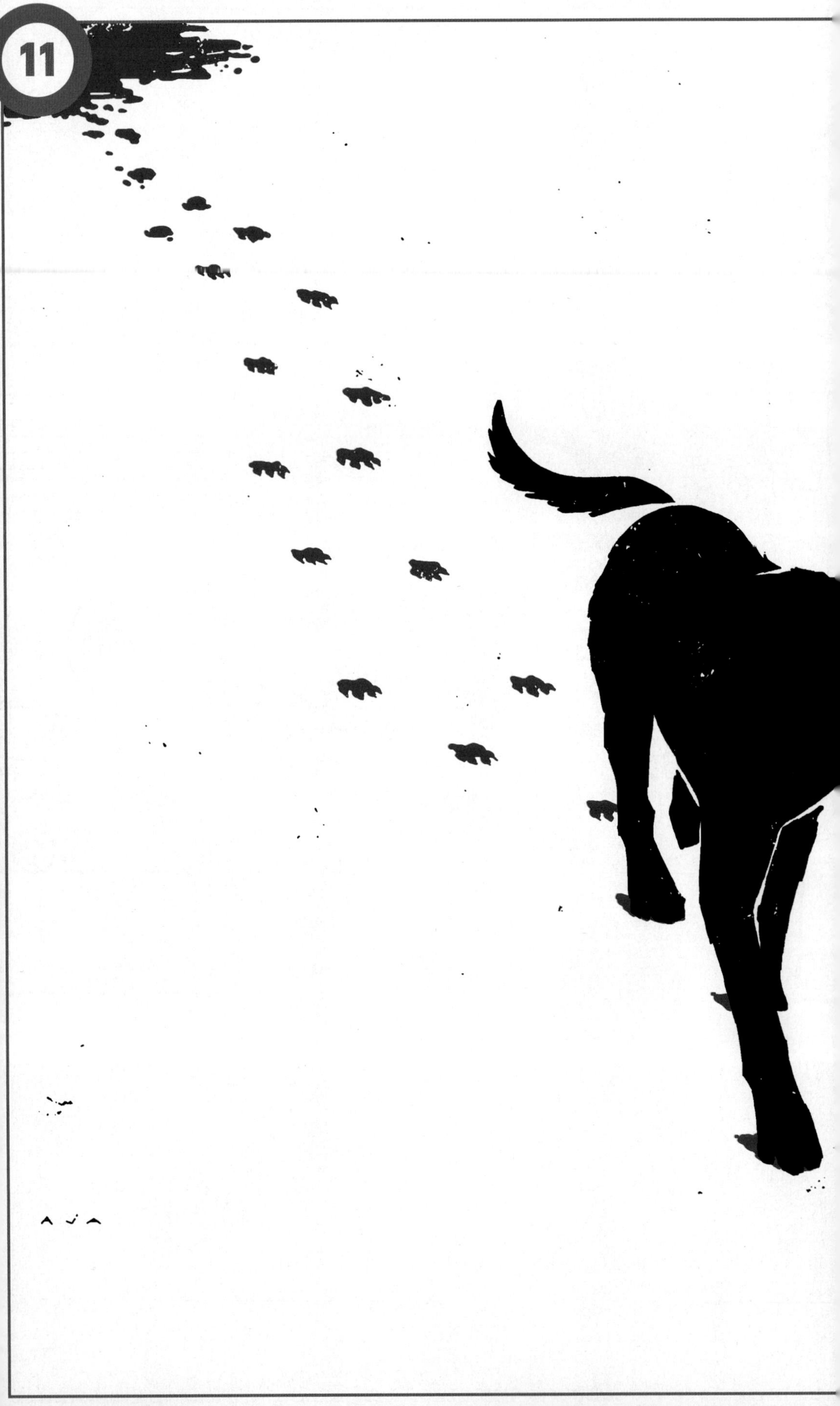

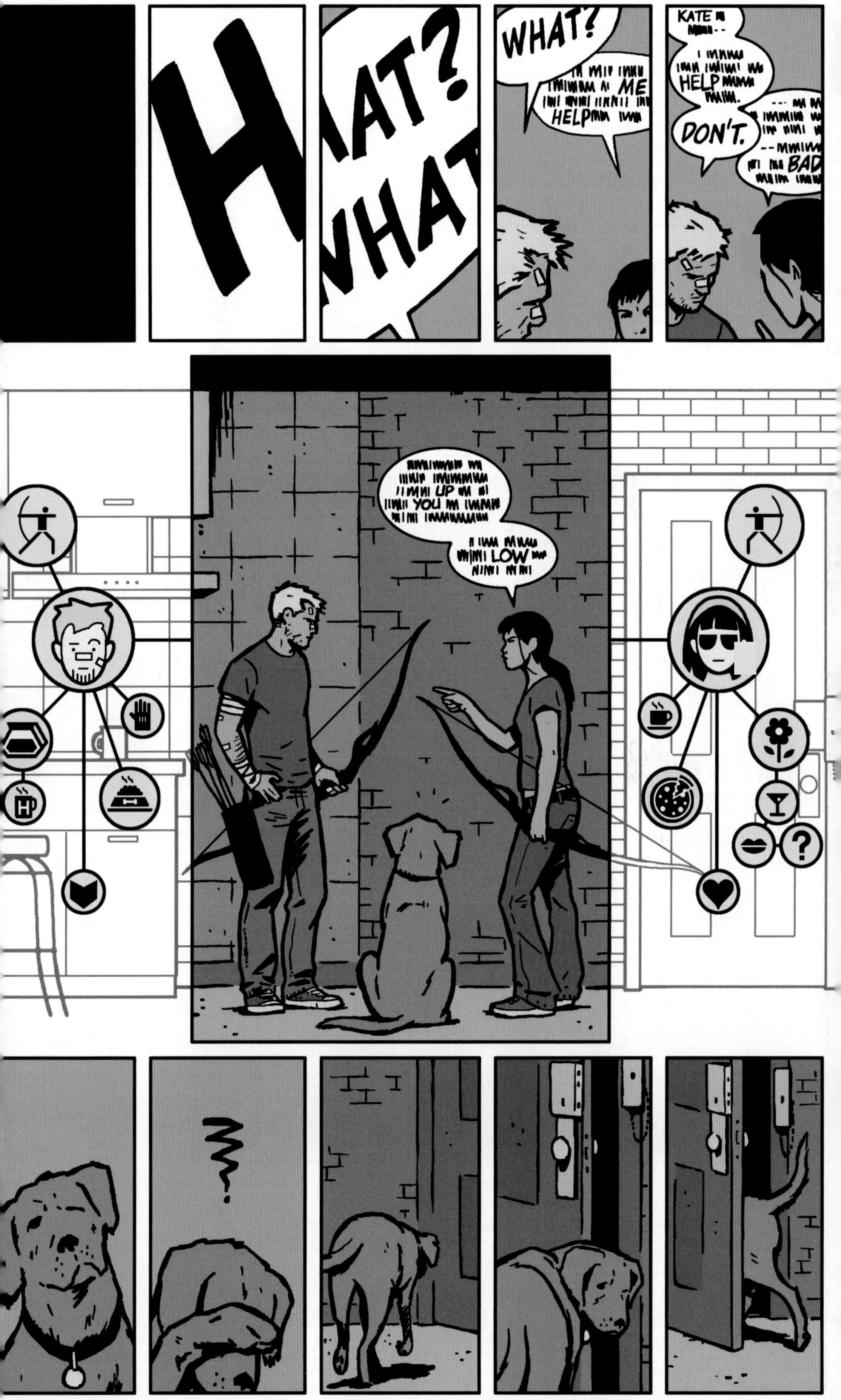
H
HAT? WHAT
WHAT?
ME
HELP
KATE
HELP
DON'T.
BAD
UP
YOU
LOW

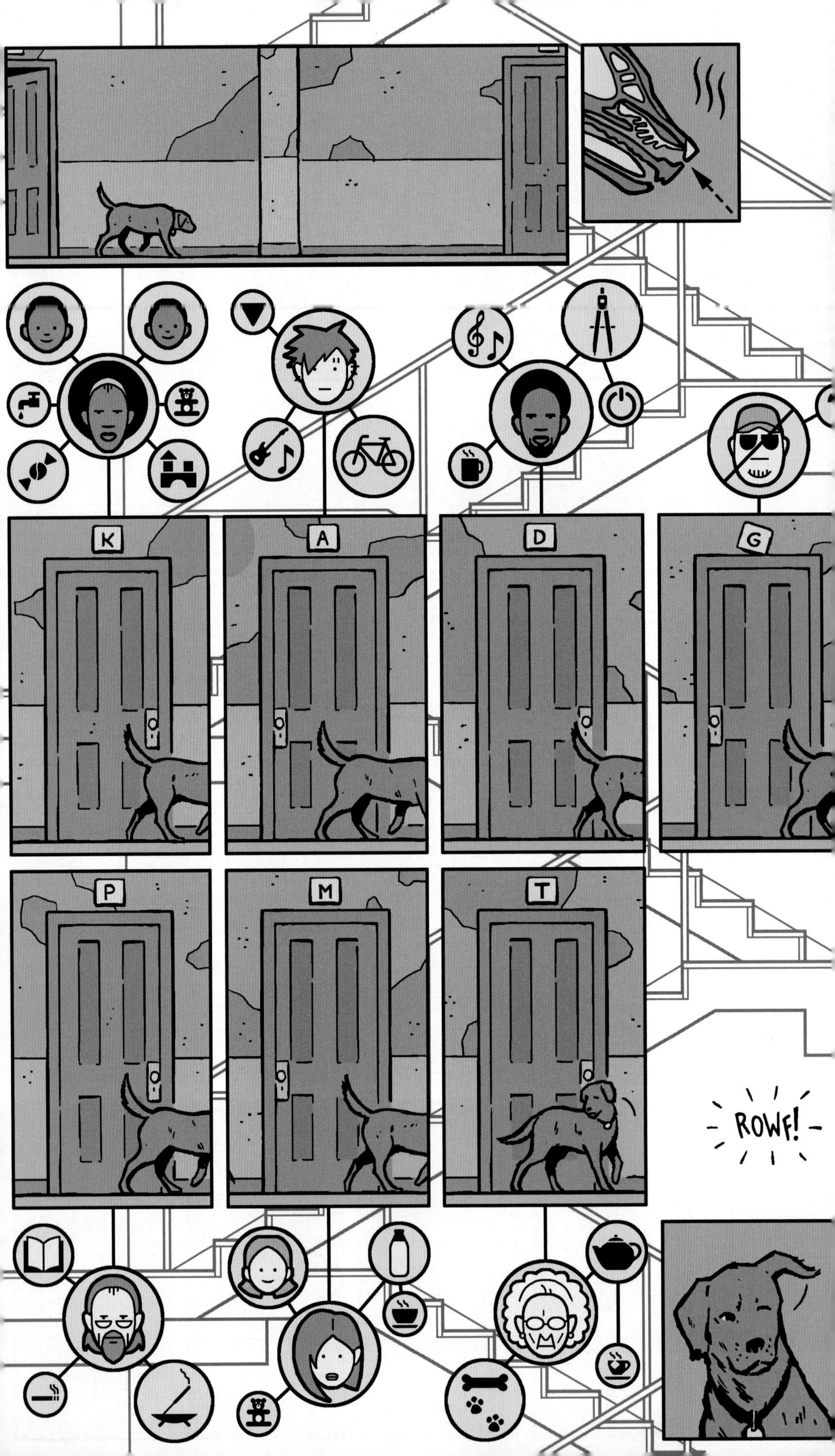
K
A
D
G
P
M
T
ROWF!

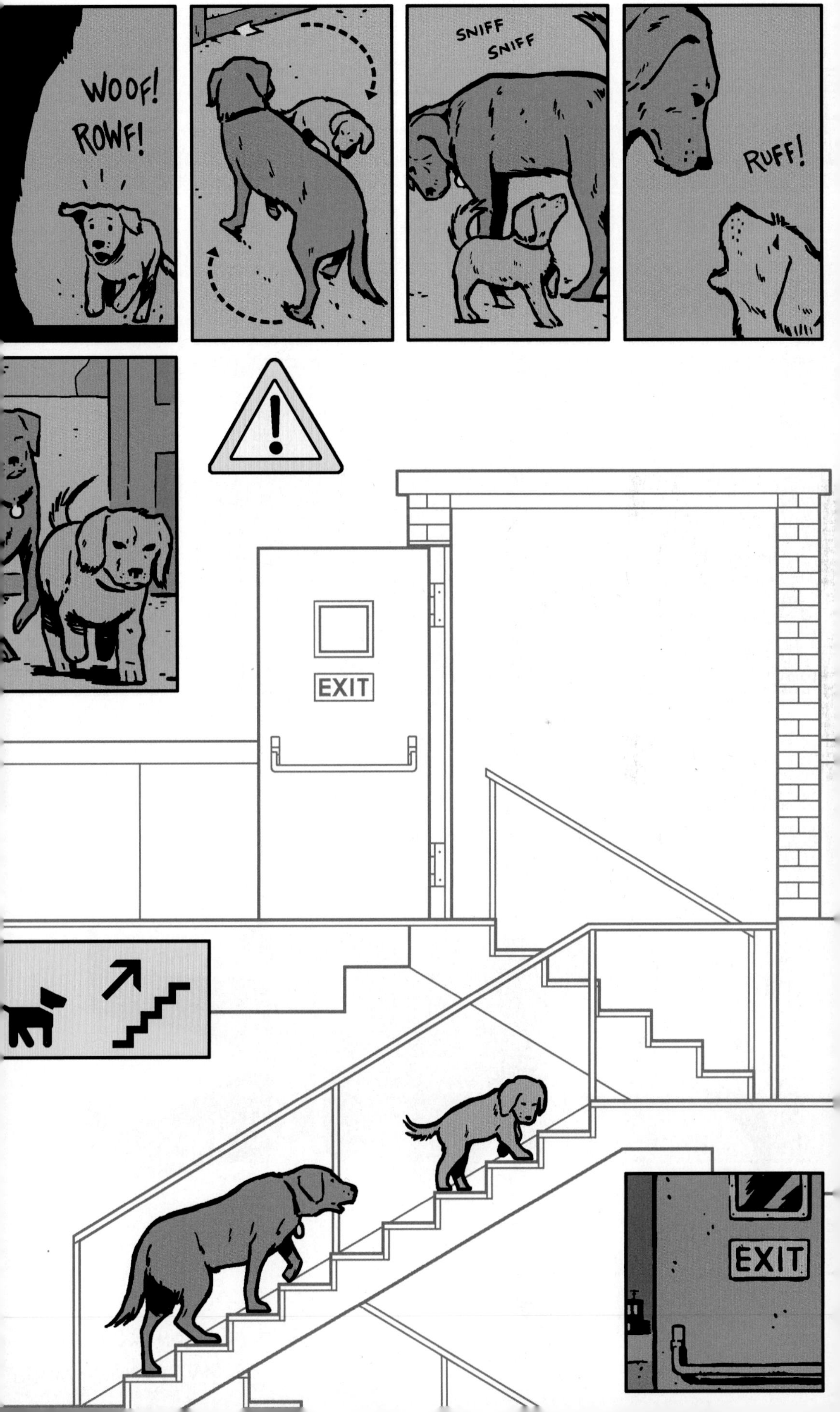
WOOF!
ROWF!
SNIFF
SNIFF
RUFF!
EXIT
EXIT

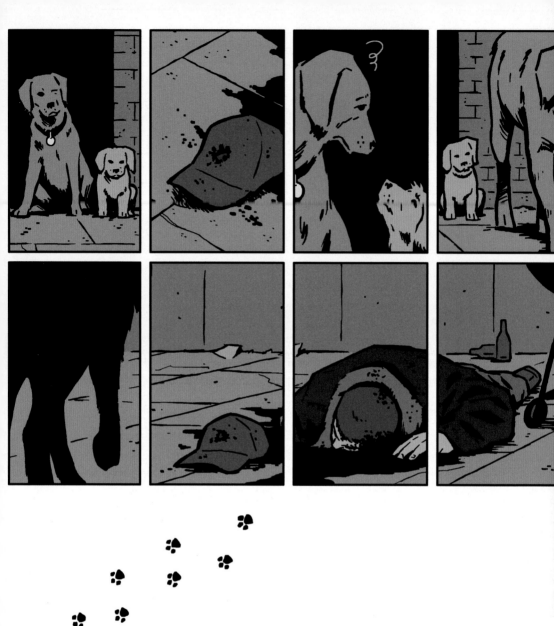

PIZZA DOG IN

PIZZA IS MY BUSINESS

BY MATT FRACTION AND DAVID AJA

WITH MATT HOLLINGSWORTH

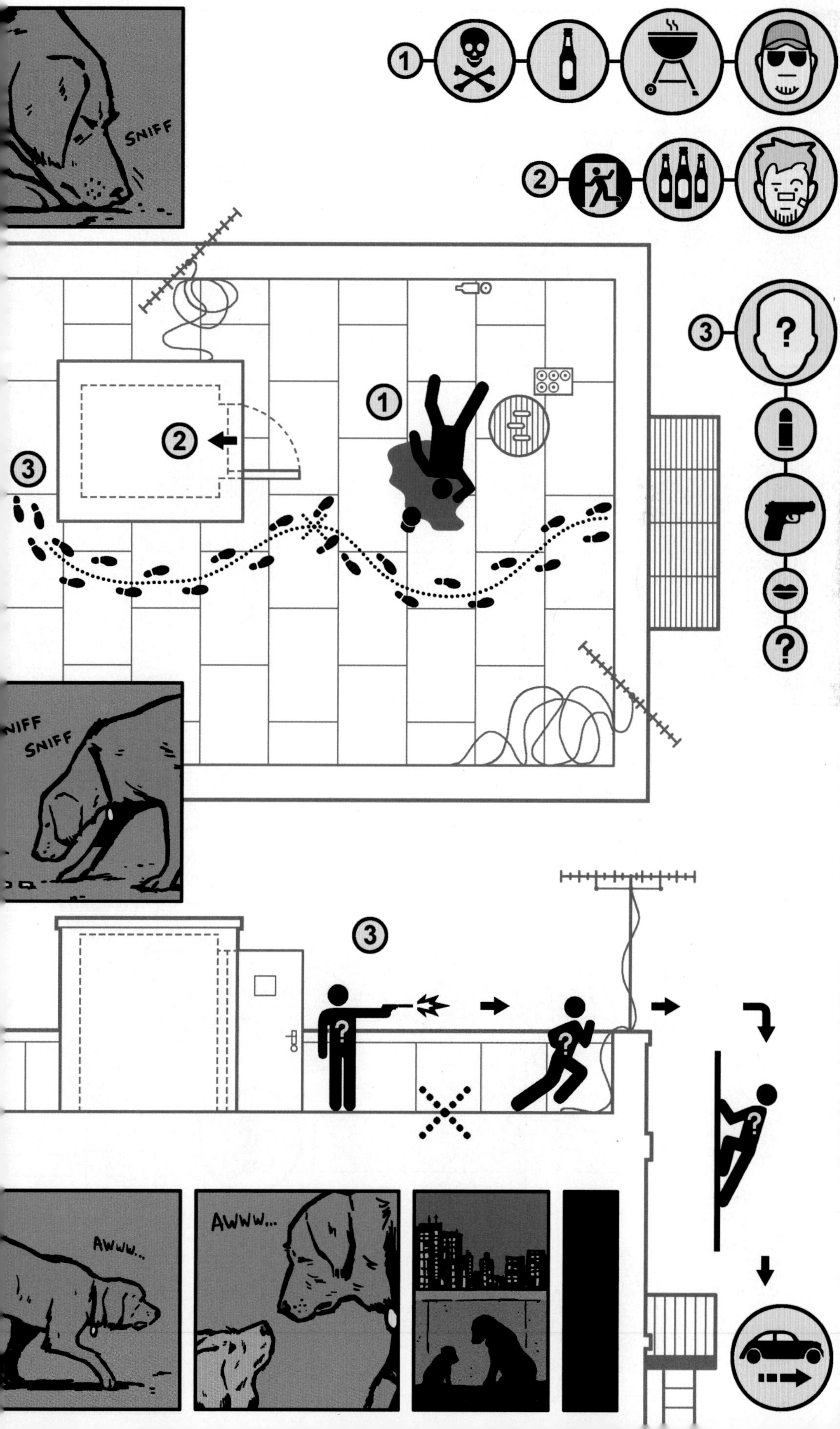
SNIFF
1
2
3
NIFF
SNIFF
AWWW...
AWWW...

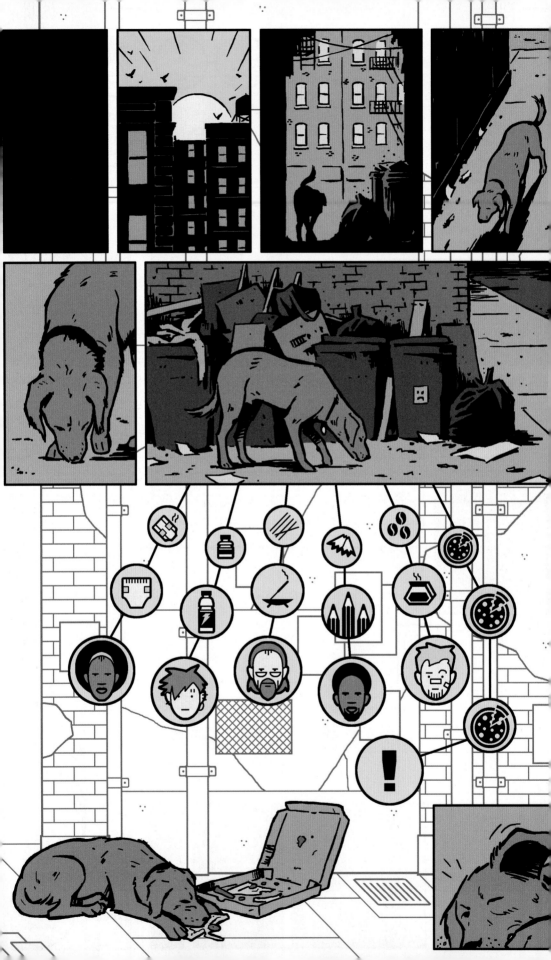

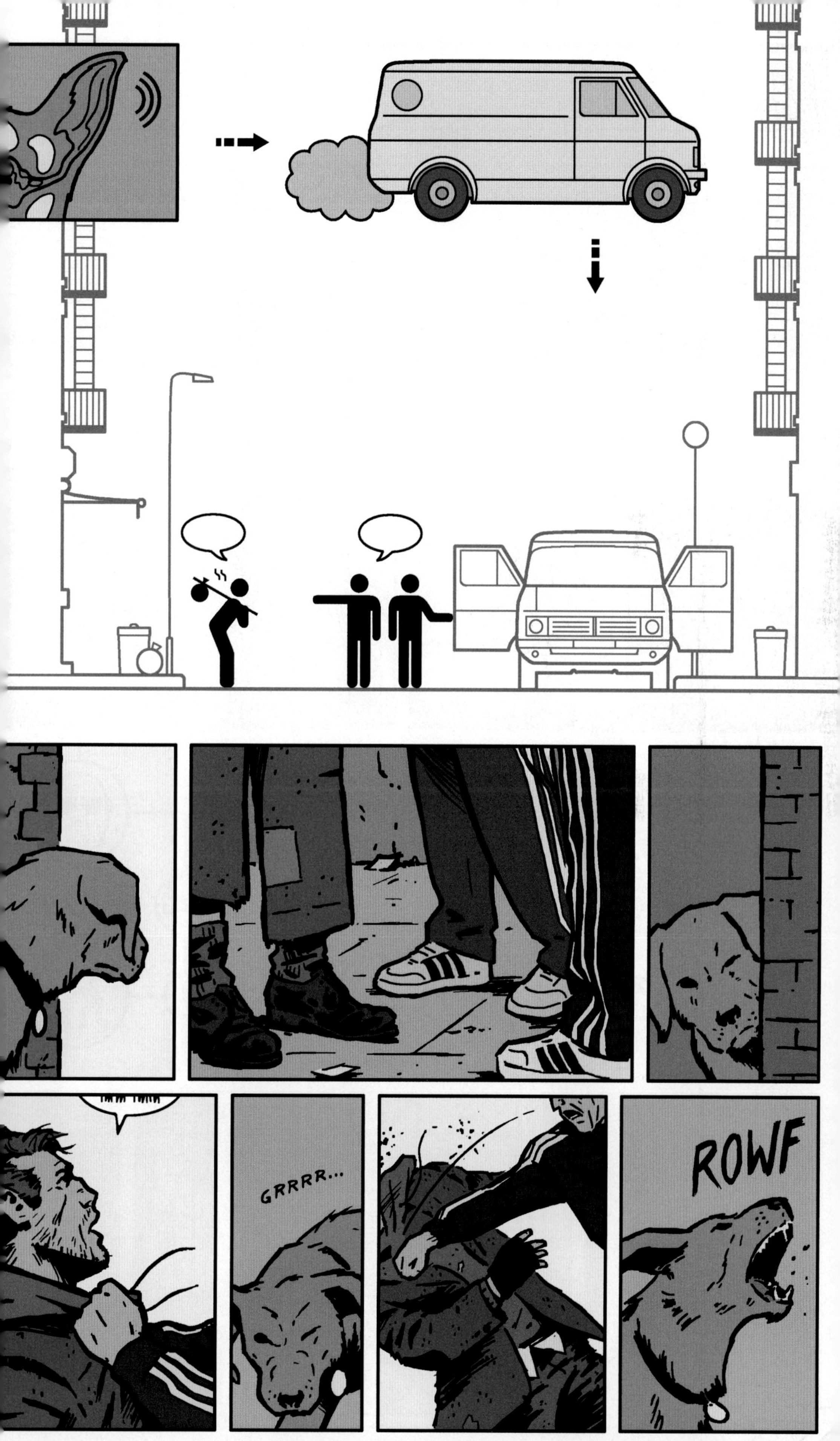
GRRRR...
ROWF

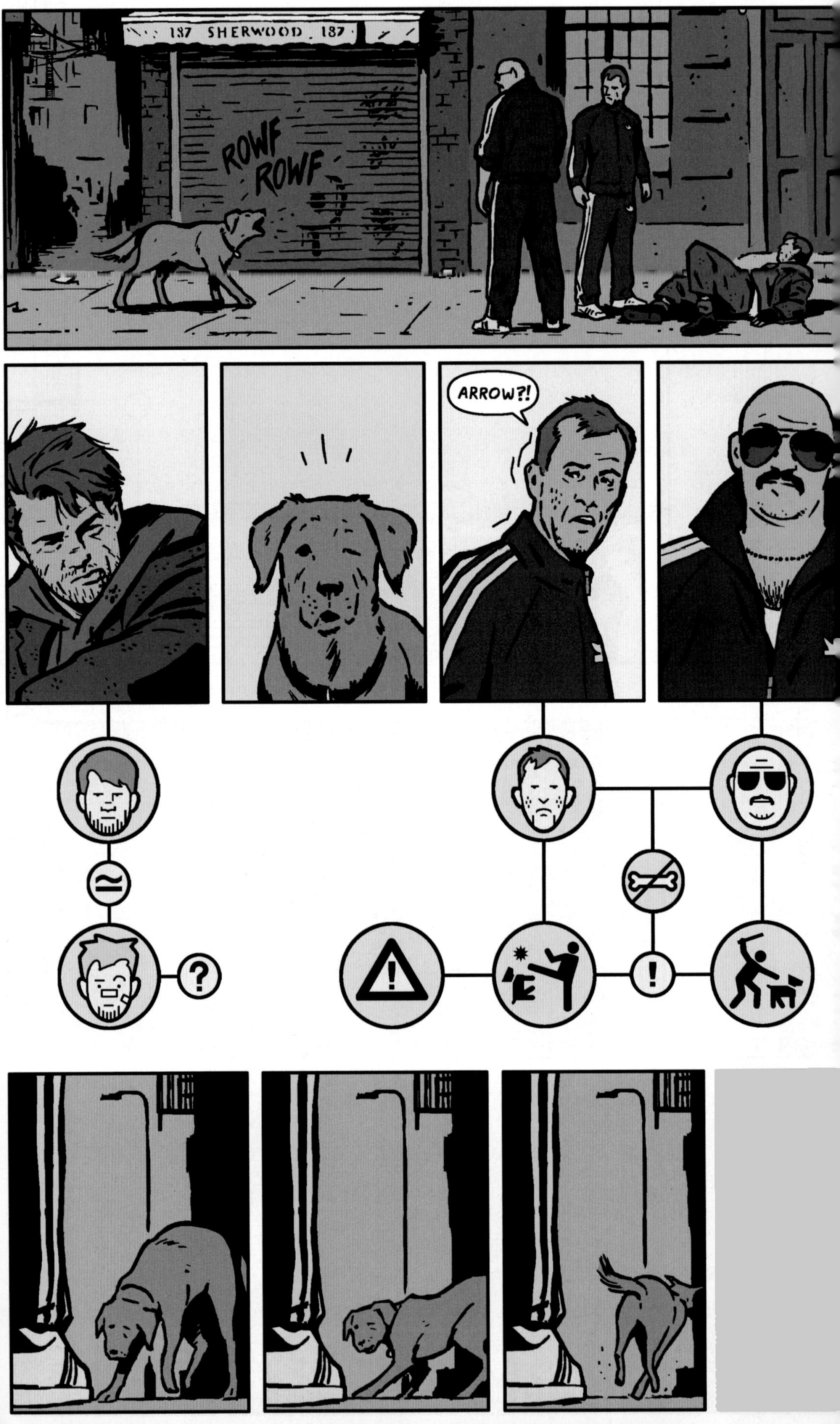

187 SHERWOOD 187
ROWF ROWF
ARROW?!

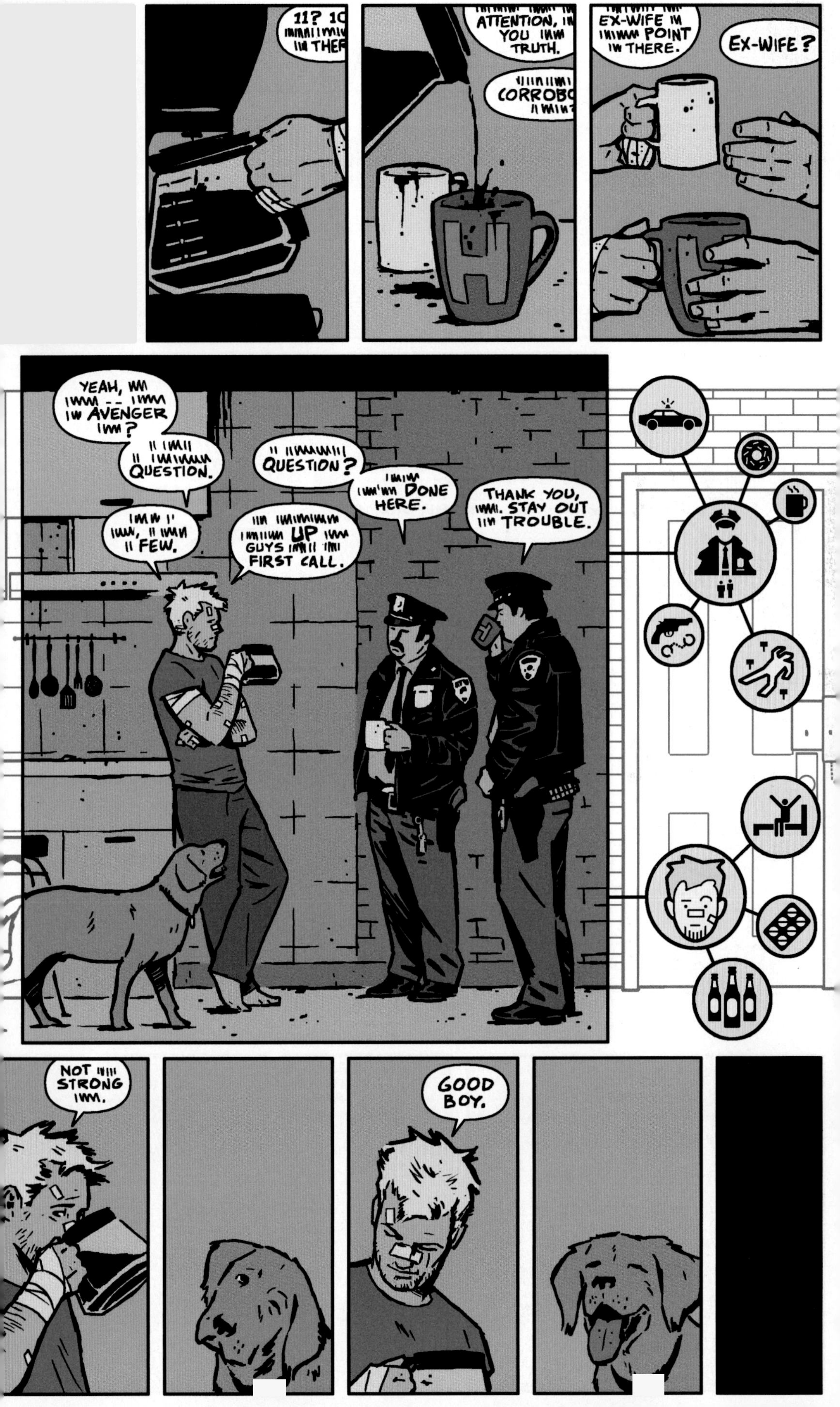

11?
ATTENTION, YOU TRUTH.
EX-WIFE POINT THERE.
EX-WIFE?
YEAH, -- AVENGER ?
QUESTION.
QUESTION?
FEW.
UP GUYS FIRST CALL.
DONE HERE.
THANK YOU, . STAY OUT TROUBLE.
NOT STRONG .
GOOD BOY.

WHAT?

I |||||| ||| COLLAR STAYS.

CURL UP? YOU |||||| ||||||| GU|| N| THERE.

COLLAR STAYS.

YE|
||||| |||
COLLAR
|| PL||

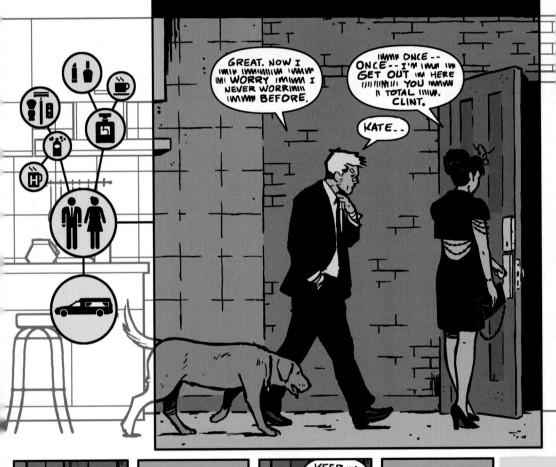

GREAT. NOW I ||||||| |||||||||||||| |||||| ||| WORRY ||||||| I NEVER WORR||||| ||||||| BEFORE.

|||||| ONCE -- ONCE -- I'M |||| || ||||||| |||||| YOU |||||| || TOTAL ||||||, CLINT.

KATE..

KEEP |||| EYE ||| |||| PLACE.

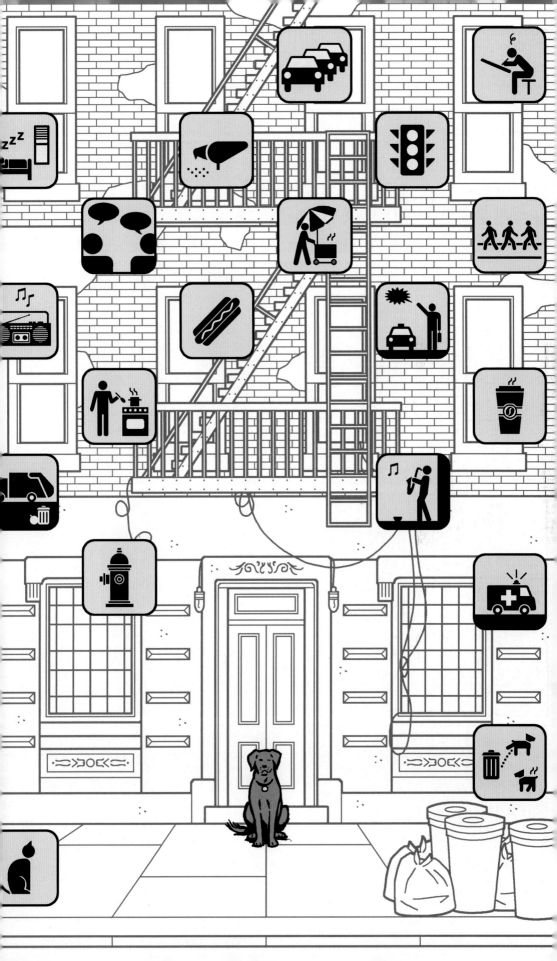

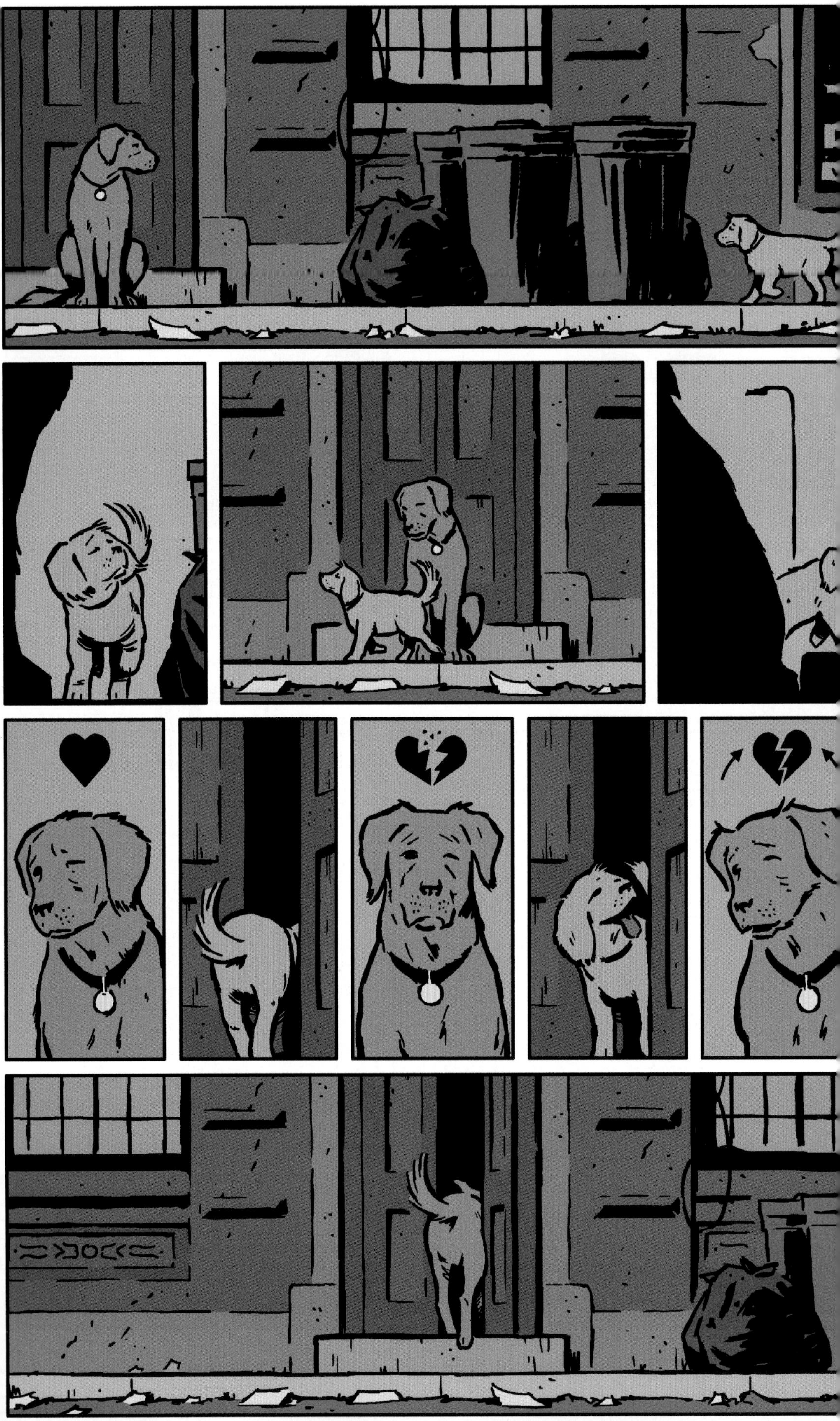

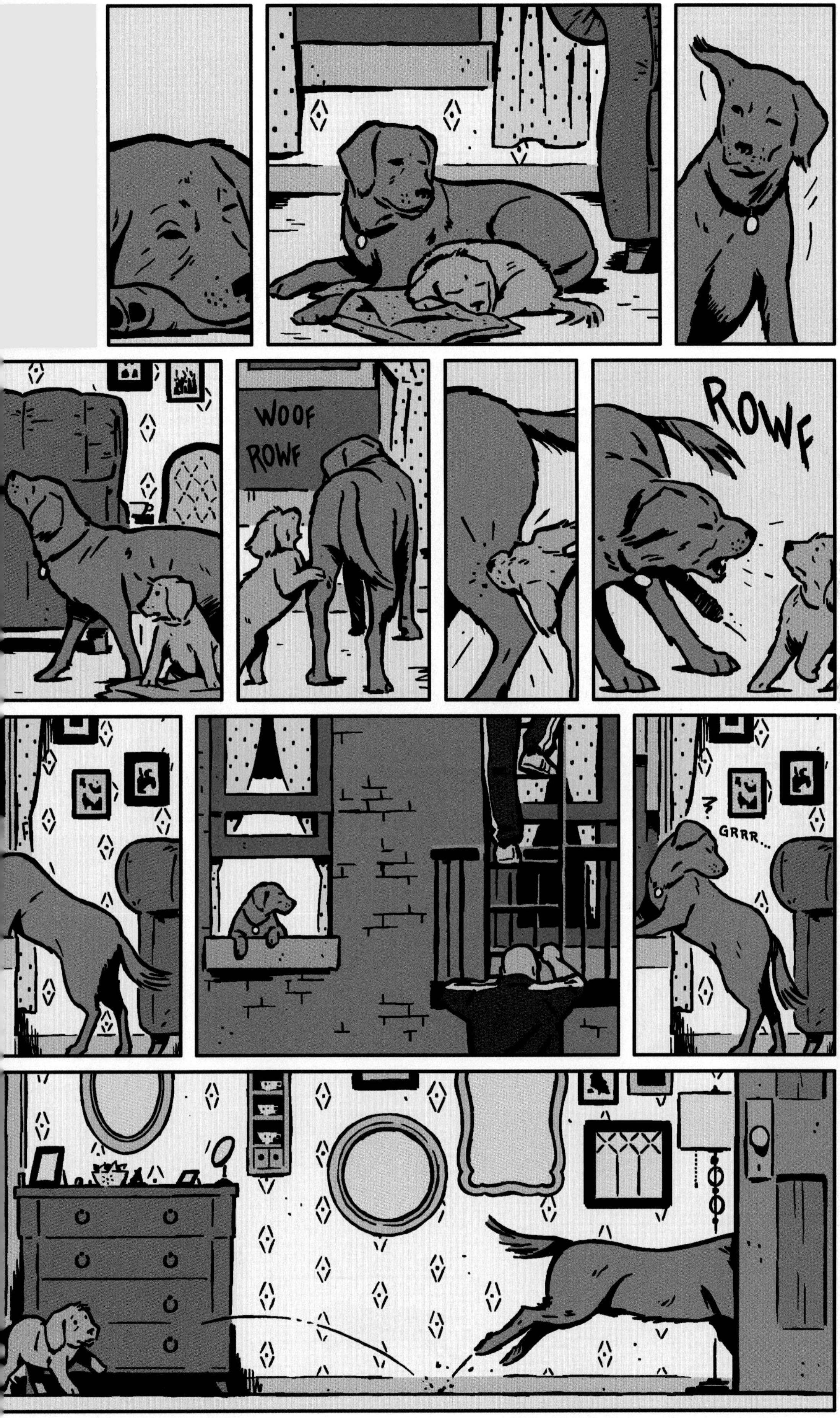
WOOF
ROWF
ROWF
?
GRRR...

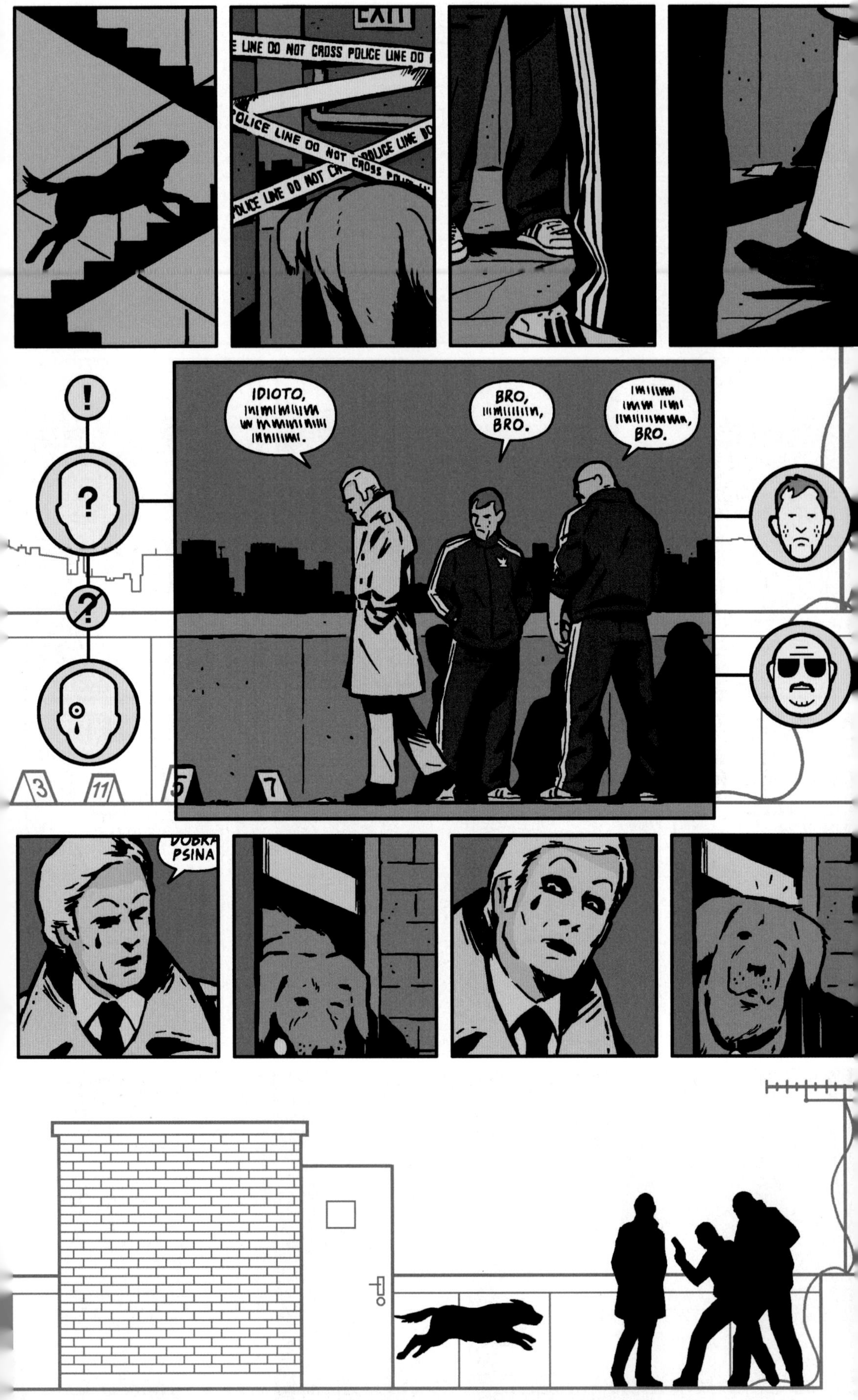

EXIT
LINE DO NOT CROSS POLICE LINE DO
POLICE LINE DO NOT CROSS
POLICE LINE DO NOT CROSS POLICE LINE DO
IDIOTO,
BRO,
BRO.
BRO.
3
11
5
7
DOBRA PSINA

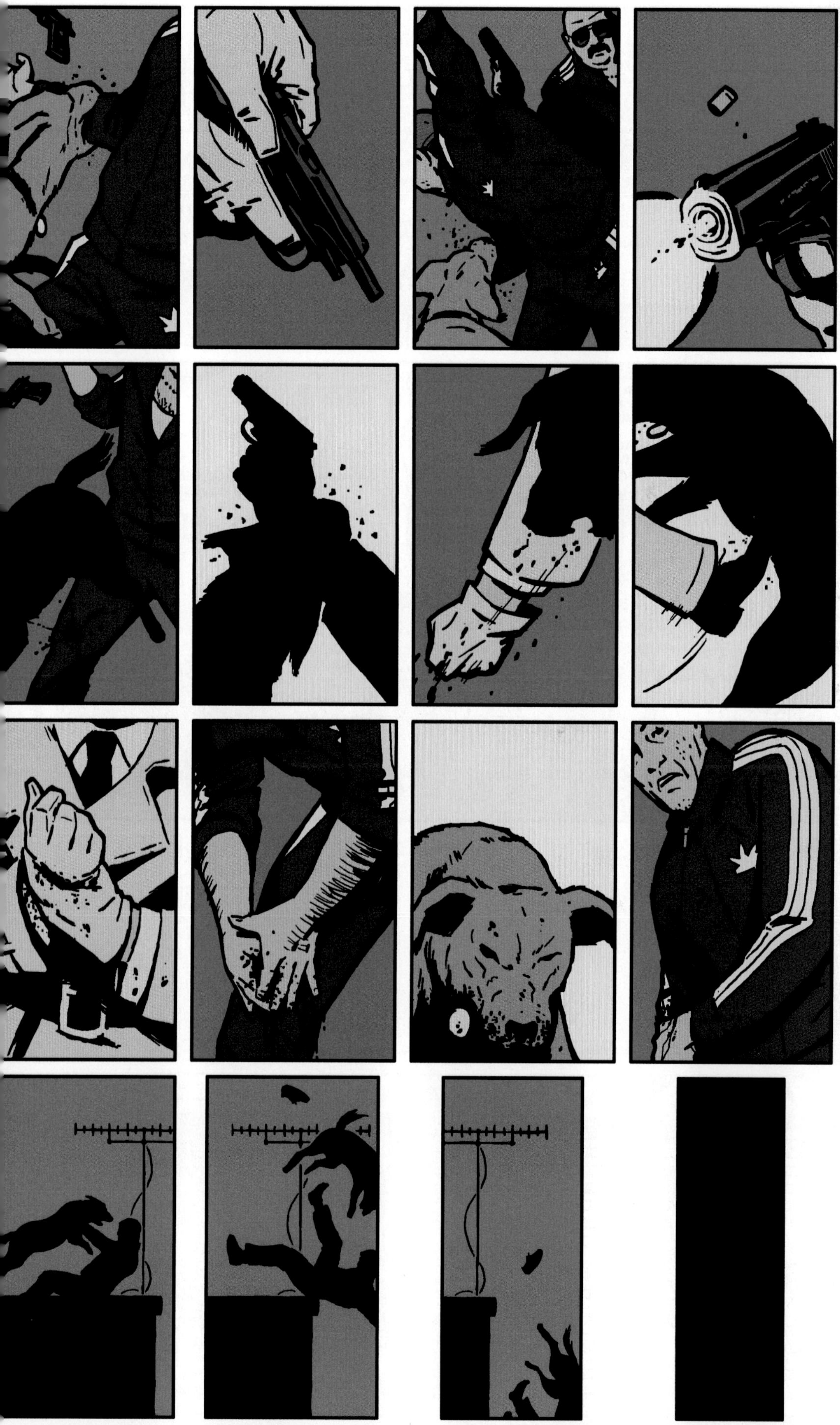

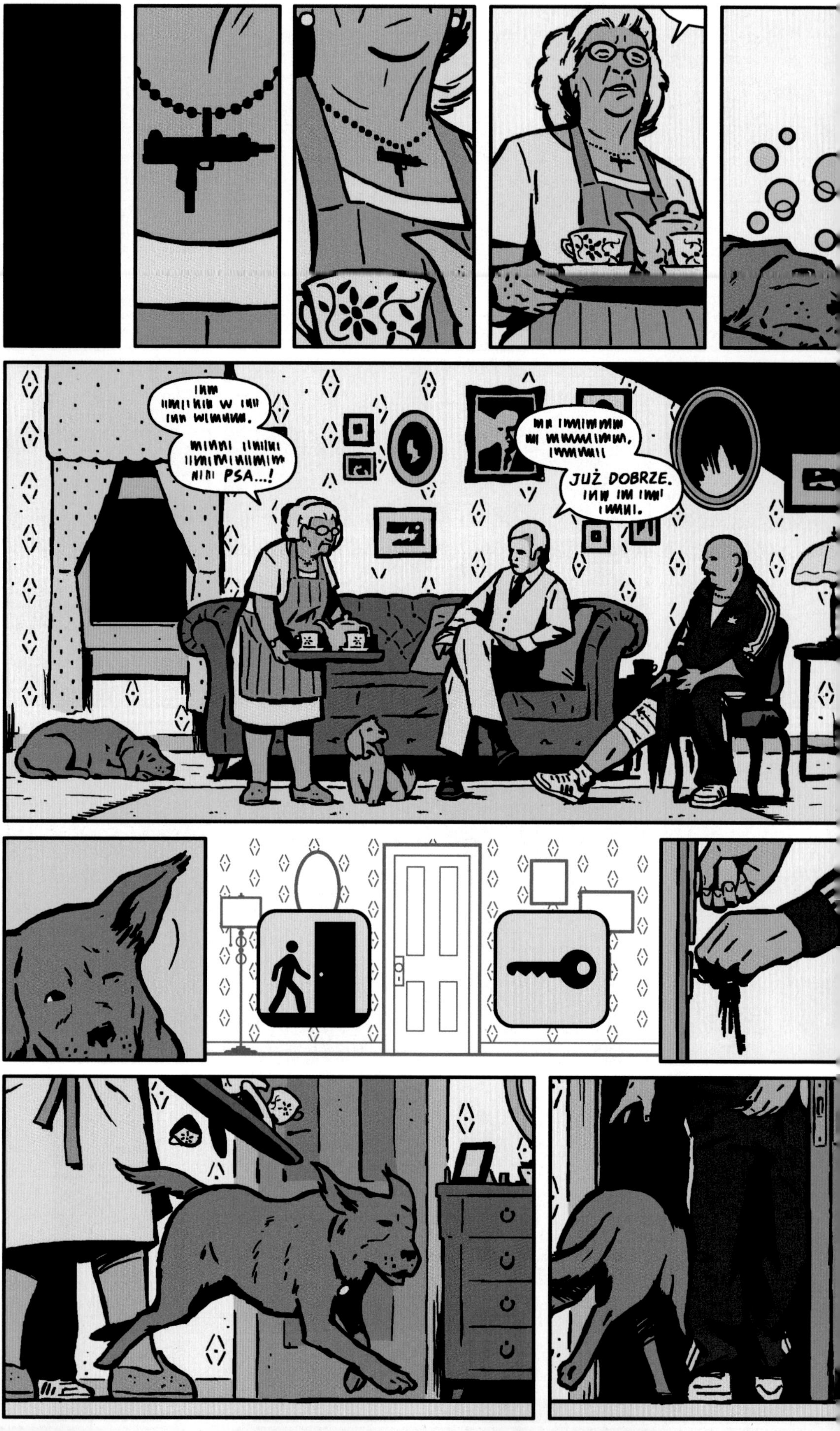
PSA...!
JUŻ DOBRZE.

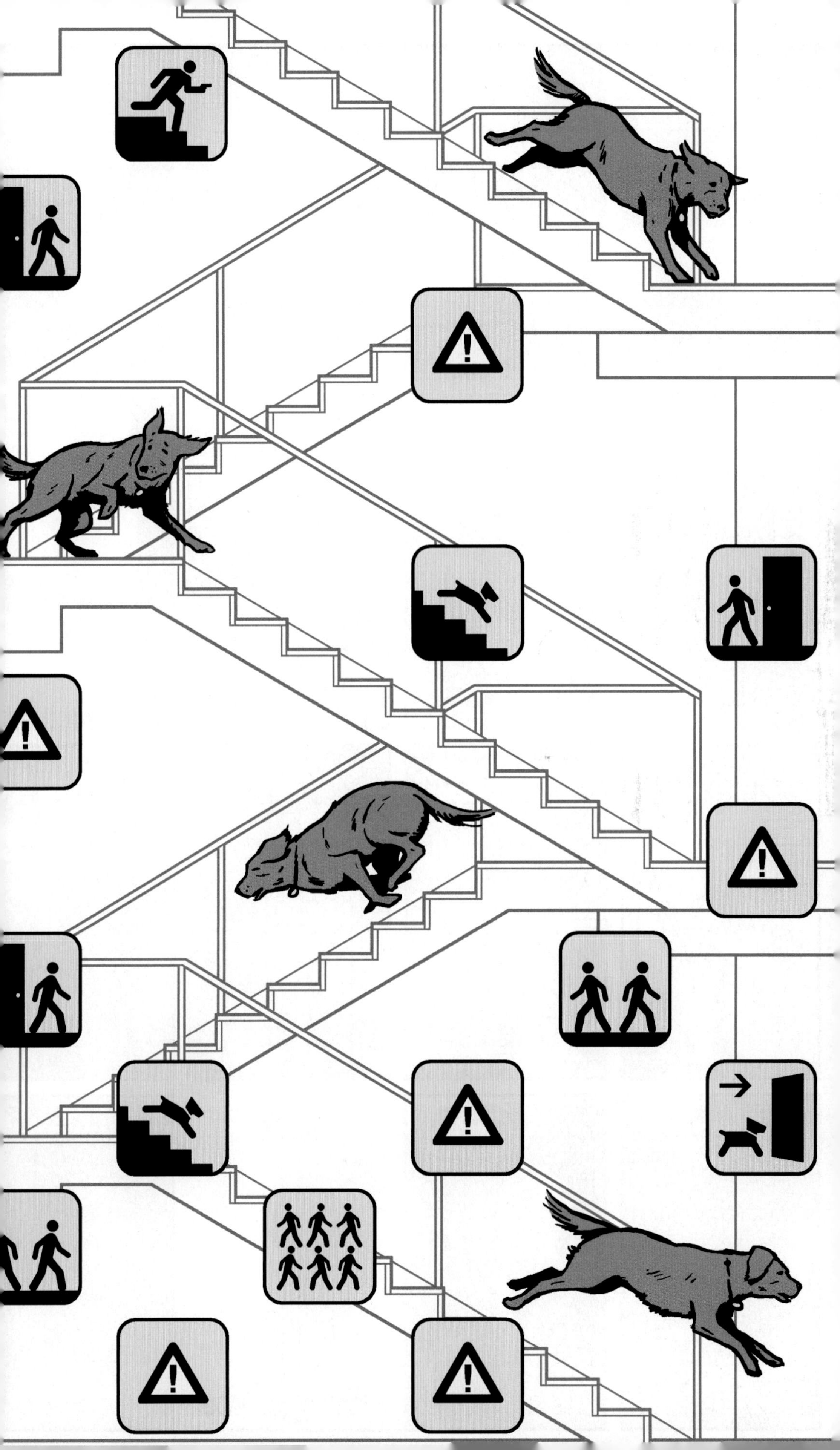

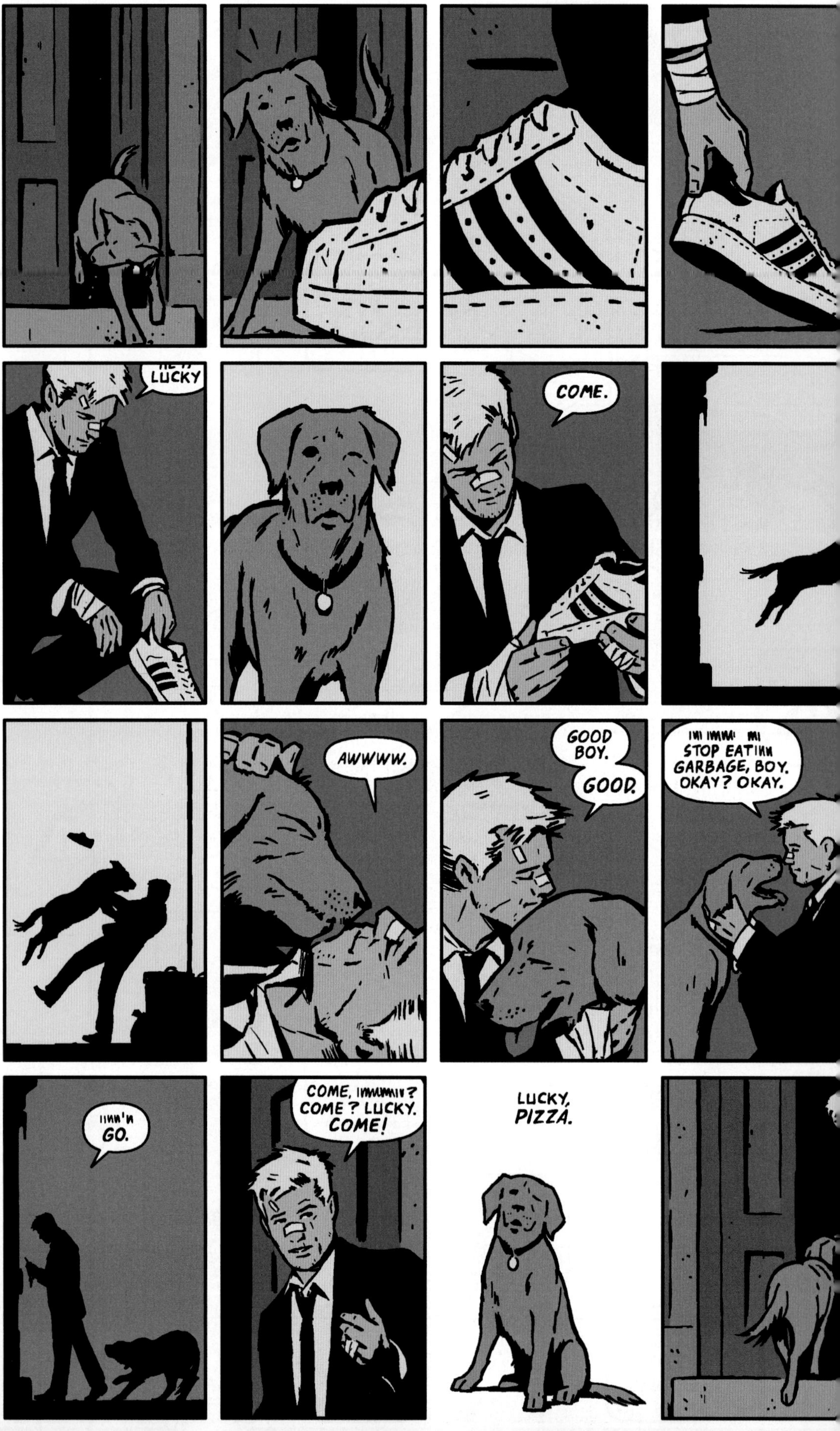
LUCKY
COME.
AWWWW.
GOOD BOY.
GOOD.
STOP EATING GARBAGE, BOY. OKAY? OKAY.
GO.
COME, COME? LUCKY. COME!
LUCKY, PIZZA.

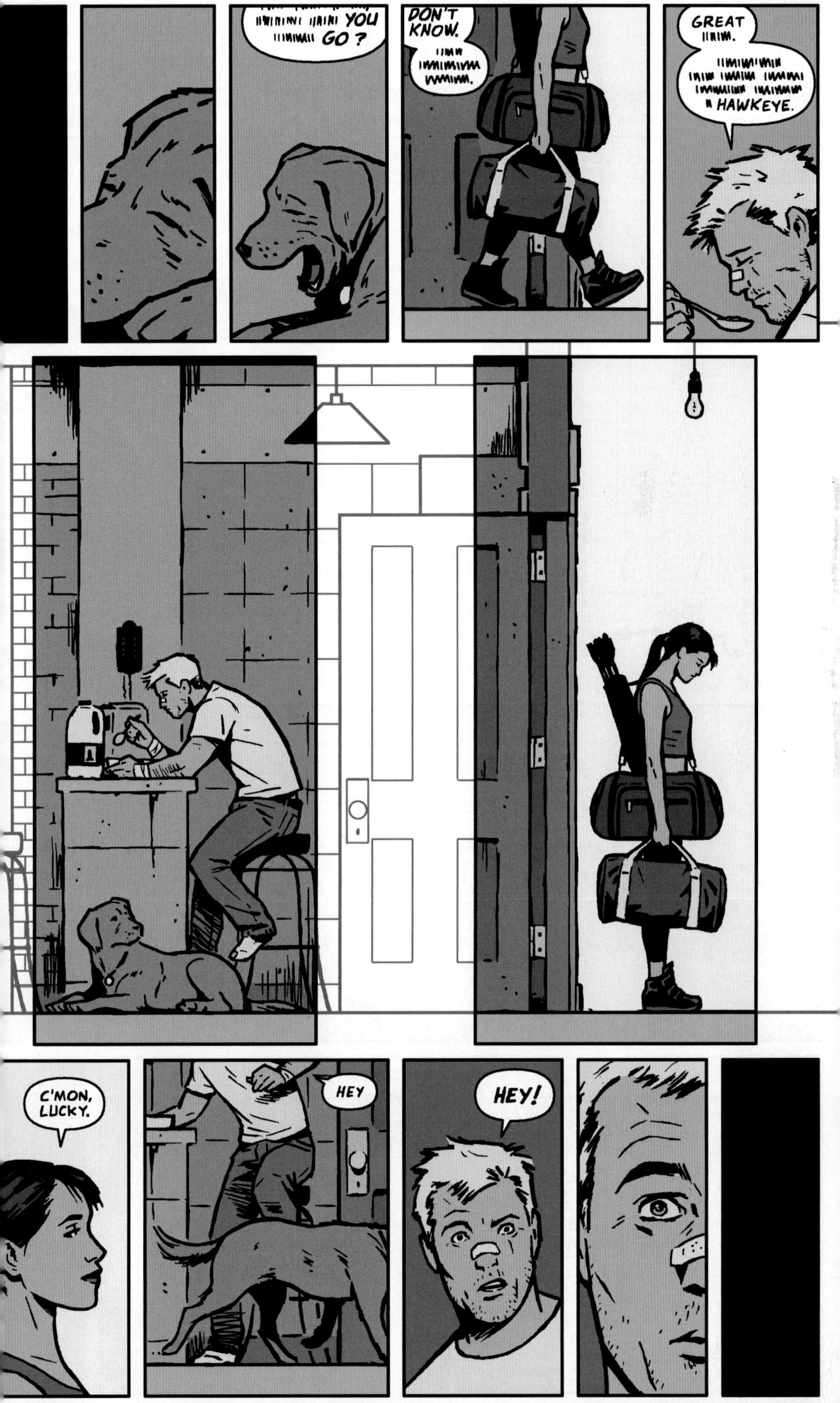
YOU GO?
DON'T KNOW.
GREAT
HAWKEYE.
C'MON, LUCKY.
HEY
HEY!

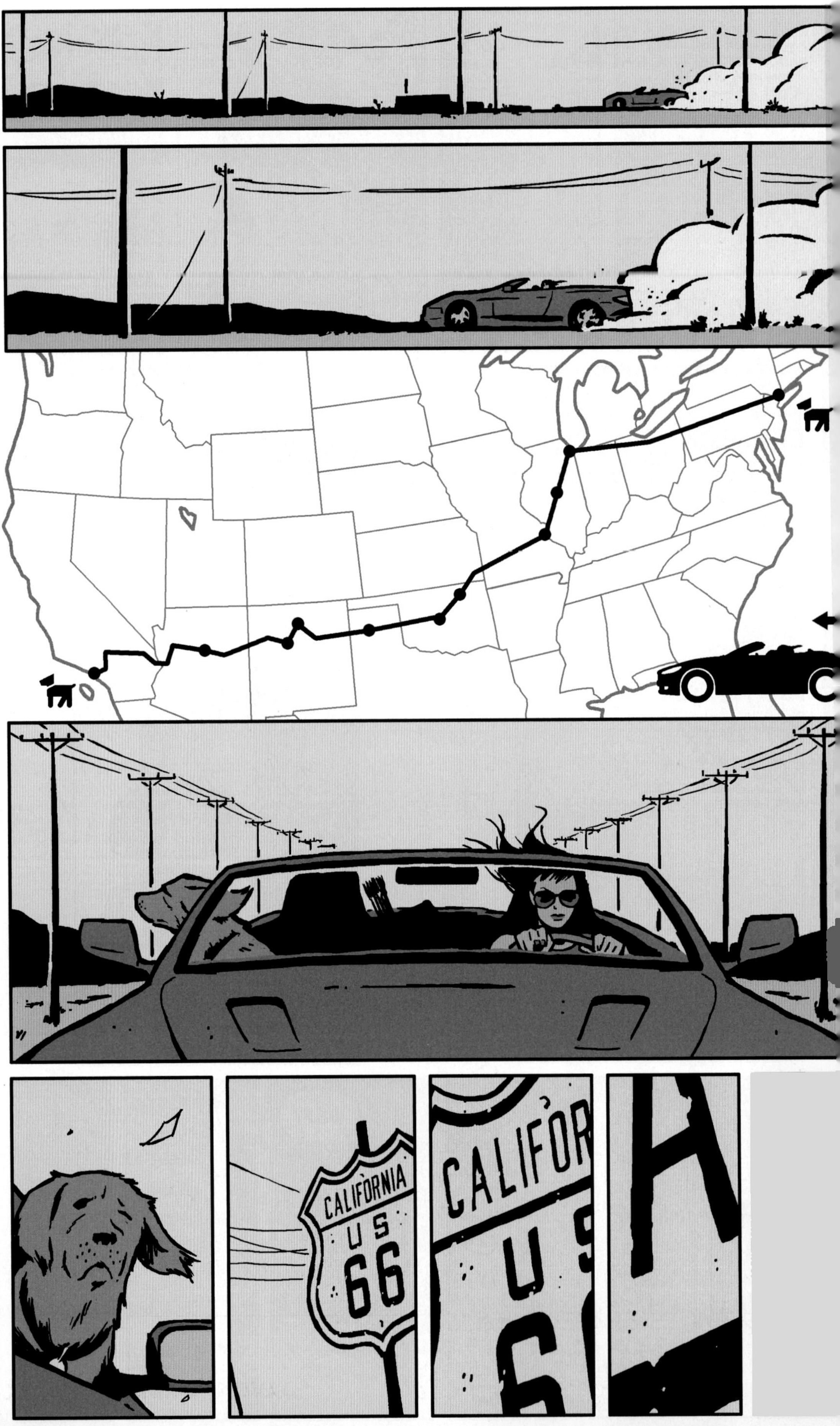
CALIFORNIA
US
66
CALIFOR
U

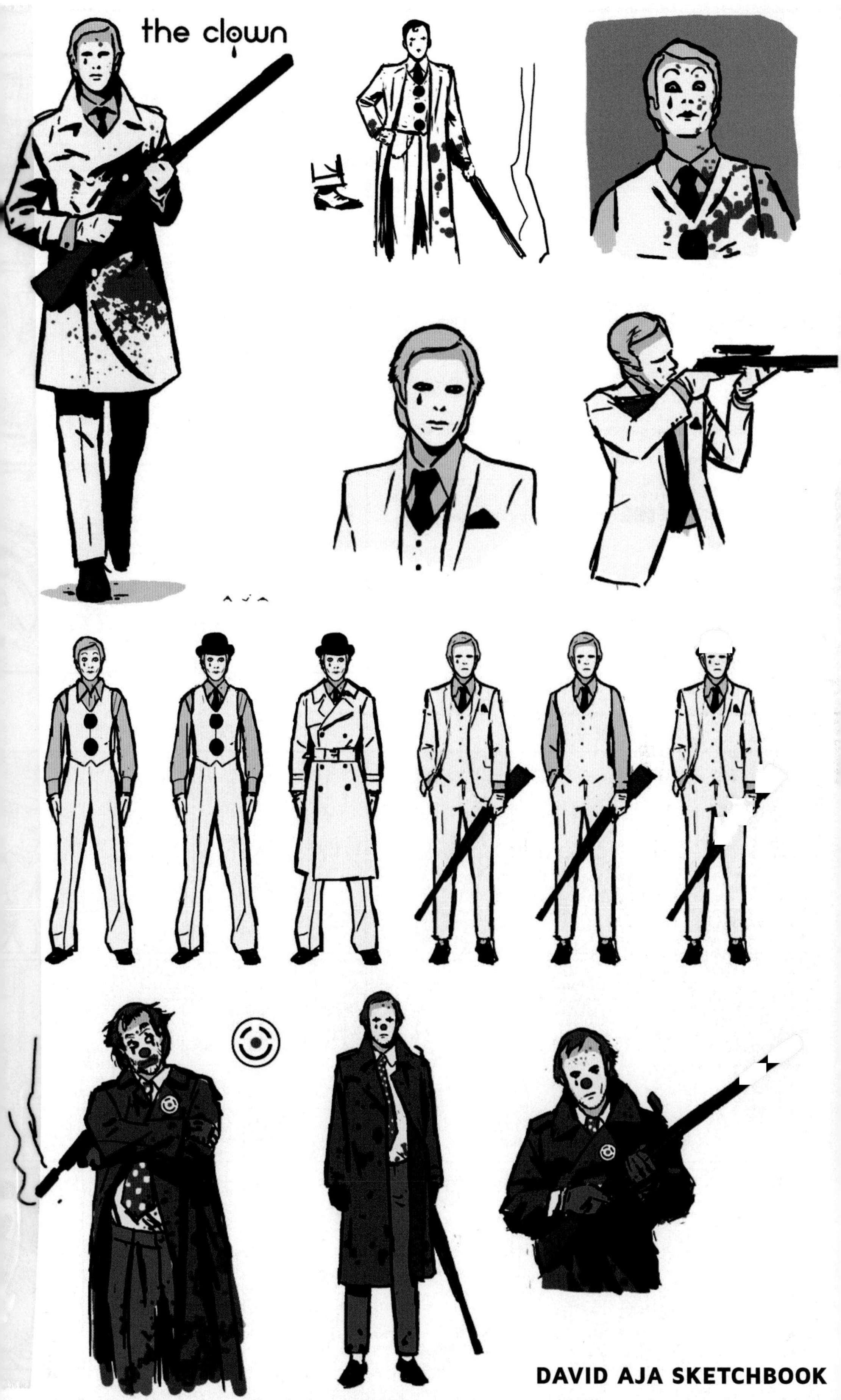
the clown
AJA

DAVID AJA SKETCHBOOK

PAGE NINE

CLINT and CHERRY, lit by Kate's TAILLIGHTS, stare at their wheelman leaving them out to dry.

They look at each other.

CLINT stomps across the street, CHERRY waiting in the shadows. A TRACKSUIT stands outside, not noticing. A couple other STRIPPERS, a few PATRONS mill about the front door of the club. We can all but hear the OONTZ OONTZ music from within.

The TRACKSUIT is bro-ing at one of the strippers as CLINT stomps up, shouting HEY ADIDAS —

— and PUNCHES THE [redacted] out of him, knocking the big guy off his stool.

The guy GETS UP in time for CLINT to HIT HIM BACK TOWARDS THE DOOR with that stool, hard —

ISSUE 8, PAGE 9 LAYOUTS

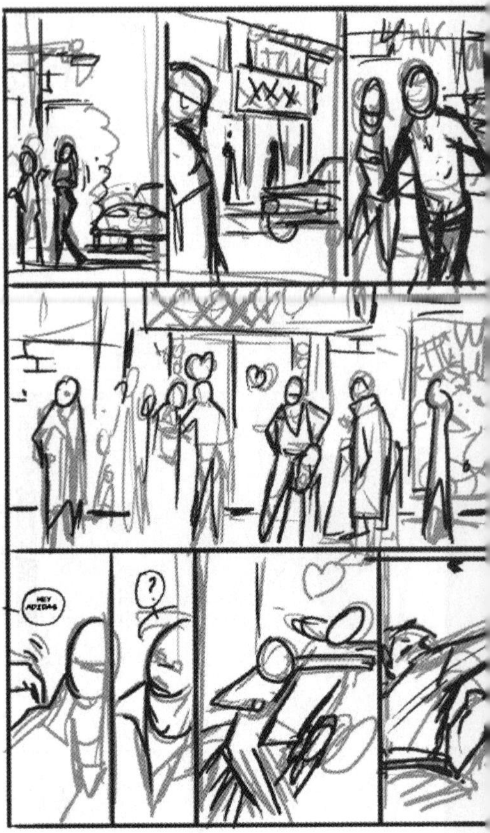
XXX
HEY ADIDAS

ISSUE 8, PAGE 9 PENCILS

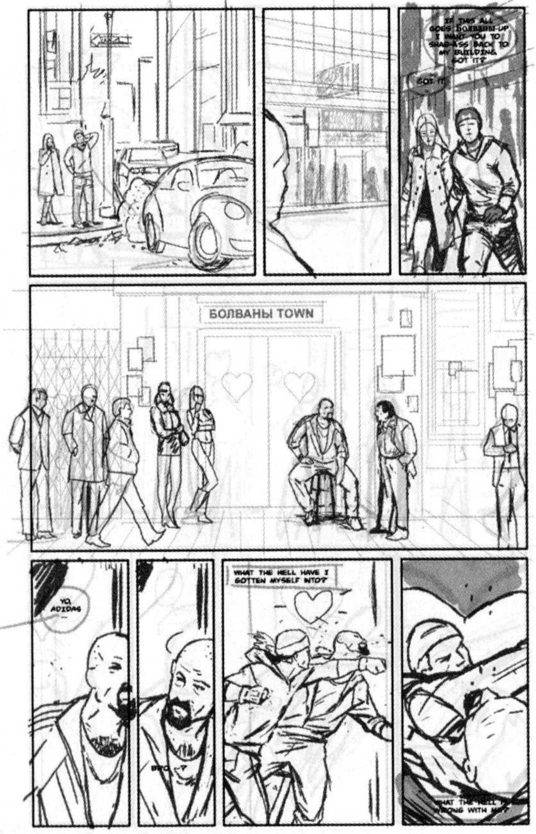
IF THIS ALL GOES БОЛВАНЫ-UP I WANT YOU TO SHAG-ASS BACK TO MY BUILDING. GOT IT?
GOT IT.
БОЛВАНЫ TOWN
YO, ADIDAS
WHAT THE HELL HAVE I GOTTEN MYSELF INTO?

ISSUE 8, PAGE 9 PARTIAL INKS

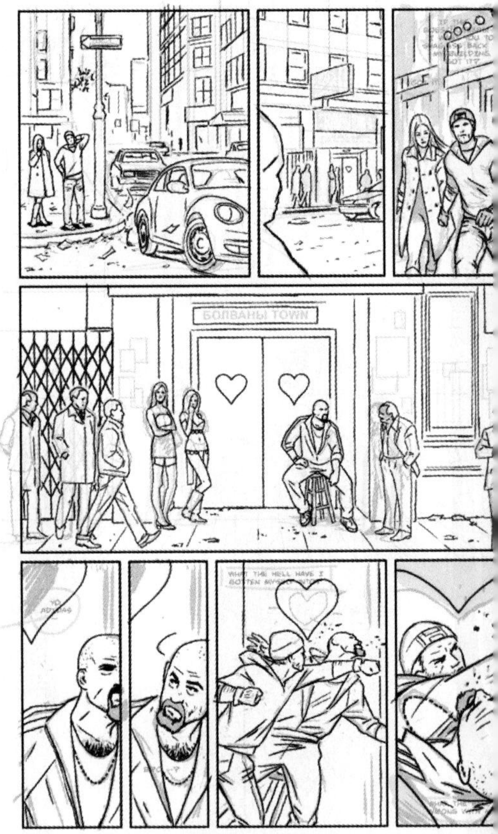
БОЛВАНЫ TOWN

ISSUE 8, PAGE 9 FINAL INKS

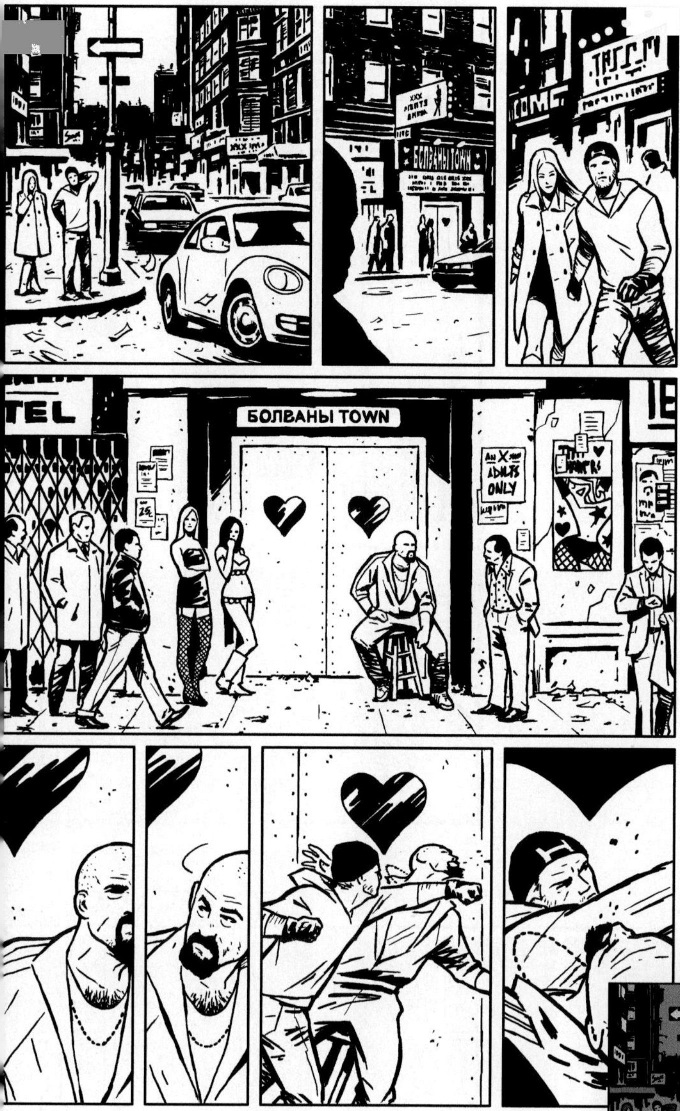
БОЛВАНЫ TOWN
TEL
ADULTS ONLY

ISSUE 8, PAGE 9 COLORS

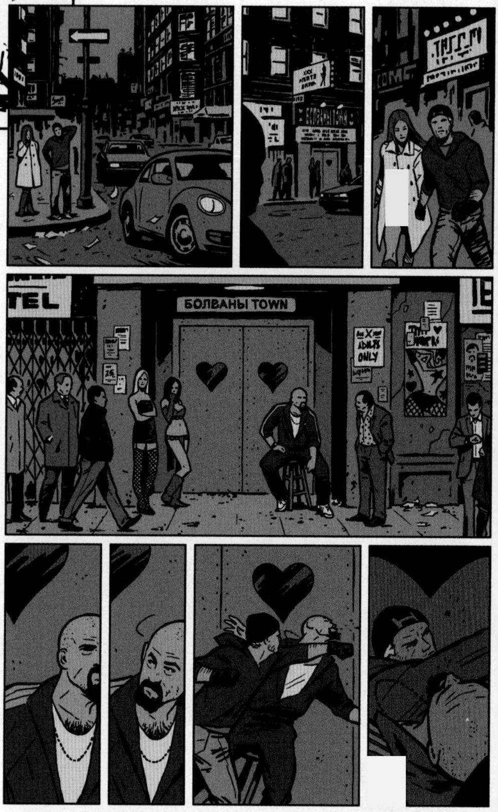
БОЛВАНЫ TOWN
TEL
ADULTS ONLY

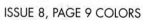

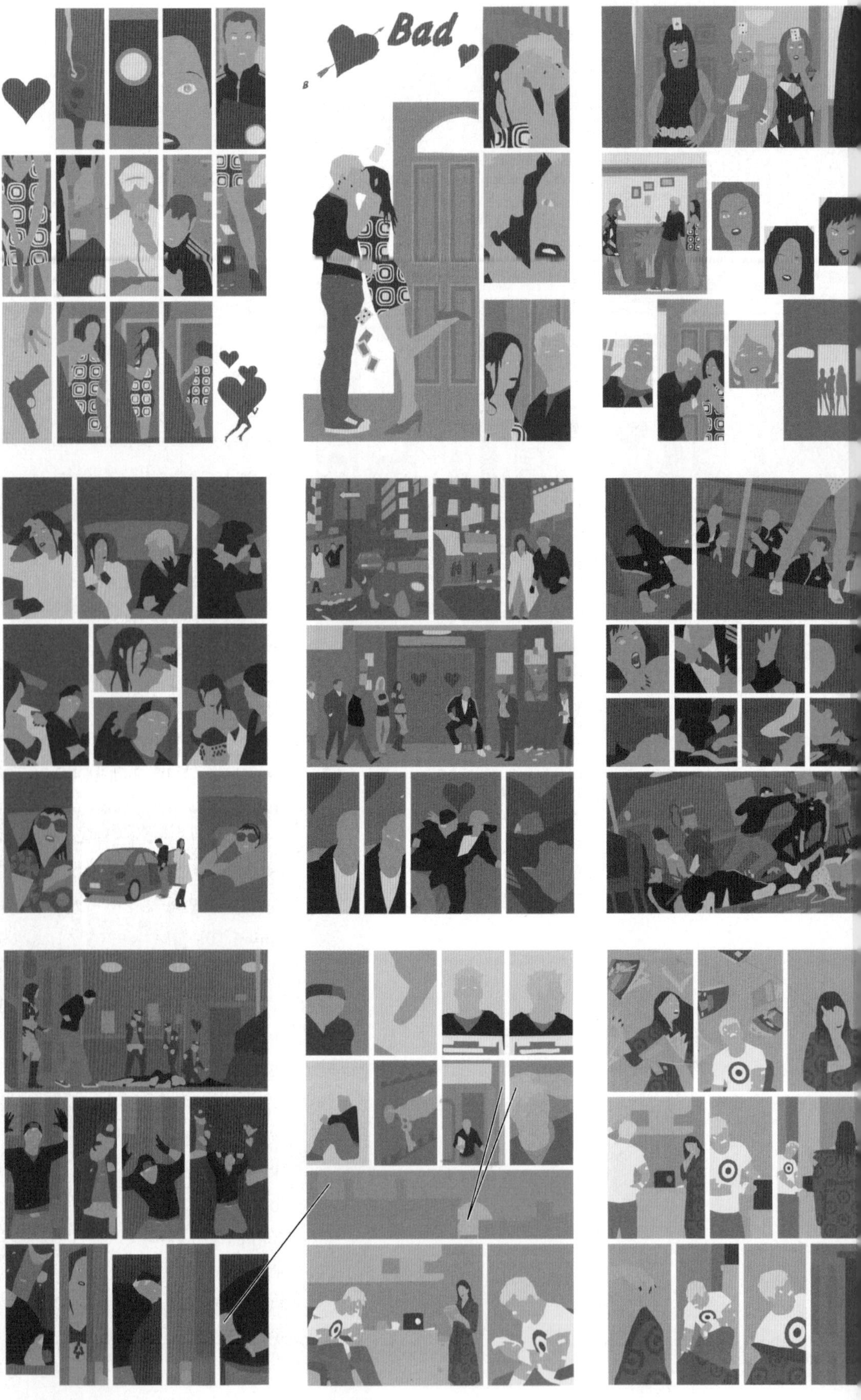
Bad

COLOR GUIDE
BY MATT HOLLINGSWORTH

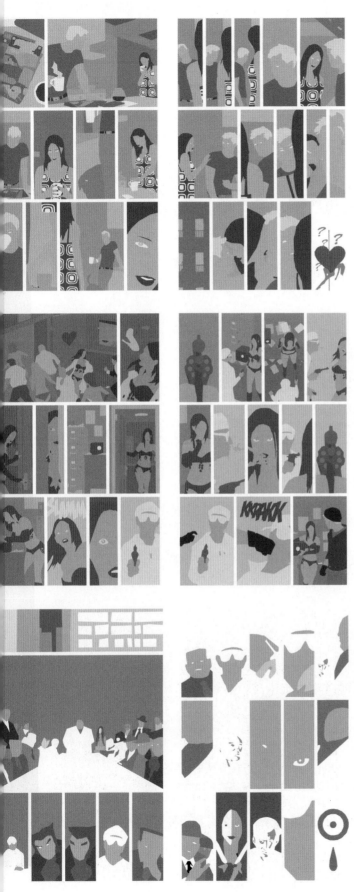

"Hawkeye is colored with minimalism in mind. Generally, as few colors as possible are used across the issue. Colors will reappear on pages across the book. You can see some examples I marked where the flesh tone from one scene is used as the sky color on the following scene and the hair color is carried over to be the color of the sun. The colors sometimes appear different because of the surrounding colors, which affect the way our eyes see that color. Color is a contextual thing.

"The book is colored as one whole unit rather than as separate pages. I work by laying out the entire issue on my second monitor. I pull a page to my main monitor and do a rough layout of the colors I want to use, then put the page back into the layout and pull another page and repeat that. Once I have the basic rough colors laid out for the entire issue, I go back and refine the colors over and over, usually minimizing the amount of colors I have more and more, distilling it down to a pretty minimal amount of colors. I don't often go monochromatic. It's usually a 2-3 color scheme with variations within those colors. I'm constantly looking at the entire issue to see how it's sitting as a whole. I will rough it in and then let it sit for a day or so and see what I think of it with fresh eyes. Well, when time allows, that is!"

—Matt Hollingsworth

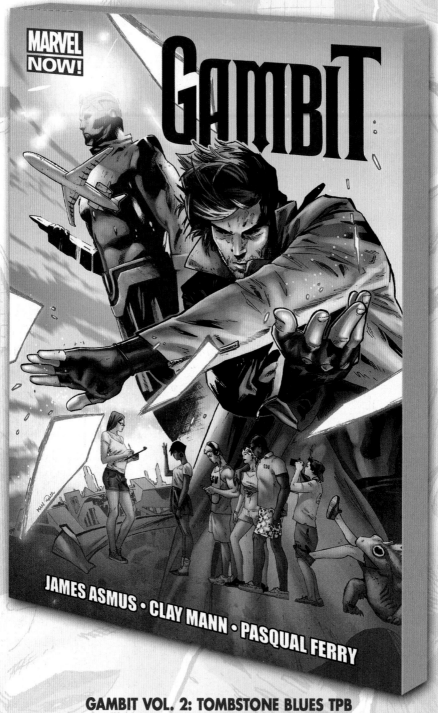

"ITS LIVED UP TO AND SURPASSED MY EXPECTATION." – *iFanboy.com*

MARVEL NOW!

GAMBIT

JAMES ASMUS • CLAY MANN • PASQUAL FERRY

GAMBIT VOL. 2: TOMBSTONE BLUES TPB
978-0-7851-6548-4 • APR130722

"FIVE OUT OF FIVE – PICK THIS BOOK UP" – *GeeksUnleashed.*

MARVEL NOW!

© 2013 MARVEL